THE 4 GOSPELS

Study Notes by Michael Keene

Good News New Testament
Second Edition

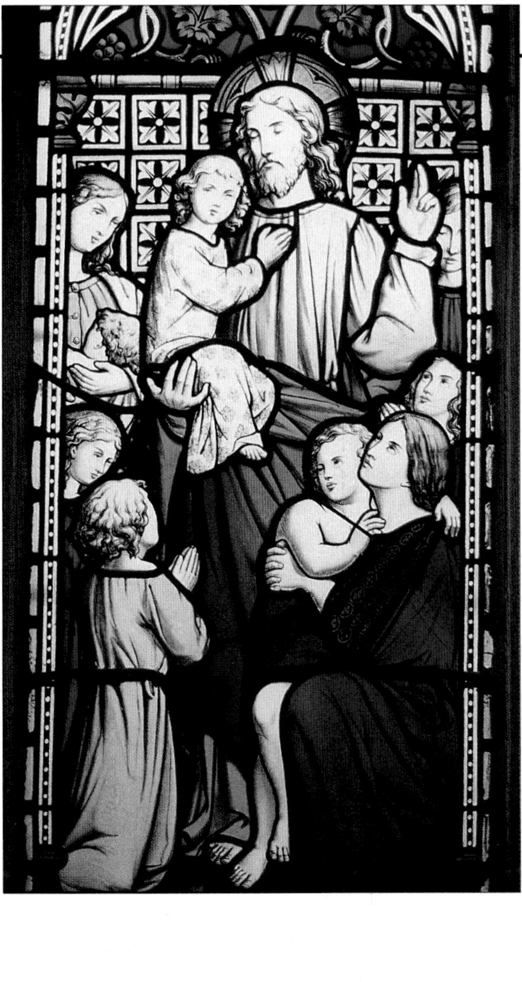

Collins Educational
An Imprint of Harper Collins*Publishers*

Contents

Introducing the Four Gospels

There are four Gospels in the New Testament. Three of them – Matthew, Mark and Luke – tell a similar story. So similar, in fact, that they have been called the Synoptic Gospels. This means that 'they see together' as they look at the life of Jesus. Two of them – Matthew and Luke – begin with the story of the birth of Jesus, although they tell rather different stories. Matthew tells the story from the viewpoint of Joseph, the father of Jesus, and includes the story of the Wise Men visiting the young Jesus. Luke looks at events through the eyes of Mary and tells us about the shepherds who visited Jesus just after he was born. Mark does not mention the birth of Jesus.

In their descriptions of the life of Jesus, Matthew, Mark and Luke also tell similar stories. Each of them shows how Jesus chose twelve disciples and taught them about God. He also taught the people who followed him. Often he used parables (stories with a religious meaning) to do this. Two of the most well-known parables are the Good Samaritan and the Prodigal Son. The Synoptic Gospels also tell how Jesus healed those who were blind, deaf and dumb, as well as people who had dreadful illnesses such as skin disease. Jesus also performed miracles to show that he had power over nature. These included walking on water, calming a storm and feeding a large crowd of people with five loaves and two fish.

The fourth Gospel – John – is very different from the other three. There are no parables in this Gospel and only a few miracles. Instead, John concentrates on the teachings of Jesus, and most of these teachings are not found in the other Gospels. All four Gospels, however, agree that Jesus was very popular with the people. It was the religious leaders who did not like the work that he was doing. Through the help of one of his disciples, Judas Iscariot, his enemies were able to bring about his death. This is the most important part of the life-story of Jesus in the Gospels. He died on a cross in Jerusalem. The Gospels go on to describe how, three days later, God brought him back from the dead. This event is called the Resurrection and is the most important part of the Christian faith.

How to Use This Book

There are four Gospels in the Bible – Matthew, Mark, Luke and John. Each Gospel is divided into many chapters. There are, for instance, 28 chapters in Matthew's Gospel whilst Mark's Gospel has 16. Each chapter is then divided into shorter sections called verses. You can find your way around this book by looking at this sample page:

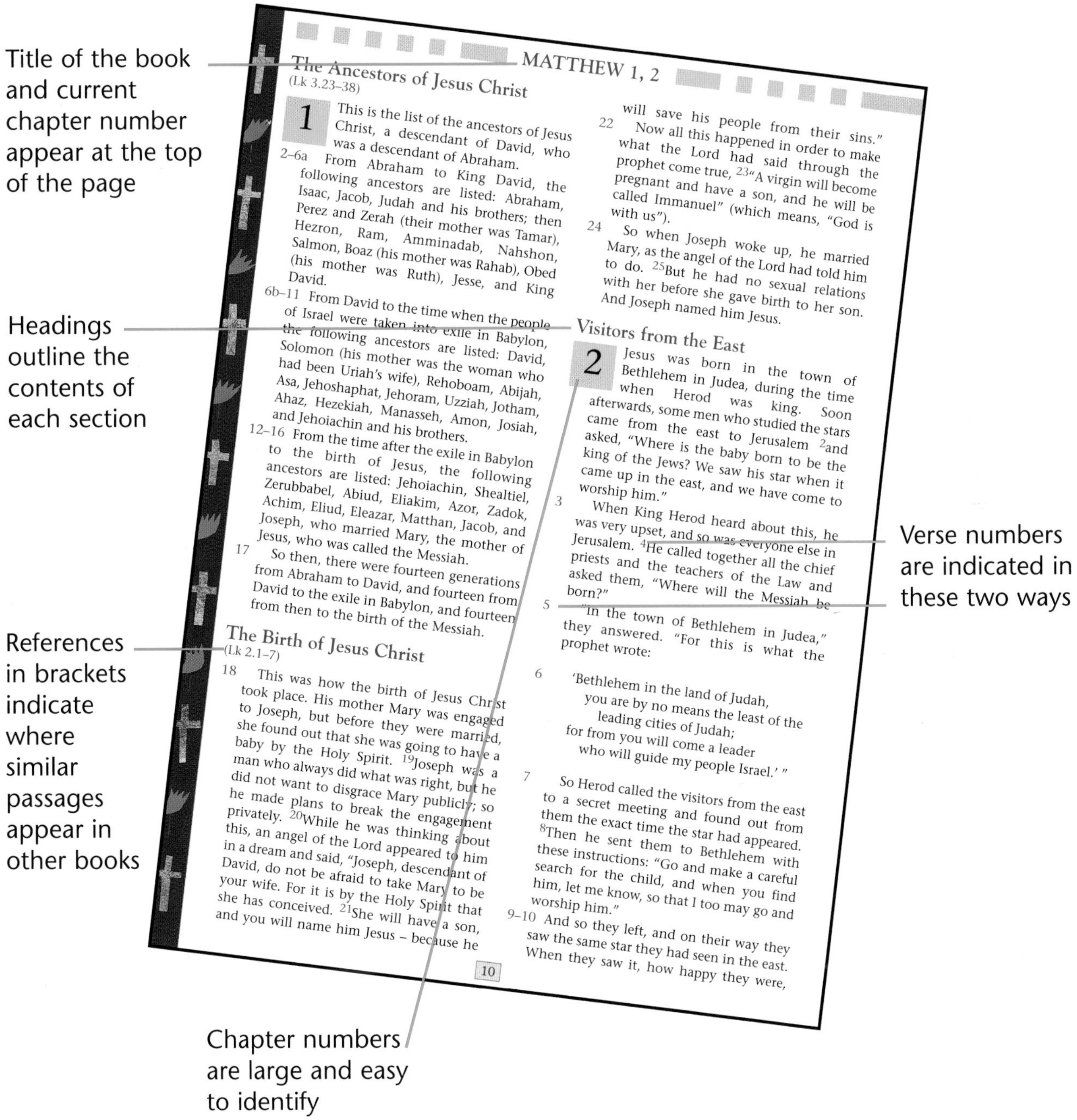

The Parables of Jesus

Jesus taught his followers by telling stories which had a religious meaning on top of the obvious meaning of the story. These stories are known as the parables. The four Gospels record around 40 different parables, as this table shows:

	Matthew	Mark	Luke
The lamp under a bowl	5.14–15	4.21–22	8.16, 11.33
The two house builders	7.24–27		6.47–49
The cloth and the wineskins	9.16–17	2.21–22	5.36–39
The sower and the soils	13.3–9, 18–23	4.3–9, 13–20	8.5–8, 11–15
The weeds	13.24–30, 36–43		
The mustard seed	13.31–32	4.30–32	13.18–19
The yeast	13.33		13.20–21
The hidden treasure	13.44		
The pearl	13.45–46		
The net	13.47–50		
The lost sheep	18.12–14		15.4–7
The unforgiving servant	18.21–34		
The workers in the vineyard	20.1–16		
The two sons	21.28–32		
The tenants in the vineyard	21.33–44	12.1–11	20.9–18
The feast	22.2–14		14.16–24
The faithful or the unfaithful servant	24.45–51		12.42–48
The ten young women	25.1–13		
The three servants	25.14–30		19.11–27
The sheep and goats	25.31–46		
The growing seed		4.26–29	
The watchful servants	24.42–44		12.35–40
The money and the moneylender			7.41–43
The good Samaritan			10.30–37
The friend in need			11.5–8
The rich fool			12.16–21
The unfruitful fig tree			13.6–9
The tower and the king			14.28–33
The lost coin			15.8–10
The lost son			15.11–32
The clever manager			16.1–8
The rich man and Lazarus			16.19–31
The widow and the judge			18.2–8
The Pharisee and the tax collector			18.10–14

The Miracles of Jesus

Jesus performed many acts which caused people to stop and wonder. These acts are known as the miracles, and fall into three categories, as this table shows:

	Matthew	Mark	Luke	John
a) Jesus heals the sick				
A man with skin disease	8.1–4	1.40–45	5.12–16	
The Roman officer's servant	8.5–13		7.1–10	
The disciple's mother-in-law	8.14–17	1.29–34	4.38–41	
The men with demons	8.28–34	5.1–20	8.26–39	
A paralysed man	9.1–7	2.1–12	5.17–26	
A woman with bleeding	9.20–22	5.25–29	8.43–48	
Two blind men	9.27–31			
A man who could not speak	9.32–34			
A man with a paralysed hand	12.9–14	3.1–6	6.6–11	
A blind and mute man	12.22		11.14–15	
The daughter with a demon	15.21–28	7.24–30		
The boy with a demon	17.14–21	9.14–29	9.37–43	
The blind men	20.29–34	10.46–52	18.35–43	
A deaf-mute		7.31–37		
A man with an evil spirit		1.21–28	4.31–37	
A blind man		8.22–26		
A crippled woman			13.10–17	
A man with swollen limbs			14.1–6	
Ten men with skin disease			17.11–19	
The High Priest's servant			22.49–51	
An official's son				4.43–54
A sick man				5.1–18
A man born blind				9.1–12
b) Jesus and nature				
Calming the storm	8.23–27	4.35–41	8.22–25	
Walking on water	14.22–33	6.45–52		6.16–21
Feeding 5,000 people	14.13–21	6.30–44	9.10–17	6.1–15
Feeding 4,000 people	15.32–38	8.1–9		
The coin in the fish's mouth	17.24–27			
The withered fig tree	21.18–22	11.12–14, 20–24		
The catch of fish			5.1–11	
Turning water into wine				2.1–11
Another catch of fish				21.1–11
c) Jesus brings the dead back to life				
Jairus' daughter	9.18–19, 23–26	5.21–24, 35–43	8.40–42,49–56	
The widow's son			7.11–17	
Lazarus				11.1–44

Places in the Four Gospels

Palestine

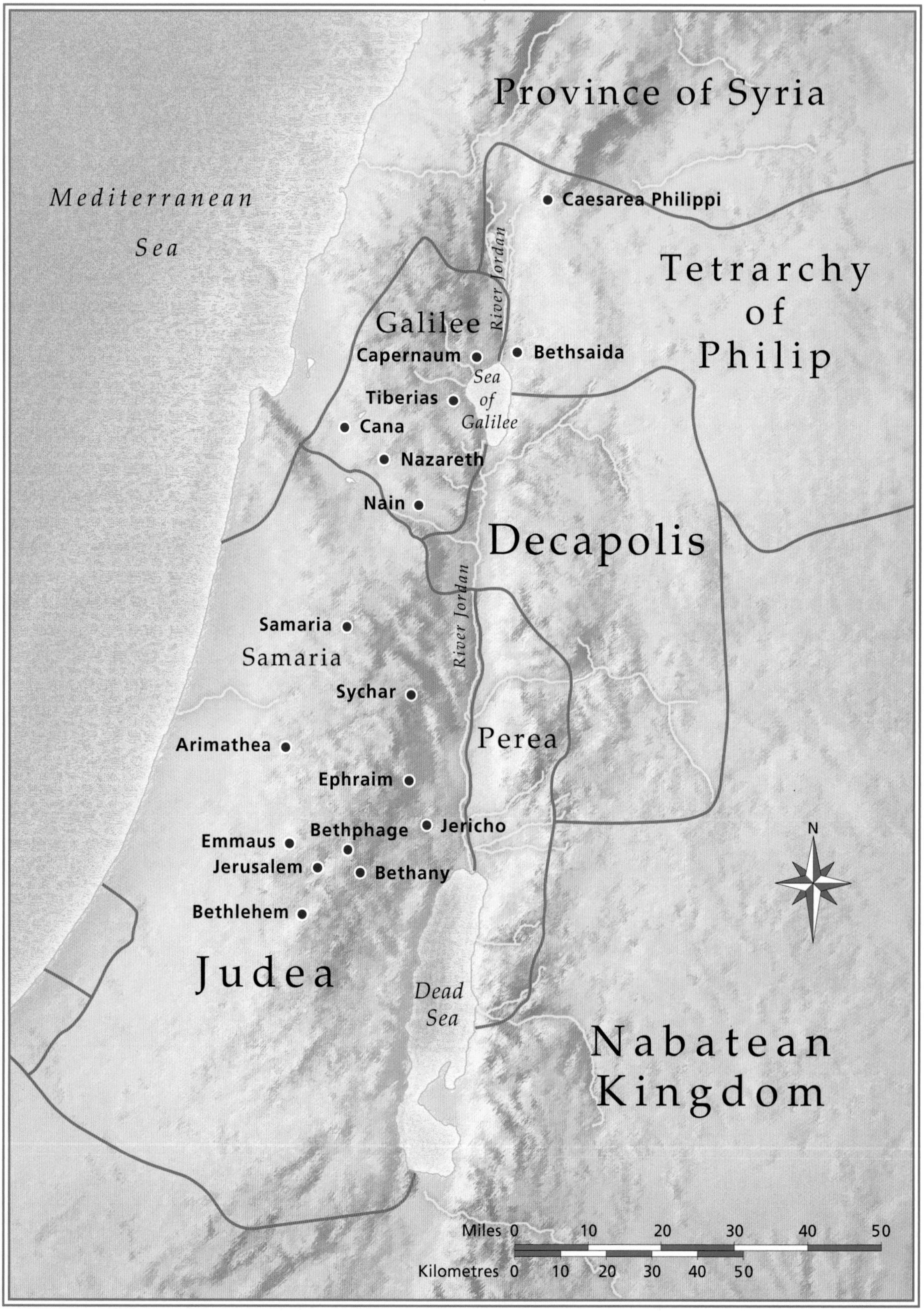

Province of Syria
Mediterranean Sea
Caesarea Philippi
River Jordan
Tetrarchy of Philip
Galilee
Capernaum
Bethsaida
Sea of Galilee
Tiberias
Cana
Nazareth
Nain
Decapolis
River Jordan
Samaria
Samaria
Sychar
Perea
Arimathea
Ephraim
Jericho
Bethphage
Emmaus
Jerusalem
Bethany
Bethlehem
N
Judea
Dead Sea
Nabatean Kingdom
Miles 0 10 20 30 40 50
Kilometres 0 10 20 30 40 50

Jerusalem

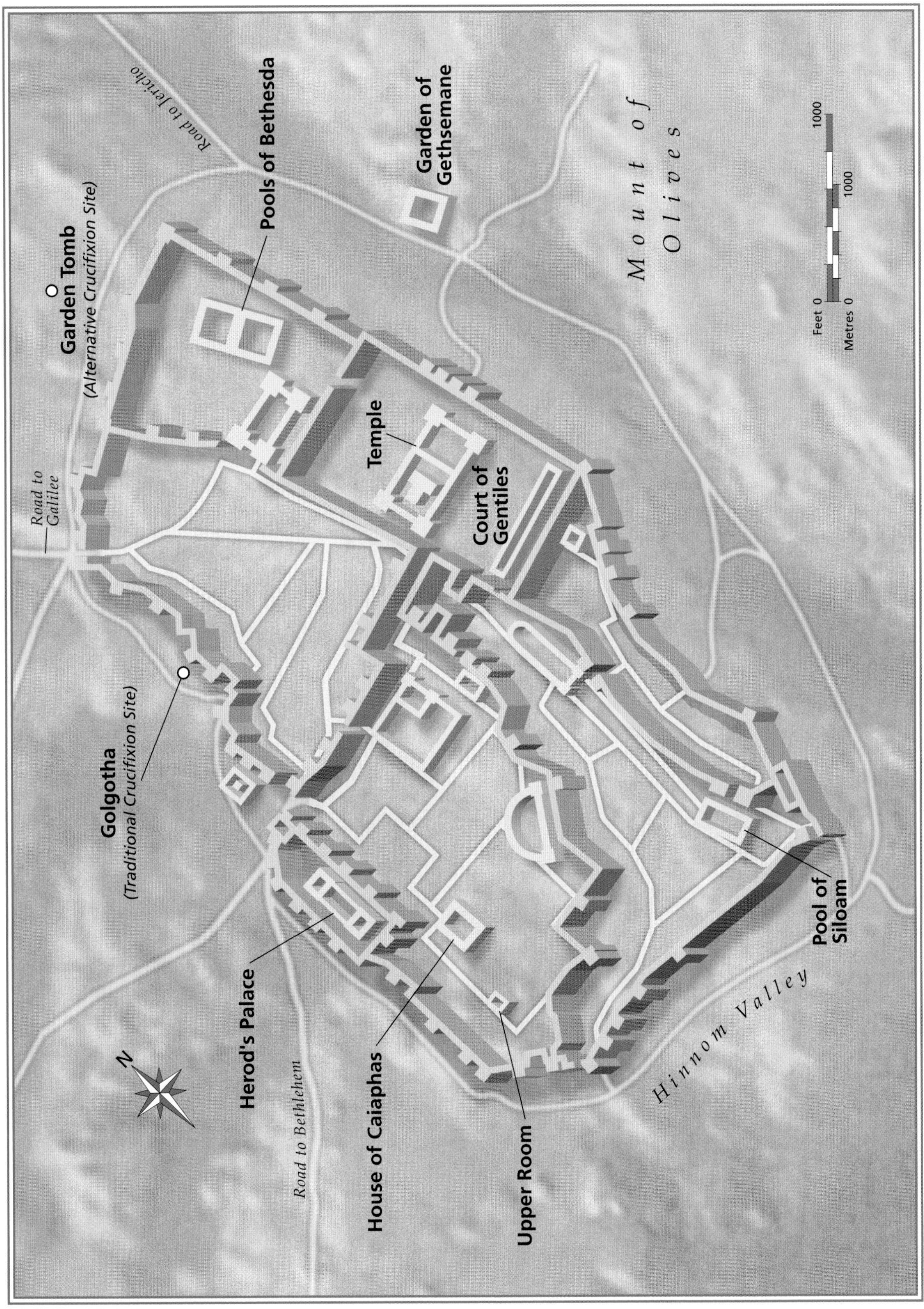
Road to Jericho
Pools of Bethesda
Garden of Gethsemane
Mount of Olives
Garden Tomb
(Alternative Crucifixion Site)
Road to Galilee
Temple
Court of Gentiles
Golgotha
(Traditional Crucifixion Site)
Herod's Palace
House of Caiaphas
Upper Room
Road to Bethlehem
Hinnom Valley
Pool of Siloam
Feet 0 1000
Metres 0 1000
N

Events in the Four Gospels

The Life of Jesus

(all dates are approximate)

5/4 BCE	Jesus born in Bethlehem
7/8 CE	Jesus visits the Temple with his parents
25 CE	John the Baptist begins his work Jesus begins his work Jesus is baptized by John the Baptist
26/27 CE	John the Baptist is put in prison by Herod the Great
27/28 CE	John the Baptist dies
29/30 CE	Jesus visits Jerusalem Jesus is arrested Pontius Pilate condemns Jesus Jesus dies Jesus comes back to life Jesus leaves earth

Rulers in Rome and Palestine

37 BCE	Herod the Great is appointed by Rome to rule Palestine
27 BCE	Augustus becomes Emperor of Rome
4 BCE	Herod the Great dies
6 CE	Roman governors begin to rule over Palestine
14 CE	Augustus dies
18 CE	Caiaphas becomes High Priest
26/36 CE	Pontius Pilate is governor of Palestine

The Gospel According to Matthew

This is the longest of the four Gospels. Although it is placed first in the New Testament it was not the first Gospel to be written. The Gospel starts, as Luke's Gospel does, with the birth of Jesus in a stable. Matthew, the writer, was one of the disciples of Jesus.

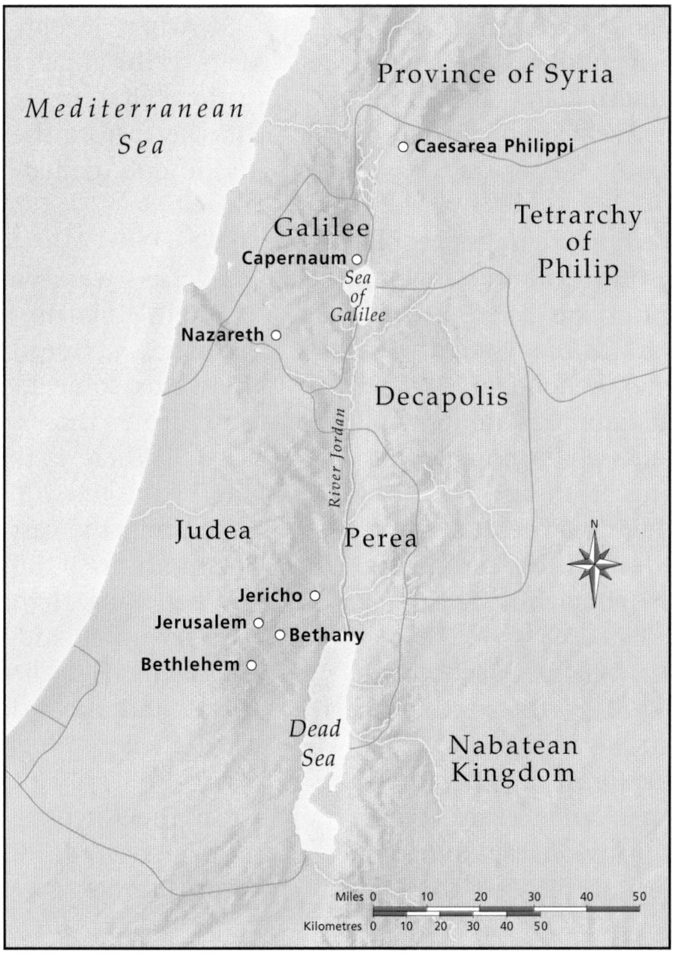

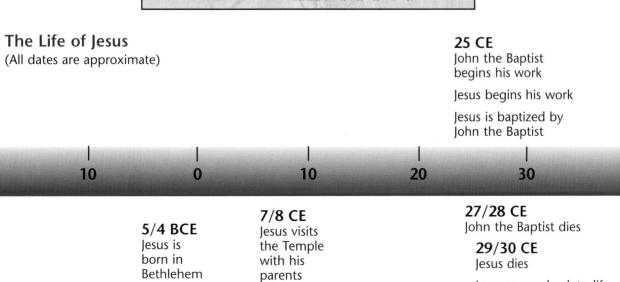

The Life of Jesus

(All dates are approximate)

10 | 0 | 10 | 20 | 30

5/4 BCE
Jesus is born in Bethlehem

7/8 CE
Jesus visits the Temple with his parents

25 CE
John the Baptist begins his work

Jesus begins his work

Jesus is baptized by John the Baptist

27/28 CE
John the Baptist dies

29/30 CE
Jesus dies

Jesus comes back to life

The Ancestors of Jesus Christ
(Lk 3.23–38)

1 This is the list of the ancestors of Jesus
Christ, a descendant of David, who
was a descendant of Abraham.
2–6a From Abraham to King David, the
following ancestors are listed: Abraham,
Isaac, Jacob, Judah and his brothers; then
Perez and Zerah (their mother was Tamar),
Hezron, Ram, Amminadab, Nahshon,
Salmon, Boaz (his mother was Rahab), Obed
(his mother was Ruth), Jesse, and King
David.
6b–11 From David to the time when the people
of Israel were taken into exile in Babylon,
the following ancestors are listed: David,
Solomon (his mother was the woman who
had been Uriah's wife), Rehoboam, Abijah,
Asa, Jehoshaphat, Jehoram, Uzziah, Jotham,
Ahaz, Hezekiah, Manasseh, Amon, Josiah,
and Jehoiachin and his brothers.
12–16 From the time after the exile in Babylon
to the birth of Jesus, the following
ancestors are listed: Jehoiachin, Shealtiel,
Zerubbabel, Abiud, Eliakim, Azor, Zadok,
Achim, Eliud, Eleazar, Matthan, Jacob, and
Joseph, who married Mary, the mother of
Jesus, who was called the Messiah.
17 So then, there were fourteen generations
from Abraham to David, and fourteen from
David to the exile in Babylon, and fourteen
from then to the birth of the Messiah.

The Birth of Jesus Christ
(Lk 2.1–7)

18 This was how the birth of Jesus Christ
took place. His mother Mary was engaged
to Joseph, but before they were married,
she found out that she was going to have a
baby by the Holy Spirit. [19]Joseph was a
man who always did what was right, but he
did not want to disgrace Mary publicly; so
he made plans to break the engagement
privately. [20]While he was thinking about
this, an angel of the Lord appeared to him
in a dream and said, "Joseph, descendant of
David, do not be afraid to take Mary to be
your wife. For it is by the Holy Spirit that
she has conceived. [21]She will have a son,
and you will name him Jesus – because he
will save his people from their sins."
22 Now all this happened in order to make
what the Lord had said through the
prophet come true, [23]"A virgin will become
pregnant and have a son, and he will be
called Immanuel" (which means, "God is
with us").
24 So when Joseph woke up, he married
Mary, as the angel of the Lord had told him
to do. [25]But he had no sexual relations
with her before she gave birth to her son.
And Joseph named him Jesus.

Visitors from the East

2 Jesus was born in the town of
Bethlehem in Judea, during the time
when Herod was king. Soon
afterwards, some men who studied the stars
came from the east to Jerusalem [2]and
asked, "Where is the baby born to be the
king of the Jews? We saw his star when it
came up in the east, and we have come to
worship him."
3 When King Herod heard about this, he
was very upset, and so was everyone else in
Jerusalem. [4]He called together all the chief
priests and the teachers of the Law and
asked them, "Where will the Messiah be
born?"
5 "In the town of Bethlehem in Judea,"
they answered. "For this is what the
prophet wrote:

6 'Bethlehem in the land of Judah,
you are by no means the least of the
leading cities of Judah;
for from you will come a leader
who will guide my people Israel.' "

7 So Herod called the visitors from the east
to a secret meeting and found out from
them the exact time the star had appeared.
[8]Then he sent them to Bethlehem with
these instructions: "Go and make a careful
search for the child, and when you find
him, let me know, so that I too may go and
worship him."
9–10 And so they left, and on their way they
saw the same star they had seen in the east.
When they saw it, how happy they were,

what joy was theirs! It went ahead of them
until it stopped over the place where the
child was. 11They went into the house, and
when they saw the child with his mother
Mary, they knelt down and worshipped
him. They brought out their gifts of gold,
frankincense, and myrrh, and presented
them to him.
12 Then they returned to their country by
another road, since God had warned them
in a dream not to go back to Herod.

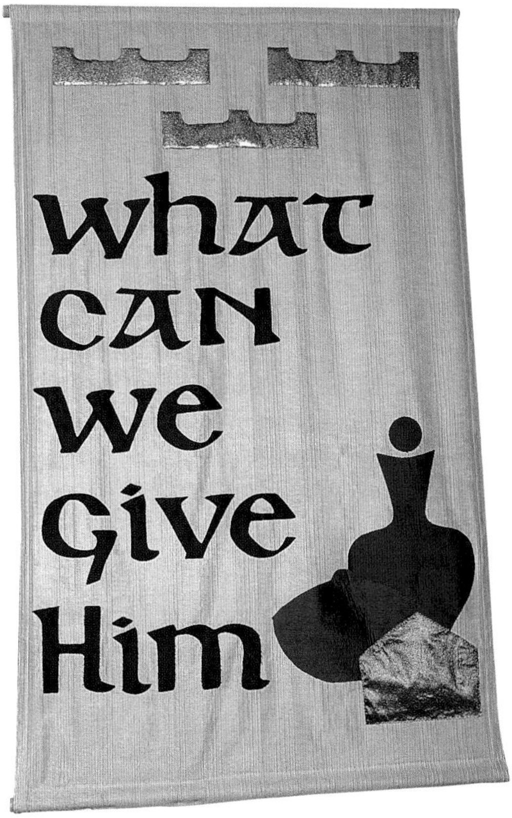

The Wise Men brought gifts to the baby Jesus.

The Escape to Egypt

13 After they had left, an angel of the Lord
appeared in a dream to Joseph and said,
"Herod will be looking for the child in
order to kill him. So get up, take the child
and his mother and escape to Egypt, and
stay there until I tell you to leave."
14 Joseph got up, took the child and his
mother, and left during the night for
Egypt, 15where he stayed until Herod died.
This was done to make what the Lord had
said through the prophet come true, "I
called my Son out of Egypt."

The Killing of the Children

16 When Herod realized that the visitors
from the east had tricked him, he was
furious. He gave orders to kill all the boys
in Bethlehem and its neighbourhood who
were two years old and younger – this was
done in accordance with what he had
learned from the visitors about the time
when the star had appeared.
17 In this way what the prophet Jeremiah
had said came true:

18 "A sound is heard in Ramah,
the sound of bitter weeping.
Rachel is crying for her children;
she refuses to be comforted,
for they are dead."

The Return from Egypt

19 After Herod died, an angel of the Lord
appeared in a dream to Joseph in Egypt
20and said, "Get up, take the child and his
mother, and go back to the land of Israel,
because those who tried to kill the child are
dead." 21So Joseph got up, took the child
and his mother, and went back to Israel.
22 But when Joseph heard that Archelaus
had succeeded his father Herod as king of
Judea, he was afraid to go there. He was
given more instructions in a dream, so he
went to the province of Galilee 23and
made his home in a town named Nazareth.
And so what the prophets had said came
true: "He will be called a Nazarene."

The Preaching of John the Baptist

(Mk 1.1–8; Lk 3.1–18; Jn 1.19–28)

3 At that time John the Baptist came to
the desert of Judea and started
preaching. 2"Turn away from your
sins," he said, "because the Kingdom of
heaven is near!" 3John was the man the
prophet Isaiah was talking about when he
said:

"Someone is shouting in the desert,
'Prepare a road for the Lord;
make a straight path for him to
travel!' "

4 John's clothes were made of camel's hair;
he wore a leather belt round his waist, and
his food was locusts and wild honey.
5People came to him from Jerusalem, from
the whole province of Judea, and from all
the country near the River Jordan. 6They
confessed their sins, and he baptized them
in the Jordan.
7 When John saw many Pharisees and
Sadducees coming to him to be baptized, he
said to them, "You snakes – who told you
that you could escape from the punishment
God is about to send? 8Do those things that
will show that you have turned from your
sins. 9And don't think you can escape
punishment by saying that Abraham is your
ancestor. I tell you that God can take these
stones and make descendants for Abraham!
10The axe is ready to cut down the trees at
the roots; every tree that does not bear good
fruit will be cut down and thrown in the fire.
11I baptize you with water to show that you
have repented,
but the one
who will come
after me will
baptize you
with the Holy
Spirit and fire.
He is much
greater than I
am; and I
am not good
enough even
to carry his
sandals. 12He
has his
winnowing
shovel with
him to thresh
out all the
grain. He will
gather his
wheat into his
barn, but he
will burn the
chaff in a fire
that never goes
out."

John baptized Jesus in the River Jordan.

The Baptism of Jesus
(Mk 1.9–11; Lk 3.21–22)

13 At that time Jesus arrived from Galilee
and came to John at the Jordan to be
baptized by him. 14But John tried to make
him change his mind. "I ought to be
baptized by you," John said, "and yet you
have come to me!"
15 But Jesus answered him, "Let it be so for
now. For in this way we shall do all that
God requires." So John agreed.
16 As soon as Jesus was baptized, he came
up out of the water. Then heaven was
opened to him, and he saw the Spirit of
God coming down like a dove and
alighting on him. 17Then a voice said from
heaven, "This is my own dear Son, with
whom I am pleased."

The Temptation of Jesus
(Mk 1.12–13; Lk 4.1–13)

4 Then the Spirit led Jesus
into the desert to be
tempted by the Devil.
2After spending 40 days and
nights without food, Jesus was
hungry. 3Then the Devil came to
him and said, "If you are God's
Son, order these stones to turn
into bread."
4 But Jesus answered, "The
scripture says, 'Human beings
cannot live on bread alone, but
need every word that God
speaks.' "
5 Then the Devil took Jesus to
Jerusalem, the Holy City, set
him on the highest point of the
Temple, 6and said to him, "If
you are God's Son, throw
yourself down, for the scripture
says:

'God will give orders to his
angels about you;
they will hold you up
with their hands,
so that not even your feet
will be hurt on the
stones.' "

7 Jesus answered, "But the scripture also
says, 'Do not put the Lord your God to the
test.' "
8 Then the Devil took Jesus to a very high
mountain and showed him all the
kingdoms of the world in
all their greatness. 9"All
this I will give you," the
Devil said, "if you kneel
down and worship me."
10 Then Jesus answered,
"Go away, Satan! The
scripture says, 'Worship
the Lord your God and
serve only him!' "
11 Then the Devil left
Jesus; and angels came and
helped him.

Jesus Begins his Work in Galilee

(Mk 1.14–15; Lk 4.14–15)

12 When Jesus heard
that John had been put
in prison, he went away
to Galilee. 13He did not stay
in Nazareth, but went to live in
Capernaum, a town by Lake Galilee, in the
territory of Zebulun and Naphtali. 14This
was done to make what the prophet Isaiah
had said come true:

15 "Land of Zebulun and land of Naphtali,
on the road to the sea, on the other
side of the Jordan,
Galilee, land of the Gentiles!
16 The people who live in darkness
will see a great light.
On those who live in the dark land of
death
the light will shine."

17 From that time Jesus began to preach his
message: "Turn away from your sins,
because the Kingdom of heaven is near!"

Jesus Calls Four Fishermen

(Mk 1.16–20; Lk 5.1–11)

18 As Jesus walked along the shore of Lake
Galilee, he saw two brothers who were
fishermen, Simon (called Peter) and his
brother Andrew, catching fish in the lake
with a net. 19Jesus said to them, "Come
with me, and I will teach you to catch
people." 20At once they left their nets and
went with him.

Jesus called Simon and Andrew to follow him.

21 He went on and saw two other brothers,
James and John, the sons of Zebedee. They
were in their boat with their father
Zebedee, getting their nets ready. Jesus
called them, 22and at once they left the
boat and their father, and went with him.

Jesus Teaches, Preaches, and Heals

(Lk 6.17–19)

23 Jesus went all over Galilee, teaching in
the synagogues, preaching the Good News
about the Kingdom, and healing people
who had all kinds of disease and sickness.
24The news about him spread through the
whole country of Syria, so that people
brought to him all those who were sick,
suffering from all kinds of diseases and
disorders: people with demons, and
epileptics, and paralytics – and Jesus healed
them all. 25Large crowds followed him
from Galilee and the Ten Towns, from
Jerusalem, Judea, and the land on the other
side of the Jordan.

THE SERMON ON THE MOUNT
5.1—7.29

5 Jesus saw the crowds and went up a hill, where he sat down. His disciples gathered round him, [2]and he began to teach them:

True Happiness
(Lk 6.20–23)

3 "Happy are those who know they are
spiritually poor;
the Kingdom of heaven belongs to
them!
4 Happy are those who mourn;
God will comfort them!
5 Happy are those who are humble;
they will receive what God has
promised!
6 Happy are those whose greatest desire is
to do what God requires;
God will satisfy them fully!
7 Happy are those who are merciful to
others;
God will be merciful to them!
8 Happy are the pure in heart;
they will see God!
9 Happy are those who work for peace;
God will call them his children!
10 Happy are those who are persecuted
because they do what God requires;
the Kingdom of heaven belongs to
them!

11 "Happy are you when people insult you and persecute you and tell all kinds of evil lies against you because you are my followers. [12]Be happy and glad, for a great reward is kept for you in heaven. This is how the prophets who lived before you were persecuted.

Salt and Light
(Mk 9.50; Lk 14.34–35)

13 "You are like salt for the whole human race. But if salt loses its saltiness, there is no way to make it salty again. It has become worthless, so it is thrown out and people trample on it.

14 "You are like light for the whole world. A city built on a hill cannot be hidden. [15]No one lights a lamp and puts it under a bowl; instead he puts it on the lampstand, where it gives light for everyone in the house. [16]In the same way your light must shine before people, so that they will see the good things you do and praise your Father in heaven.

Teaching about the Law

17 "Do not think that I have come to do away with the Law of Moses and the teachings of the prophets. I have not come to do away with them, but to make their teachings come true. [18]Remember that as long as heaven and earth last, not the least point nor the smallest detail of the Law will be done away with – not until the end of all things.[a] [19]So then, whoever disobeys even the least important of the commandments and teaches others to do the same, will be least in the Kingdom of heaven. On the other hand, whoever obeys the Law and teaches others to do the same, will be great in the Kingdom of heaven. [20]I tell you, then, that you will be able to enter the Kingdom of heaven only if you are more faithful than the teachers of the Law and the Pharisees in doing what God requires.

Teaching about Anger
(Lk 12.57–59)

21 "You have heard that people were told in the past, 'Do not commit murder; anyone who does will be brought to trial.' [22]But now I tell you: whoever is angry[b] with his brother will be brought to trial, whoever calls his brother 'You good-for-nothing!' will be brought before the Council, and whoever calls his brother a worthless fool will be in danger of going to the fire of hell. [23]So if you are about to offer your gift to God at the altar and there you remember that your brother has something against you, [24]leave your gift there in front of the altar, go at once and make peace with your brother, and then come back and offer your gift to God.

[a] **5.18** the end of all things; *or* all its teachings come true.
[b] **5.22** whoever is angry; *some manuscripts have* whoever without cause is angry

25 "If someone brings a lawsuit against you
and takes you to court, settle the dispute
with him while there is time, before you get
to court. Once you are there, he will hand
you over to the judge, who will hand you
over to the police, and you will be put in
jail. [26]There you will stay, I tell you, until
you pay the last penny of your fine.

Teaching about Adultery

27 "You have heard that it was said, 'Do not
commit adultery.' [28]But now I tell you:
anyone who looks at a woman and wants to
possess her is guilty of committing adultery
with her in his heart. [29]So if your right eye
causes you to sin, take it out and throw it
away! It is much better for you to lose a part
of your body than to have your whole body
thrown into hell. [30]If your right hand
causes you to sin, cut it off and throw it
away! It is much better for you to lose one
of your limbs than for your whole body to
go to hell.

Teaching about Divorce

(Mt 19.9; Mk 10.11–12; Lk 16.18)

31 "It was also said, 'Anyone who divorces
his wife must give her a written notice of
divorce.' [32]But now I tell you: if a man
divorces his wife, for any cause other than
her unfaithfulness, then he is guilty of
making her commit adultery if she marries
again; and the man who marries her
commits adultery also.

Teaching about Vows

33 "You have also heard that people were
told in the past, 'Do not break your
promise, but do what you have vowed to
the Lord to do.' [34]But now I tell you: do
not use any vow when you make a
promise. Do not swear by heaven, for it is
God's throne; [35]nor by earth, for it is the
resting place for his feet; nor by
Jerusalem, for it is the city of the great
King. [36]Do not even swear by your head,
because you cannot make a single hair
white or black. [37]Just say 'Yes' or 'No' –
anything else you say comes from the Evil
One.

Teaching about Revenge

(Lk 6.29–30)

38 "You have heard that it was said, 'An eye
for an eye, and a tooth for a tooth.' [39]But
now I tell you: do not take revenge on
someone who wrongs you. If anyone slaps
you on the right cheek, let him slap your left
cheek too. [40]And if someone takes you to
court to sue you for your shirt, let him have
your coat as well. [41]And if one of the
occupation troops forces you to carry his
pack one kilometre, carry it two kilometres.
[42]When someone asks you for something,
give it to him; when someone wants to
borrow something, lend it to him.

Love for Enemies

(Lk 6.27–28, 32–36)

43 "You have heard that it was said, 'Love
your friends, hate your enemies.' [44]But now
I tell you: love your enemies and pray for
those who persecute you, [45]so that you
may become the children of your Father in
heaven. For he makes his sun to shine on
bad and good people alike, and gives rain to
those who do good and to those who do
evil. [46]Why should God reward you if you
love only the people who love you? Even
the tax collectors do that! [47]And if you
speak only to your friends, have you done
anything out of the ordinary? Even the
pagans do that! [48]You must be perfect – just
as your Father in heaven is perfect!

Teaching about Charity

6 "Make certain you do not perform your
religious duties in public so that people
will see what you do. If you do these
things publicly, you will not have any
reward from your Father in heaven.
2 "So when you give something to a needy
person, do not make a big show of it, as the
hypocrites do in the houses of worship and
on the streets. They do it so that people will
praise them. I assure you, they have already
been paid in full. [3]But when you help a
needy person, do it in such a way that even
your closest friend will not know about it.
[4]Then it will be a private matter. And your
Father, who sees what you do in private, will
reward you.

Jesus taught his disciples how they should pray.

Teaching about Prayer

(Lk 11.2–4)

5 "When you pray, do not be like the hypocrites! They love to stand up and pray in the houses of worship and on the street corners, so that everyone will see them. I assure you, they have already been paid in
full. 6But when you pray, go to your room, close the door, and pray to your Father, who is unseen. And your Father, who sees what you do in private, will reward you.
7 "When you pray, do not use a lot of meaningless words, as the pagans do, who think that their gods will hear them
because their prayers are long. 8Do not be like them. Your Father already knows what
you need before you ask him. 9This, then,
is how you should pray:

'Our Father in heaven:
May your holy name be honoured;
10 may your Kingdom come;
may your will be done on earth as it is in heaven.
11 Give us today the food we need.[a]
12 Forgive us the wrongs we have done,
as we forgive the wrongs that others have done to us.
13 Do not bring us to hard testing,
but keep us safe from the Evil One.'[b]

14 "If you forgive others the wrongs they have done to you, your Father in heaven
will also forgive you. 15But if you do not forgive others, then your Father will not forgive the wrongs you have done.

Teaching about Fasting

16 "And when you fast, do not put on a sad face as the hypocrites do. They neglect their appearance so that everyone will see that they are fasting. I assure you, they
have already been paid in full. 17When
you go without food, wash your face and
comb your hair, 18so that others cannot
know that you are fasting – only your Father, who is unseen, will know. And your Father, who sees what you do in private, will reward you.

Riches in Heaven

(Lk 12.33–34)

19 "Do not store up riches for yourselves here on earth, where moths and rust destroy, and robbers break in and steal.
20Instead, store up riches for yourselves in heaven, where moths and rust cannot destroy, and robbers cannot break in and
steal. 21For your heart will always be where your riches are.

The Light of the Body

(Lk 11.34–36)

22 "The eyes are like a lamp for the body. If your eyes are sound, your whole body will
be full of light; 23but if your eyes are no good, your body will be in darkness. So if the light in you is darkness, how terribly dark it will be!

God and Possessions

(Lk 16.13; 12.22–31)

24 "No one can be a slave of two masters; he will hate one and love the other; he will be loyal to one and despise the other. You cannot serve both God and money.
25 "This is why I tell you not to be worried about the food and drink you need in order

[a] **6.11** we need; *or* for today; *or* for tomorrow.

[b] **6.13** *Some manuscripts add* For yours is the kingdom, and the power, and the glory for ever. Amen.

to stay alive, or about clothes for your
body. After all, isn't life worth more than
food? And isn't the body worth more than
clothes? [26]Look at the birds: they do not
sow seeds, gather a harvest and put it in
barns; yet your Father in heaven takes care
of them! Aren't you worth much more than
birds? [27]Can any of you live a bit longer[a]
by worrying about it?
28 "And why worry about clothes? Look
how the wild flowers grow: they do not
work or make clothes for themselves. [29]But
I tell you that not even King Solomon with
all his wealth had clothes as beautiful as
one of these flowers. [30]It is God who
clothes the wild grass – grass that is here
today and gone tomorrow, burnt up in the
oven. Won't he be all the more sure to
clothe you? How little faith you have!
31 "So do not start worrying: 'Where will
my food come from? or my drink? or my
clothes?' [32](These are the things the pagans
are always concerned about.) Your Father in
heaven knows that you need all these
things. [33]Instead, be concerned above
everything else with the Kingdom of God
and with what he requires of you, and he
will provide you with all these other things.
[34]So do not worry about tomorrow; it will
have enough worries of its own. There is no
need to add to the troubles each day brings.

Judging Others
(Lk 6.37–38, 41–42)

7 "Do not judge
others, so that God
will not judge you,
[2]for God will judge you
in the same way as you
judge others, and he
will apply to you the
same rules you apply to
others. [3]Why, then, do
you look at the speck in
your brother's eye, and
pay no attention to the
log in your own eye?
[4]How dare you say to your brother, 'Please,
let me take that speck out of your eye,'
when you have a log in your own eye? [5]You
hypocrite! First take the log out of your
own eye, and then you will be able to see
clearly to take the speck out of your
brother's eye.
6 "Do not give what is holy to dogs – they
will only turn and attack you. Do not
throw your pearls in front of pigs – they
will only trample them underfoot.

Ask, Seek, Knock
(Lk 11.9–13)

7 "Ask, and you will receive; seek, and you
will find; knock, and the door will be
opened to you. [8]For everyone who asks will
receive, and anyone who seeks will find,
and the door will be opened to those who
knock. [9]Would any of you who are fathers
give your son a stone when he asks for
bread? [10]Or would you give him a snake
when he asks for a fish? [11]Bad as you are,
you know how to give good things to your
children. How much more, then, will your
Father in heaven give good things to those
who ask him!
12 "Do for others what you want them to
do for you: this is the meaning of the Law
of Moses and of the teachings of the
prophets.

Jesus said that as a father listens to his children when they seek help, so God too listens to his people.

[a] **6.27** live a bit longer; *or* grow a bit taller.

The Narrow Gate
(Lk 13.24)

13 "Go in through the narrow gate, because
the gate to hell is wide and the road that
leads to it is easy, and there are many who
travel it. 14But the gate to life is narrow and
the way that leads to it is hard, and there
are few people who find it.

A Tree and its Fruit
(Lk 6.43–44)

15 "Be on your guard against false prophets;
they come to you looking like sheep on the
outside, but on the inside they are really
like wild wolves. 16You will know them by
what they do. Thorn bushes do not bear
grapes, and briars do not bear figs. 17A
healthy tree bears good fruit, but a poor
tree bears bad fruit. 18A healthy tree cannot
bear bad fruit, and a poor tree cannot bear
good fruit. 19And any tree that does not
bear good fruit is cut down and thrown in
the fire. 20So then, you will know the false
prophets by what they do.

I Never Knew You
(Lk 13.25–27)

21 "Not everyone who calls me 'Lord, Lord'
will enter the Kingdom of heaven, but only
those who do what my Father in heaven
wants them to do. 22When Judgement Day
comes, many will say to me, 'Lord, Lord! In
your name we spoke God's message, by
your name we drove out many demons and
performed many miracles!' 23Then I will
say to them, 'I never knew you. Get away
from me, you wicked people!'

The Two House Builders
(Lk 6.47–49)

24 "So then, anyone who hears these words
of mine and obeys them is like a wise man
who built his house on rock. 25The rain
poured down, the rivers overflowed, and
the wind blew hard against that house. But
it did not fall, because it was built on rock.
26 "But anyone who hears these words of
mine and does not obey them is like a
foolish man who built his house on sand.
27The rain poured down, the rivers
overflowed, the wind blew hard against
that house, and it fell. And what a terrible
fall that was!"

The Authority of Jesus

28 When Jesus finished saying these things,
the crowd was amazed at the way he
taught. 29He wasn't like the teachers of the
Law; instead, he taught with authority.

Jesus Heals a Man
(Mk 1.40–45; Lk 5.12–16)

8 When Jesus came down from the hill,
large crowds followed him. 2Then a
man suffering from a dreaded skin
disease came to him, knelt down before
him, and said, "Sir, if you want to, you can
make me clean."[a]
3 Jesus stretched out his hand and touched
him. "I do want to," he answered. "Be
clean!" At once the man was healed of his
disease. 4Then Jesus said to him, "Listen!
Don't tell anyone, but go straight to the
priest and let him examine you; then in
order to prove to everyone that you are
cured, offer the sacrifice that Moses
ordered."

Jesus Heals a Roman Officer's Servant
(Lk 7.1–10)

5 When Jesus entered Capernaum, a Roman
officer met him and begged for help: 6"Sir,
my servant is sick in bed at home, unable
to move and suffering terribly."
7 "I will go and make him well," Jesus said.
8 "Oh no, sir," answered the officer. "I do
not deserve to have you come into my
house. Just give the order, and my servant
will get well. 9I, too, am a man under the
authority of superior officers, and I have
soldiers under me. I order this one, 'Go!'
and he goes; and I order that one, 'Come!'
and he comes; and I order my slave, 'Do
this!' and he does it."
10 When Jesus heard this, he was surprised
and said to the people following him, "I tell
you, I have never found anyone in Israel
with faith like this. 11I assure you that
many will come from the east and the west

[a] **8.2** MAKE ME CLEAN: *This disease was considered to make a person ritually unclean.*

and sit down with Abraham, Isaac, and
Jacob at the feast in the Kingdom of heaven.
12But those who should be in the Kingdom
will be thrown out into the darkness, where
they will cry and grind their teeth." 13Then
Jesus said to the officer, "Go home, and
what you believe will be done for you."
And the officer's servant was healed that
very moment.

Jesus Heals Many People
(Mk 1.29–34; Lk 4.38–41)

14 Jesus went to Peter's home, and there he
saw Peter's mother-in-law sick in bed with a
fever. 15He touched her hand; the fever left
her, and she got up and began to wait on
him.
16 When evening came, people brought to
Jesus many who had demons in them. Jesus
drove out the evil spirits with a word and
healed all who were sick. 17He did this to
make what the prophet Isaiah had said
come true, "He himself took our sickness
and carried away our diseases."

The Would-be Followers of Jesus
(Lk 9.57–62)

18 When Jesus noticed the crowd round
him, he ordered his disciples to go to the
other side of the lake. 19A teacher of the
Law came to him. "Teacher," he said, "I am
ready to go with you wherever you go."
20 Jesus answered him, "Foxes have holes,
and birds have nests, but the Son of Man
has nowhere to lie down and rest."
21 Another man, who was a disciple, said,
"Sir, first let me go back and bury my
father."
22 "Follow me," Jesus answered, "and let the
dead bury their own dead."

Jesus Calms a Storm
(Mk 4.35–41; Lk 8.22–25)

23 Jesus got into a boat, and his disciples
went with him. 24Suddenly a fierce storm
hit the lake, and the boat was in danger of
sinking. But Jesus was asleep. 25The
disciples went to him and woke him up.
"Save us, Lord!" they said. "We are about
to die!"
26 "Why are you so frightened?" Jesus
answered. "How little faith you have!"
Then he got up and ordered the winds
and the waves to stop, and there was a
great calm.
27 Everyone was amazed. "What kind of
man is this?" they said. "Even the winds
and the waves obey him!"

Jesus Heals Two Men with Demons
(Mk 5.1–20; Lk 8.26–39)

28 When Jesus came to the territory of
Gadara on the other side of the lake, he
was met by two men who came out of the
burial caves there. These men had demons
in them and were so fierce that no one
dared travel on that road. 29At once they
screamed, "What do you want with us,
you Son of God? Have you come to
punish us before the right time?"
30 Not far away there was a large herd of
pigs feeding. 31So the demons begged
Jesus, "If you are going to drive us out,
send us into that herd of pigs."
32 "Go," Jesus told them; so they left and
went off into the pigs. The whole herd
rushed down the side of the cliff into the
lake and was drowned.
33 The men who had been taking care of
the pigs ran away and went into the town,
where they told the whole story and what
had happened to the men with the
demons. 34So everyone from the town
went out to meet Jesus; and when they
saw him, they begged him to leave their
territory.

Jesus Heals a Paralysed Man
(Mk 2.1–12; Lk 5.17–26)

9 Jesus got into the boat and went back
across the lake to his own town,[a]
2where some people brought to him
a paralysed man, lying on a bed. When
Jesus saw how much faith they had, he
said to the paralysed man, "Courage, my
son! Your sins are forgiven."
3 Then some teachers of the Law said to
themselves, "This man is speaking
blasphemy!"

[a] **9.1** HIS OWN TOWN: *Capernaum (see 4.13).*

4 Jesus perceived what they were thinking,
so he said, "Why are you thinking such evil
things? [5]Is it easier to say, 'Your sins are
forgiven,' or to say, 'Get up and walk'? [6]I
will prove to you, then, that the Son of
Man has authority on earth to forgive sins."
So he said to the paralysed man, "Get up,
pick up your bed, and go home!"
7 The man got up and went home. [8]When
the people saw it, they were afraid, and
praised God for giving such authority to
people.

Jesus Calls Matthew

(Mk 2.13–17; Lk 5.27–32)

9 Jesus left that place, and as he walked
along, he saw a tax collector, named
Matthew, sitting in his office. He said to
him, "Follow me."

Matthew got up and followed him.

10 While Jesus was having a meal in
Matthew's house,[a] many tax collectors and
other outcasts came and joined Jesus and
his disciples at the table. [11]Some Pharisees
saw this and asked his disciples, "Why does
your teacher eat with such people?"
12 Jesus heard them and answered, "People
who are well do not need a doctor, but only
those who are sick. [13]Go and find out what
is meant by the scripture that says: 'It is
kindness that I want, not animal sacrifices.'
I have not come to call respectable people,
but outcasts."

The Question about Fasting

(Mk 2.18–22; Lk 5.33–39)

14 Then the followers of John the Baptist
came to Jesus, asking, "Why is it that we
and the Pharisees fast often, but your
disciples don't fast at all?"
15 Jesus answered, "Do you expect the
guests at a wedding party to be sad as long
as the bridegroom is with them? Of course
not! But the day will come when the
bridegroom will be taken away from them,
and then they will fast.
16 "No one patches up an old coat with a
piece of new cloth, for the new patch will
shrink and make an even bigger hole in the
coat. [17]Nor does anyone pour new wine
into used wineskins, for the skins will burst,
the wine will pour out, and the skins will be
ruined. Instead, new wine is poured into
fresh wineskins, and both will keep in good
condition."

The Official's Daughter and the Woman who Touched Jesus' Cloak

(Mk 5.21–43; Lk 8.40–56)

18 While Jesus was saying this, a Jewish
official came to him, knelt down before
him, and said, "My daughter has just died;
but come and place your hands on her, and
she will live."
19 So Jesus got up and followed him, and
his disciples went along with him.
20 A woman who had suffered from severe
bleeding for twelve years came up behind
Jesus and touched the edge of his cloak.
[21]She said to herself, "If I only touch his
cloak, I will get well."
22 Jesus turned round and saw her, and
said, "Courage, my daughter! Your faith has
made you well." At that very moment the
woman became well.
23 Then Jesus went into the official's house.
When he saw the musicians for the funeral
and the people all stirred up, [24]he said,
"Get out, everybody! The little girl is not
dead – she is only sleeping!" Then they all
laughed at him. [25]But as soon as the people
had been put out, Jesus went into the girl's
room and took hold of her hand, and she
got up. [26]The news about this spread all
over that part of the country.

Jesus Heals Two Blind Men

27 Jesus left that place, and as he walked
along, two blind men started following
him. "Take pity on us, Son of David!" they
shouted.
28 When Jesus had gone indoors, the two
blind men came to him, and he asked
them, "Do you believe that I can heal you?"

"Yes, sir!" they answered.

29 Then Jesus touched their eyes and said,
"Let it happen, then, just as you believe!" –
[30]and their sight was restored. Jesus spoke
sternly to them, "Don't tell this to
anyone!"

[a] **9.10** in Matthew's house; *or* in his (*that is,* Jesus') house.

Jesus healed two blind men.

31 But they left and spread the news about
Jesus all over that part of the country.

Jesus Heals a Man who could not Speak

32 As the men were leaving, some people
brought to Jesus a man who could not talk
because he had a demon. [33]But as soon as
the demon was driven out, the man started
talking, and everyone was amazed. "We
have never seen anything like this in
Israel!" they exclaimed.
34 But the Pharisees said, "It is the chief of
the demons who gives Jesus the power to
drive out demons."

Jesus has Pity for the People

35 Jesus went round visiting all the towns
and villages. He taught in the synagogues,
preached the Good News about the
Kingdom, and healed people with every
kind of disease and sickness. [36]As he saw
the crowds, his heart was filled with pity
for them, because they were worried and
helpless, like sheep without a shepherd.
[37]So he said to his disciples, "The harvest is
large, but there are few workers to gather it
in. [38]Pray to the owner of the harvest that
he will send out workers to gather in his
harvest."

The Twelve Apostles

(Mk 3.13–19; Lk 6.12–16)

10 Jesus called his twelve disciples
together and gave them authority to
drive out evil spirits and to heal every
disease and every sickness. [2]These are the
names of the twelve apostles: first, Simon
(called Peter) and his brother Andrew;
James and his brother John, the sons of
Zebedee; [3]Philip and Bartholomew;
Thomas and Matthew, the tax collector;
James son of Alphaeus, and Thaddaeus;
[4]Simon the Patriot, and Judas Iscariot, who
betrayed Jesus.

The Mission of the Twelve

(Mk 6.7–13; Lk 9.1–6)

5 These twelve men were sent out by Jesus
with the following instructions: "Do not go
to any Gentile territory or any Samaritan
towns. [6]Instead, you are to go to the lost
sheep of the people of Israel. [7]Go and
preach, 'The Kingdom of heaven is near!'
[8]Heal the sick, bring the dead back to life,
heal those who suffer from dreaded skin
diseases, and drive out demons. You have
received without paying, so give without
being paid. [9]Do not carry any gold, silver,
or copper money in your pockets; [10]do not
carry a beggar's bag for the journey or an
extra shirt or shoes or a stick. Workers
should be given what they need.
11 "When you come to a town or village, go
in and look for someone who is willing to
welcome you, and stay with him until you
leave that place. [12]When you go into a
house, say, 'Peace be with you.' [13]If the
people in that house welcome you, let your
greeting of peace remain; but if they do not
welcome you, then take back your greeting.
[14]And if some home or town will not
welcome you or listen to you, then leave
that place and shake the dust off your feet.

[15]I assure you that on the Judgement Day
God will show more mercy to the people of
Sodom and Gomorrah than to the people of
that town!

Coming Persecutions

(Mk 13.9–13; Lk 21.12–17)

16 "Listen! I am sending you out just like
sheep to a pack of wolves. You must be as
cautious as snakes and as gentle as doves.
[17]Watch out, for there will be those who
will arrest you and take you to court, and
they will whip you in the synagogues.
[18]For my sake you will be brought to trial
before rulers and kings, to tell the Good
News to them and to the Gentiles. [19]When
they bring you to trial, do not worry about
what you are going to say or how you will
say it; when the time comes, you will be
given what you will say. [20]For the words
you will speak will not be yours; they will
come from the Spirit of your Father
speaking through you.
21 "Men will hand over their own brothers
to be put to death, and fathers will do the
same to their children; children will turn
against their parents and have them put to
death. [22]Everyone will hate you because of
me. But whoever holds out to the end will be
saved. [23]When they persecute you in one
town, run away to another one. I assure you
that you will not finish your work in all the
towns of Israel before the Son of Man comes.
24 "No pupil is greater than his teacher; no
slave is greater than his master. [25]So a pupil
should be satisfied to become like his
teacher, and a slave like his master. If the
head of the family is called Beelzebul, the
members of the family will be called even
worse names!

Whom to Fear

(Lk 12.2–7)

26 "So do not be afraid of people. Whatever
is now covered up will be uncovered, and
every secret will be made known. [27]What I
am telling you in the dark you must repeat
in broad daylight, and what you have
heard in private you must announce from
the housetops. [28]Do not be afraid of those
who kill the body but cannot kill the soul;
rather be afraid of God, who can destroy
both body and soul in hell. [29]For only a
penny you can buy two sparrows, yet not
one sparrow falls to the ground without
your Father's consent. [30]As for you, even
the hairs of your head have all been
counted. [31]So do not be afraid; you are
worth much more than many sparrows!

Confessing and Rejecting Christ

(Lk 12.8–9)

32 "For those who declare publicly that
they belong to me, I will do the same before
my Father in heaven. [33]But if anyone
rejects me publicly, I will reject him before
my Father in heaven.

Not Peace, but a Sword

(Lk 12.51–53; 14.26–27)

34 "Do not think that I have come to bring
peace to the world. No, I did not come to
bring peace, but a sword. [35]I came to set
sons against their fathers, daughters against
their mothers, daughters-in-law against
their mothers-in-law; [36]your worst enemies
will be the members of your own family.
37 "Those who love their father or mother
more than me are not fit to be my disciples;
those who love their son or daughter more
than me are not fit to be my disciples.
[38]Those who do not take up their cross and
follow in my steps are not fit to be my
disciples. [39]Those who try to gain their
own life will lose it; but those who lose
their life for my sake will gain it.

Rewards

(Mk 9.41)

40 "Whoever welcomes you welcomes me;
and whoever welcomes me welcomes the
one who sent me. [41]Whoever welcomes
God's messenger because he is God's
messenger, will share in his reward. And
whoever welcomes a good man because he
is good, will share in his reward. [42]You can
be sure that whoever gives even a drink of
cold water to one of the least of these my
followers because he is my follower, will
certainly receive a reward."

The Messengers from John the Baptist
(Lk 7.18–35)

11 When Jesus finished giving these
instructions to his twelve disciples, he
left that place and went off to teach
and preach in the towns near there.
2 When John the Baptist heard in prison
about the things that Christ was doing, he
sent some of his disciples to him. [3]"Tell us,"
they asked Jesus, "are you the one John said
was going to come, or should we expect
someone else?"
4 Jesus answered, "Go back and tell John
what you are hearing and seeing: [5]the blind
can see, the lame can walk, those who
suffer from dreaded skin diseases are made
clean,[a] the deaf hear, the dead are brought
back to life, and the Good News is preached
to the poor. [6]How happy are those who
have no doubts about me!"
7 While John's disciples were leaving, Jesus
spoke about him to the crowds: "When you
went out to John in the desert, what did
you expect to see? A blade of grass bending
in the wind? [8]What did you go out to see?
A man dressed up in fancy clothes? People
who dress like that live in palaces! [9]Tell me,
what did you go out to see? A prophet? Yes
indeed, but you saw much more than a
prophet. [10]For John is the one of whom the
scripture says: 'God said, I will send my
messenger ahead of you to open the way
for you.' [11]I assure you that John the
Baptist is greater than anyone who has ever
lived. But the one who is least in the
Kingdom of heaven is greater than John.
[12]From the time John preached his
message until this very day the Kingdom of
heaven has suffered violent attacks,[b] and
violent men try to seize it. [13]Until the time
of John all the prophets and the Law of
Moses spoke about the Kingdom; [14]and if
you are willing to believe their message,
John is Elijah, whose coming was
predicted. [15]Listen, then, if you have ears!
16 "Now, to what can I compare the people
of this day? They are like children sitting
in the market place. One group shouts to
the other, [17]'We played wedding music for
you, but you wouldn't dance! We sang
funeral songs, but you wouldn't cry!'
[18]When John came, he fasted and drank
no wine, and everyone said, 'He has a
demon in him!' [19]When the Son of Man
came, he ate and drank, and everyone
said, 'Look at this man! He is a glutton and
a drinker, a friend of tax collectors and
other outcasts!' God's wisdom, however, is
shown to be true by its results."

The Unbelieving Towns
(Lk 10.13–15)

20 The people in the towns where Jesus
had performed most of his miracles did
not turn from their sins, so he reproached
those towns. [21]"How terrible it will be for
you, Chorazin! How terrible for you too,
Bethsaida! If the miracles which were
performed in you had been performed in
Tyre and Sidon, the people there would
long ago have put on sackcloth and
sprinkled ashes on themselves, to show
that they had turned from their sins! [22]I
assure you that on the Judgement Day
God will show more mercy to the people
of Tyre and Sidon than to you! [23]And as
for you, Capernaum! Did you want to lift
yourself up to heaven? You will be thrown
down to hell! If the miracles which were
performed in you had been performed in
Sodom, it would still be in existence
today! [24]You can be sure that on the
Judgement Day God will show more
mercy to Sodom than to you!"

Come to Me and Rest
(Lk 10.21–22)

25 At that time Jesus said, "Father, Lord of
heaven and earth! I thank you because you
have shown to the unlearned what you
have hidden from the wise and learned.
[26]Yes, Father, this was how you wanted it to
happen.
27 "My Father has given me all things. No
one knows the Son except the Father, and
no one knows the Father except the Son
and those to whom the Son chooses to
reveal him.

[a] **11.5** MADE CLEAN: *See 8.2.*
[b] **11.12** has suffered violent attacks; *or* has been coming violently.

28 "Come to me, all of you who are tired
from carrying heavy loads, and I will give
you rest. [29]Take my yoke and put it on you,
and learn from me, because I am gentle and
humble in spirit; and you will find rest.
[30]For the yoke I will give you is easy, and the
load I will put on you is light."

The Question about the Sabbath
(Mk 2.23–28; Lk 6.1–5)

12 Not long afterwards Jesus was walking
through some cornfields on the
Sabbath. His disciples were hungry, so
they began to pick ears of corn and eat the
grain. [2]When the Pharisees saw this, they
said to Jesus, "Look, it is against our Law for
your disciples to do this on the Sabbath!"
3 Jesus answered, "Have you never read
what David did that time when he and his
men were hungry? [4]He went into the
house of God, and he and his men ate the
bread offered to God, even though it was
against the Law for them to eat it – only
the priests were allowed to eat that bread.
[5]Or have you not read in the Law of Moses
that every Sabbath the priests in the
Temple actually break the Sabbath law, yet
they are not guilty? [6]I tell you that there is
something here greater than the Temple.
[7]The scripture says, 'It is kindness that I
want, not animal sacrifices.' If you really
knew what this means, you would not
condemn people who are not guilty; [8]for
the Son of Man is Lord of the Sabbath."

The Man with a Paralysed Hand
(Mk 3.1–6; Lk 6.6–11)

9 Jesus left that place and went to a
synagogue, [10]where there was a man who
had a paralysed hand. Some people were
there who wanted to accuse Jesus of doing
wrong, so they asked him, "Is it against our
Law to heal on the Sabbath?"
11 Jesus answered, "What if one of you has
a sheep and it falls into a deep hole on the
Sabbath? Will you not take hold of it and
lift it out? [12]And a human being is worth
much more than a sheep! So then, our Law
does allow us to help someone on the
Sabbath." [13]Then he said to the man with
the paralysed hand, "Stretch out your
hand."

He stretched it out, and it became well
again, just like the other one. [14]Then the
Pharisees left and made plans to kill Jesus.

Jesus told the parable of the sheep to teach people to respect others.

God's Chosen Servant

15 When Jesus heard about the plot against
him, he went away from that place; and
large crowds followed him. He healed all
those who were ill [16]and gave them orders
not to tell others about him. [17]He did this
so as to make what God had said through
the prophet Isaiah come true:

18 "Here is my servant, whom I have chosen,
the one I love, and with whom I am pleased.
I will send my Spirit upon him,
and he will announce my judgement to the nations.
19 He will not argue or shout,
or make loud speeches in the streets.
20 He will not break off a bent reed,
or put out a flickering lamp.

He will persist until he causes justice to
triumph,
21 and in him all peoples will put their
hope."

Jesus and Beelzebul

(Mk 3.20–30; Lk 11.14–23)

22 Then some people brought to Jesus a
man who was blind and could not talk
because he had a demon. Jesus healed the
man, so that he was able to talk and see.
23The crowds were all amazed at what Jesus
had done. "Could he be the Son of David?"
they asked.
24 When the Pharisees heard this, they
replied, "He drives out demons only
because their ruler Beelzebul gives him
power to do so."
25 Jesus knew what they were thinking, so
he said to them, "Any country that divides
itself into groups which fight each other
will not last very long. And any town or
family that divides itself into groups which
fight each other will fall apart. 26So if one
group is fighting another in Satan's
kingdom, this means that it is already
divided into groups and will soon fall apart!
27You say that I drive out demons because
Beelzebul gives me the power to do so. Well,
then, who gives your followers the power to
drive them out? What your own followers
do proves that you are wrong! 28No, it is not
Beelzebul, but God's Spirit, who gives me
the power to drive out demons, which
proves that the Kingdom of God has already
come upon you.
29 "No one can break into a strong man's
house and take away his belongings unless
he first ties up the strong man; then he can
plunder his house.
30 "Anyone who is not for me is really
against me; anyone who does not help me
gather is really scattering. 31And so I tell
you that people can be forgiven any sin and
any evil thing they say;[a] but whoever says
evil things against the Holy Spirit will not
be forgiven. 32Anyone who says something
against the Son of Man can be forgiven; but
whoever says something against the Holy
Spirit will not be forgiven – now or ever.

A Tree and its Fruit

(Lk 6.43–45)

33 "To have good fruit you must have a
healthy tree; if you have a poor tree, you
will have bad fruit. A tree is known by the
kind of fruit it bears. 34You snakes – how
can you say good things when you are evil?
For the mouth speaks what the heart is full
of. 35A good person brings good things out
of a treasure of good things; a bad person
brings bad things out of a treasure of bad
things.
36 "You can be sure that on Judgement Day
everyone will have to give account of every
useless word he has ever spoken. 37Your
words will be used to judge you – to declare
you either innocent or guilty."

The Demand for a Miracle

(Mk 8.11–12; Lk 11.29–32)

38 Then some teachers of the Law and some
Pharisees spoke up. "Teacher," they said,
"we want to see you perform a miracle."
39 "How evil and godless are the people of
this day!" Jesus exclaimed. "You ask me for
a miracle? No! The only miracle you will be
given is the miracle of the prophet Jonah.
40In the same way that Jonah spent three
days and nights in the big fish, so will the
Son of Man spend three days and nights in
the depths of the earth. 41On Judgement
Day the people of Nineveh will stand up
and accuse you, because they turned from
their sins when they heard Jonah preach;
and I tell you that there is something here
greater than Jonah! 42On Judgement Day
the Queen of Sheba will stand up and
accuse you, because she travelled all the
way from her country to listen to King
Solomon's wise teaching; and I assure you
that there is something here greater than
Solomon!

The Return of the Evil Spirit

(Lk 11.24–26)

43 "When an evil spirit goes out of a person,
it travels over dry country looking for a
place to rest. If it can't find one, 44it says to
itself, 'I will go back to my house.' So it goes
back and finds the house empty, clean, and

[a] **12.31** evil thing they say; *or* evil thing they say against God.

all tidy. [45]Then it goes out and brings along
seven other spirits even worse than itself,
and they come and live there. So when it is
all over, that person is in a worse state than
he was at the beginning. This is what will
happen to the evil people of this day."

Jesus' Mother and Brothers

(Mk 3.31–35; Lk 8.19–21)

46 Jesus was still talking to the people when
his mother and brothers arrived. They
stood outside, asking to speak with him.
[47]So one of the people there said to him,
"Look, your mother and brothers are
standing outside, and they want to speak
with you."[a]
48 Jesus answered, "Who is my mother?
Who are my brothers?" [49]Then he pointed
to his disciples and said, "Look! Here are
my mother and my brothers! [50]Whoever
does what my Father in heaven wants him
to do is my brother, my sister, and my
mother."

The Parable of the Sower

(Mk 4.1–9; Lk 8.4–8)

13 That same day Jesus left the house and
went to the lakeside, where he sat
down to teach. [2]The crowd that
gathered round him was so large that he
got into a boat and sat in it, while the
crowd stood on the shore. [3]He used
parables to tell them many things.

"Once there was a man who went out to
sow corn. [4]As he scattered the seed in the
field, some of it fell along the path, and the
birds came and ate it up. [5]Some of it fell on
rocky ground, where there was little soil.
The seeds soon sprouted, because the soil
wasn't deep. [6]But when the sun came up, it
burnt the young plants; and because the
roots had not grown deep enough, the
plants soon dried up. [7]Some of the seed fell
among thorn bushes, which grew up and
choked the plants. [8]But some seeds fell in
good soil, and the plants produced corn;
some produced a hundred grains, others
sixty, and others thirty."
9 And Jesus concluded, "Listen, then, if
you have ears!"

The Purpose of the Parables

(Mk 4.10–12; Lk 8.9–10)

10 Then the disciples came to Jesus and
asked him, "Why do you use parables when
you talk to the people?"
11 Jesus answered, "The knowledge about
the secrets of the Kingdom of heaven has
been given to you, but not to them. [12]For
the person who has something will be given
more, so that he will have more than
enough; but the person who has nothing
will have taken away from him even the
little he has. [13]The reason I use parables in
talking to them is that they look, but do not
see, and they listen, but do not hear or
understand. [14]So the prophecy of Isaiah
applies to them:

'This people will listen and listen, but
not understand;
they will look and look, but not see,
15 because their minds are dull,
and they have stopped up their ears
and have closed their eyes.
Otherwise, their eyes would see,
their ears would hear,
their minds would understand,
and they would turn to me, says God,
and I would heal them.'

16 "As for you, how fortunate you are!
Your eyes see and your ears hear. [17]I assure
you that many prophets and many of
God's people wanted very much to see
what you see, but they could not, and to
hear what you hear, but they did not.

Jesus Explains the Parable of the Sower

(Mk 4.13–20; Lk 8.11–15)

18 "Listen, then, and learn what the parable
of the sower means. [19]Those who hear the
message about the Kingdom but do not
understand it are like the seeds that fell
along the path. The Evil One comes and
snatches away what was sown in them.
[20]The seeds that fell on rocky ground stand
for those who receive the message gladly as
soon as they hear it. [21]But it does not sink
deep into them, and they don't last long. So

[a] **12.47** *Some manuscripts do not have verse 47.*

when trouble or persecution comes because
of the message, they give up at once. [22]The
seeds that fell among thorn bushes stand for
those who hear the message; but the worries
about this life and the love for riches choke
the message, and they don't bear fruit.
[23]And the seeds sown in the good soil stand
for those who hear the message and
understand it: they bear fruit, some as much
as a hundred, others sixty, and others
thirty."

The Parable of the Weeds

24 Jesus told them another parable: "The
Kingdom of heaven is like this. A man
sowed good seed in his field. [25]One night,
when everyone was asleep, an enemy
came and sowed weeds among the wheat
and went away. [26]When the plants grew
and the ears of corn began to form, then
the weeds showed up. [27]The man's
servants came to him and said, 'Sir, it was
good seed you sowed in your field; where
did the weeds come from?' [28]'It was some
enemy who did this,' he answered. 'Do
you want us to go and pull up the weeds?'
they asked him. [29]'No,' he answered,
'because as you gather the weeds you
might pull up some of the wheat along
with them. [30]Let the wheat and the weeds
both grow together until harvest. Then I
will tell the harvest workers to pull up the
weeds first, tie them in bundles and burn
them, and then to gather in the wheat
and put it in my barn.' "

The Parable of the Mustard Seed

(Mk 4.30–32; Lk 13.18–19)

31 Jesus told them another parable: "The
Kingdom of heaven is like this. A man
takes a mustard seed and sows it in his
field. [32]It is the smallest of all seeds, but
when it grows up, it is the biggest of all
plants. It becomes a tree, so that birds
come and make their nests in its
branches."

The Parable of the Yeast

(Lk 13.20–21)

33 Jesus told them still another parable: "The
Kingdom of heaven is like this. A woman
takes some yeast and mixes it with forty
litres of flour until the whole batch of
dough rises."

Jesus' Use of Parables

(Mk 4.33–34)

34 Jesus used parables to tell all these things
to the crowds; he would not say a thing to
them without using a parable. [35]He did
this to make what the prophet had said
come true:

"I will use parables when I speak to
them;
I will tell them things unknown
since the creation of the world."

Jesus Explains the Parable of the Weeds

36 When Jesus had left the crowd and gone
indoors, his disciples came to him and said,
"Tell us what the parable about the weeds
in the field means."
37 Jesus answered, "The man who sowed
the good seed is the Son of Man; [38]the field
is the world; the good seed is the people
who belong to the Kingdom; the weeds are
the people who belong to the Evil One;
[39]and the enemy who sowed the weeds is
the Devil. The harvest is the end of the age,
and the harvest workers are angels. [40]Just
as the weeds are gathered up and burnt in
the fire, so the same thing will happen at
the end of the age: [41]the Son of Man will
send out his angels to gather up out of his
Kingdom all those who cause people to sin
and all others who do evil things, [42]and
they will throw them into the fiery
furnace, where they will cry and grind their
teeth. [43]Then God's people will shine like
the sun in their Father's Kingdom. Listen,
then, if you have ears!

The Parable of the Hidden Treasure

44 "The Kingdom of heaven is like this. A
man happens to find a treasure hidden in a
field. He covers it up again, and is so happy
that he goes and sells everything he has,
and then goes back and buys that field.

The Parable of the Pearl

45 "Also, the Kingdom of heaven is like this.
A man is looking for fine pearls, [46]and
when he finds one that is unusually fine,
he goes and sells everything he has, and
buys that pearl.

The Parable of the Net

47 "Also, the Kingdom of heaven is like
this. Some fishermen throw their net out in
the lake and catch all kinds of fish. [48]When
the net is full, they pull it to shore and sit
down to divide the fish: the good ones go
into their buckets, the worthless ones are
thrown away. [49]It will be like this at the
end of the age: the angels will go out and
gather up the evil people from among the
good [50]and will throw them into the fiery
furnace, where they will cry and grind their
teeth.

New Truths and Old

51 "Do you understand these things?" Jesus
asked them.

"Yes," they answered.

52 So he replied, "This means, then, that
every teacher of the Law who becomes a
disciple in the Kingdom of heaven is like
the owner of a house who takes new and
old things out of his storeroom."

Jesus is Rejected at Nazareth

(Mk 6.1–6; Lk 4.16–30)

53 When Jesus finished telling these
parables, he left that place [54]and went back
to his home town. He taught in the
synagogue, and those who heard him were
amazed. "Where did he get such wisdom?"
they asked. "And what about his miracles?
[55]Isn't he the carpenter's son? Isn't Mary
his mother, and aren't James, Joseph,
Simon, and Judas his brothers? [56]Aren't all
his sisters living here? Where did he get all
this?" [57]And so they rejected him.

Jesus said to them, "A prophet is
respected everywhere except in his home
town and by his own family." [58]Because
they did not have faith, he did not perform
many miracles there.

The Death of John the Baptist

(Mk 6.14–29; Lk 9.7–9)

14 At that time Herod, the ruler of
Galilee, heard about Jesus. [2]"He is
really John the Baptist, who has come
back to life," he told his officials. "That is
why he has this power to perform
miracles."

3 For Herod had earlier ordered John's
arrest, and he had him chained and put in
prison. He had done this because of
Herodias, his brother Philip's wife. [4]For
some time John the Baptist had told Herod,
"It isn't right for you to be married to
Herodias!" [5]Herod wanted to kill him, but
he was afraid of the Jewish people, because
they considered John to be a prophet.

6 On Herod's birthday the daughter of
Herodias danced in front of the whole
group. Herod was so pleased [7]that he
promised her, "I swear that I will give you
anything you ask for!"

8 At her mother's suggestion she asked
him, "Give me here and now the head of
John the Baptist on a dish!"

9 The king was sad, but because of the
promise he had made in front of all his
guests he gave orders that her wish be
granted. [10]So he had John beheaded in
prison. [11]The head was brought in on a
dish and given to the girl, who took it to
her mother. [12]John's disciples came, carried
away his body, and buried it; then they
went and told Jesus.

Jesus Feeds a Great Crowd

(Mk 6.30–44; Lk 9.10–17; Jn 6.1–14)

13 When Jesus heard the news about John,
he left there in a boat and went to a lonely
place by himself. The people heard about it,
so they left their towns and followed him
by land. [14]Jesus got out of the boat, and
when he saw the large crowd, his heart was
filled with pity for them, and he healed
those who were ill.

15 That evening his disciples came to him
and said, "It is already very late, and this is
a lonely place. Send the people away and
let them go to the villages to buy food for
themselves."

16 “They don’t have to leave,” answered
Jesus. “You yourselves give them something
to eat!”
17 “All we have here are five loaves and two
fish,” they replied.
18 “Then bring them here to me,” Jesus
said. [19]He ordered the people to sit down
on the grass; then he took the five loaves
and the two fish, looked up to heaven,
and gave thanks to God. He broke the
loaves and gave them to the disciples, and
the disciples gave them to the people.
[20]Everyone ate and had enough. Then the
disciples took up twelve baskets full of
what was left over. [21]The number of men
who ate was about 5,000, not counting
the women and children.

Jesus performed the miracle of feeding the 5,000.

Jesus Walks on the Water
(Mk 6.45–52; Jn 6.15–21)

22 Then Jesus made the disciples get into
the boat and go on ahead to the other side
of the lake, while he sent the people away.
[23]After sending the people away, he went
up a hill by himself to pray. When evening
came, Jesus was there alone; [24]and by this
time the boat was far out in the lake,
tossed about by the waves, because the
wind was blowing against it.
25 Between three and six o’clock in the
morning Jesus came to the disciples,
walking on the water. [26]When they saw
him walking on the water, they were
terrified. “It’s a ghost!” they said, and
screamed with fear.
27 Jesus spoke to them at once. “Courage!”
he said. “It is I. Don’t be afraid!”
28 Then Peter spoke up. “Lord, if it is really
you, order me to come out on the water to
you.”
29 “Come!” answered Jesus. So Peter got out
of the boat and started walking on the
water to Jesus. [30]But when he noticed the
strong wind, he was afraid and started to
sink down in the water. “Save me, Lord!” he
cried.
31 At once Jesus reached out and grabbed
hold of him and said, “How little faith you
have! Why did you doubt?”
32 They both got into the boat, and the
wind died down. [33]Then the disciples in
the boat worshipped Jesus. “Truly you are
the Son of God!” they exclaimed.

Jesus Heals the Sick in Gennesaret
(Mk 6.53–56)

34 They crossed the lake and came to land
at Gennesaret, [35]where the people
recognized Jesus. So they sent for the sick
people in all the surrounding country and
brought them to Jesus. [36]They begged him
to let those who were ill at least touch the
edge of his cloak; and all who touched it
were made well.

The Teaching of the Ancestors
(Mk 7.1–13)

15 Then some Pharisees and teachers of
the Law came from Jerusalem to Jesus
and asked him, [2]“Why is it that your
disciples disobey the teaching handed
down by our ancestors? They don’t wash
their hands in the proper way before they
eat!”
3 Jesus answered, “And why do you

disobey God's command and follow your
own teaching? [4]For God said, 'Respect your
father and your mother,' and 'Whoever
curses his father or his mother is to be put
to death.' [5]But you teach that if a person
has something he could use to help his
father or mother, but says, 'This belongs to
God,' [6]he does not need to honour his
father.[a] In this way you disregard God's
command, in order to follow your own
teaching. [7]You hypocrites! How right Isaiah
was when he prophesied about you!

8 'These people, says God, honour me
with their words,
but their heart is really far away from
me.
9 It is no use for them to worship me,
because they teach human rules as
though they were my laws!' "

The Things that Make a Person Unclean

(Mk 7.14–23)

10 Then Jesus called the crowd to him and
said to them, "Listen and understand! [11]It
is not what goes into a person's mouth that
makes him ritually unclean; rather, what
comes out of it makes him unclean."
12 Then the disciples came to him and said,
"Do you know that the Pharisees had their
feelings hurt by what you said?"
13 "Every plant which my Father in heaven
did not plant will be pulled up," answered
Jesus. [14]"Don't worry about them! They are
blind leaders of the blind; and when one
blind man leads another, both fall into a
ditch."
15 Peter spoke up, "Explain this saying to
us."
16 Jesus said to them, "You are still no more
intelligent than the others. [17]Don't you
understand? Anything that goes into a
person's mouth goes into his stomach and
then on out of his body. [18]But the things
that come out of the mouth come from the
heart, and these are the things that make a
person ritually unclean. [19]For from his heart
come the evil ideas which lead him to kill,
commit adultery, and do other immoral
things; to rob, lie, and slander others.
[20]These are the things that make a person
unclean. But to eat without washing your
hands as they say you should – this doesn't
make a person unclean."

A Woman's Faith

(Mk 7.24–30)

21 Jesus left that place and went off to the
territory near the cities of Tyre and Sidon.
[22]A Canaanite woman who lived in that
region came to him. "Son of David!" she
cried out. "Have mercy on me, sir! My
daughter has a demon and is in a terrible
condition."
23 But Jesus did not say a word to her. His
disciples came to him and begged him,
"Send her away! She is following us and
making all this noise!"
24 Then Jesus replied, "I have been sent
only to the lost sheep of the people of
Israel."
25 At this the woman came and fell at his
feet. "Help me, sir!" she said.
26 Jesus answered, "It isn't right to take the
children's food and throw it to the dogs."
27 "That's true, sir," she answered; "but
even the dogs eat the leftovers that fall
from their masters' table."
28 So Jesus answered her, "You are a woman
of great faith! What you want will be done
for you." And at that very moment her
daughter was healed.

Jesus Heals Many People

29 Jesus left there and went along by Lake
Galilee. He climbed a hill and sat down.
[30]Large crowds came to him, bringing with
them the lame, the blind, the crippled, the
dumb, and many other sick people, whom
they placed at Jesus' feet; and he healed
them. [31]The people were amazed as they
saw the dumb speaking, the crippled made
whole, the lame walking, and the blind
seeing; and they praised the God of Israel.

Jesus Feeds Another Great Crowd

(Mk 8.1–10)

32 Jesus called his disciples to him and said,
"I feel sorry for these people, because they

[a] **15.6** his father; *some manuscripts have* his father or mother.

have been with me for three days and now
have nothing to eat. I don't want to send
them away without feeding them, for they
might faint on their way home."
33 The disciples asked him, "Where will we
find enough food in this desert to feed this
crowd?"
34 "How much bread have you?" Jesus
asked.
"Seven loaves," they answered, "and a
few small fish."
35 So Jesus ordered the crowd to sit down
on the ground. [36]Then he took the seven
loaves and the fish, gave thanks to God,
broke them, and gave them to the
disciples; and the disciples gave them to
the people. [37]They all ate and had enough.
Then the disciples took up seven baskets
full of pieces left over. [38]The number of
men who ate was 4,000, not counting the
women and children.
39 Then Jesus sent the people away, got
into a boat, and went to the territory of
Magadan.

The Demand for a Miracle

(Mk 8.11–13; Lk 12.54–56)

16 Some Pharisees and Sadducees who
came to Jesus wanted to trap him, so
they asked him to perform a miracle
for them, to show that God approved of
him. [2]But Jesus answered, "When the sun
is setting, you say, 'We are going to have
fine weather, because the sky is red.' [3]And
early in the morning you say, 'It is going to
rain, because the sky is red and dark.' You
can predict the weather by looking at the
sky, but you cannot interpret the signs
concerning these times![a] [4]How evil and
godless are the people of this day! You ask
me for a miracle? No! The only miracle you
will be given is the miracle of Jonah."
So he left them and went away.

The Yeast of the Pharisees and Sadducees

(Mk 8.14–21)

5 When the disciples crossed over to the
other side of the lake, they forgot to take
any bread. [6]Jesus said to them, "Take care;
be on your guard against the yeast of the
Pharisees and Sadducees."
7 They started discussing among
themselves, "He says this because we didn't
bring any bread."
8 Jesus knew what they were saying, so he
asked them, "Why are you discussing
among yourselves about not having any
bread? How little faith you have! [9]Don't
you understand yet? Don't you remember
when I broke the five loaves for the five
thousand men? How many baskets did you
fill? [10]And what about the seven loaves for
the four thousand men? How many
baskets did you fill? [11]How is it that you
don't understand that I was not talking to
you about bread? Guard yourselves from
the yeast of the Pharisees and Sadducees!"
12 Then the disciples understood that he
was not warning them to guard themselves
from the yeast used in bread but from the
teaching of the Pharisees and Sadducees.

Peter's Declaration about Jesus

(Mk 8.27–30; Lk 9.18–21)

13 Jesus went to the territory near the town
of Caesarea Philippi, where he asked his
disciples, "Who do people say the Son of
Man is?"
14 "Some say John the Baptist," they
answered. "Others say Elijah, while others
say Jeremiah or some other prophet."
15 "What about you?" he asked them.
"Who do you say I am?"
16 Simon Peter answered, "You are the
Messiah, the Son of the living God."
17 "Good for you, Simon son of John!"
answered Jesus. "For this truth did not come
to you from any human being, but it was
given to you directly by my Father in
heaven. [18]And so I tell you, Peter: you are a
rock, and on this rock foundation I will
build my church, and not even death will
ever be able to overcome it. [19]I will give you
the keys of the Kingdom of heaven; what
you prohibit on earth will be prohibited in
heaven, and what you permit on earth will
be permitted in heaven."
20 Then Jesus ordered his disciples not to
tell anyone that he was the Messiah.

[a] **16.3** *Some manuscripts do not have the words of Jesus in verses 2–3.*

Peter was Jesus' head disciple.

Jesus Speaks about his Suffering and Death
(Mk 8.31—9.1; Lk 9.22–27)

21 From that time on Jesus began to say
plainly to his disciples, "I must go to
Jerusalem and suffer much from the elders,
the chief priests, and the teachers of the Law.
I will be put to death, but three days later I
will be raised to life."
22 Peter took him aside and began to rebuke
him. "God forbid it, Lord!" he said. "That
must never happen to you!"
23 Jesus turned around and said to Peter,
"Get away from me, Satan! You are an
obstacle in my way, because these thoughts
of yours don't come from God, but from
human nature."
24 Then Jesus said to his disciples, "If anyone
wants to come with me, he must forget self,
carry his cross, and follow me. 25For
whoever wants to save his own life will lose
it; but whoever loses his life for my sake will
find it. 26Will people gain anything if they
win the whole world but lose their life? Of
course not! There is nothing they can give to
regain their life. 27For the Son of Man is
about to come in the glory of his Father with
his angels, and then he will reward each one
according to his deeds. 28I assure you that
there are some here who will not die until
they have seen the Son of Man come as
King."

The Transfiguration
(Mk 9.2–13; Lk 9.28–36)

17 Six days later Jesus took with him
Peter and the brothers James and John
and led them up a high mountain
where they were alone. 2As they looked on,
a change came over Jesus: his face was
shining like the sun, and his clothes were
dazzling white. 3Then the three disciples
saw Moses and Elijah talking with Jesus.
4So Peter spoke up and said to Jesus, "Lord,
how good it is that we are here! If you wish,
I will make three tents here, one for you,
one for Moses, and one for Elijah."
5 While he was talking, a shining cloud
came over them, and a voice from the
cloud said, "This is my own dear Son, with
whom I am pleased – listen to him!"
6 When the disciples heard the voice, they
were so terrified that they threw themselves
face downwards on the ground. 7Jesus
came to them and touched them. "Get up,"
he said. "Don't be afraid!" 8So they looked
up and saw no one there but Jesus.
9 As they came down the mountain, Jesus
ordered them, "Don't tell anyone about
this vision you have seen until the Son of
Man has been raised from death."
10 Then the disciples asked Jesus, "Why do
the teachers of the Law say that Elijah has
to come first?"
11 "Elijah is indeed coming first," answered
Jesus, "and he will get everything ready.
12But I tell you that Elijah has already come
and people did not recognize him, but
treated him just as they pleased. In the
same way they will also ill-treat the Son of
Man."
13 Then the disciples understood that he
was talking to them about John the Baptist.

Jesus Heals a Boy with a Demon
(Mk 9.14–29; Lk 9.37–43a)

14 When they returned to the crowd, a man
came to Jesus, knelt before him, 15and said,
"Sir, have mercy on my son! He is an

epileptic and has such terrible fits that he
often falls in the fire or into water. [16]I
brought him to your disciples, but they
could not heal him."

17 Jesus answered, "How unbelieving and
wrong you people are! How long must I
stay with you? How long do I have to put
up with you? Bring the boy here to me!"
[18]Jesus gave a command to the demon, and
it went out of the boy, and at that very
moment he was healed.

19 Then the disciples came to Jesus in
private and asked him, "Why couldn't we
drive the demon out?"

20 "It was because you haven't enough
faith," answered Jesus. "I assure you that if
you have faith as big as a mustard seed, you
can say to this hill, 'Go from here to there!'
and it will go. You could do anything!"[a]

Jesus Speaks Again about his Death

(Mk 9.30–32; Lk 9.43b–45)

22 When the disciples all came together in
Galilee, Jesus said to them, "The Son of Man
is about to be handed over to people [23]who
will kill him; but three days later he will be
raised to life."

The disciples became very sad.

Payment of the Temple Tax

24 When Jesus and his disciples came to
Capernaum, the collectors of the temple
tax came to Peter and asked, "Does your
teacher pay the temple tax?"

25 "Of course," Peter answered.

When Peter went into the house, Jesus
spoke up first, "Simon, what is your
opinion? Who pays duties or taxes to the
kings of this world? The citizens of the
country or the foreigners?"

26 "The foreigners," answered Peter.

"Well, then," replied Jesus, "that means
that the citizens don't have to pay. [27]But
we don't want to offend these people. So go
to the lake and drop in a line. Pull up the
first fish you hook, and in its mouth you
will find a coin worth enough for my
temple tax and yours. Take it and pay them
our taxes."

Who is the Greatest?

(Mk 9.33–37; Lk 9.46–48)

18 At that time the disciples came to
Jesus, asking, "Who is the greatest in
the Kingdom of heaven?"

2 So Jesus called a child, made him stand
in front of them, [3]and said, "I assure you
that unless you change and become like
children, you will never enter the Kingdom
of heaven. The greatest in the Kingdom of
heaven is the one who humbles himself
and becomes like this child. [5]And whoever
welcomes in my name one such child as
this, welcomes me.

Temptations to Sin

(Mk 9.42–48; Lk 17.1–2)

6 "If anyone should cause one of these
little ones to lose his faith in me, it would
be better for that person to have a large
millstone tied round his neck and be
drowned in the deep sea. [7]How terrible for
the world that there are things that make
people lose their faith! Such things will
always happen – but how terrible for the
one who causes them!

8 "If your hand or your foot makes you
lose your faith, cut it off and throw it away!
It is better for you to enter life without a
hand or a foot than to keep both hands and
both feet and be thrown into the eternal
fire. [9]And if your eye makes you lose your
faith, take it out and throw it away! It is
better for you to enter life with only one
eye than to keep both eyes and be thrown
into the fire of hell.

The Parable of the Lost Sheep

(Lk 15.3–7)

10 "See that you don't despise any of these
little ones. Their angels in heaven, I tell
you, are always in the presence of my
Father in heaven.[b]

12 "What do you think a man does who has
a hundred sheep and one of them gets lost?
He will leave the other ninety-nine grazing
on the hillside and go and look for the lost
sheep. [13]When he finds it, I tell you, he
feels far happier over this one sheep than
over the ninety-nine that did not get lost.

[a] **17.20** *Some manuscripts add verse 21:* But only prayer and fasting can drive this kind out; nothing else can *(see Mk 9.29).*

[b] **18.10** *Some manuscripts add verse 11:* For the Son of Man came to save the lost *(see Lk 19.10).*

14In just the same way your[a] Father in heaven does not want any of these little ones to be lost.

A Brother or Sister who Sins

15 "If your brother sins against you,[b] go to
him and show him his fault. But do it
privately, just between yourselves. If he
listens to you, you have won your brother
back. 16But if he will not listen to you, take
one or two other persons with you, so that
'every accusation may be upheld by the
testimony of two or more witnesses,' as the
scripture says. 17And if he will not listen to
them, then tell the whole thing to the
church. Finally, if he will not listen to the
church, treat him as though he were a
pagan or a tax collector.

Prohibiting and Permitting

18 "And so I tell all of you: what you prohibit on earth will be prohibited in heaven, and what you permit on earth will be permitted in heaven.

19 "And I tell you more: whenever two of
you on earth agree about anything you
pray for, it will be done for you by my
Father in heaven. 20For where two or three
come together in my name, I am there with
them."

The Parable of the Unforgiving Servant

21 Then Peter came to Jesus and asked, "Lord, if my brother keeps on sinning against me, how many times do I have to forgive him? Seven times?"

22 "No, not seven times," answered Jesus,
"but seventy times seven,[c] 23because the
Kingdom of heaven is like this. Once there
was a king who decided to check on his
servants' accounts. 24He had just begun to
do so when one of them was brought in
who owed him millions of pounds. 25The
servant did not have enough to pay his
debt, so the king ordered him to be sold as
a slave, with his wife and his children and
all that he had, in order to pay the debt.
26The servant fell on his knees before the
king. 'Be patient with me,' he begged, 'and
I will pay you everything!' 27The king felt
sorry for him, so he forgave him the debt
and let him go.

28 "Then the man went out and met one of
his fellow-servants who owed him a few
pounds. He grabbed him and started
choking him. 'Pay back what you owe me!'
he said. 29His fellow-servant fell down and
begged him, 'Be patient with me, and I will
pay you back!' 30But he refused; instead, he
had him thrown into jail until he should
pay the debt. 31When the other servants saw
what had happened, they were very upset
and went to the king and told him
everything. 32So he called the servant in.
'You worthless slave!' he said. 'I forgave you
the whole amount you owed me, just
because you asked me to. 33You should have
had mercy on your fellow-servant, just as I
had mercy on you.' 34The king was very
angry, and he sent the servant to jail to be
punished until he should pay back the
whole amount."

35 And Jesus concluded, "That is how my Father in heaven will treat every one of you unless you forgive your brother from your heart."

Jesus Teaches about Divorce

(Mk 10.1–12)

19 When Jesus finished saying these
things, he left Galilee and went to the
territory of Judea on the other side of
the River Jordan. 2Large crowds followed
him, and he healed them there.

3 Some Pharisees came to him and tried to trap him by asking, "Does our Law allow a man to divorce his wife for whatever reason he wishes?"

4 Jesus answered, "Haven't you read the
scripture that says that in the beginning
the Creator made people male and female?
5And God said, 'For this reason a man will
leave his father and mother and unite with
his wife, and the two will become one.' 6So
they are no longer two, but one. No human
being must separate, then, what God has
joined together."

[a] **18.14** your; *some manuscripts have* my.
[b] **18.15** *Some manuscripts do not have* against you.
[c] **18.22** seventy times seven; *or* seventy-seven times.

7 The Pharisees asked him, "Why, then, did
Moses give the law for a man to hand his
wife a divorce notice and send her away?"
8 Jesus answered, "Moses gave you
permission to divorce your wives because
you are so hard to teach. But it was not like
that at the time of creation. [9]I tell you,
then, that any man who divorces his wife
for any cause other than her unfaithfulness,
commits adultery if he marries some other
woman."
10 His disciples said to him, "If this is how it
is between a man and his wife, it is better
not to marry."
11 Jesus answered, "This teaching does not
apply to everyone, but only to those to
whom God has given it. [12]For there are
different reasons why men cannot marry:
some, because they were born that way;
others, because men made them that way;
and others do not marry for the sake of the
Kingdom of heaven. Let him who can
accept this teaching do so."

Jesus Blesses Little Children
(Mk 10.13–16; Lk 18.15–17)

13 Some people brought children to Jesus
for him to place his hands on them and to
pray for them, but the disciples scolded the
people. [14]Jesus said, "Let the children come
to me and do not stop them, because the
Kingdom of heaven belongs to such as
these."
15 He placed his hands on them and then went away.

Jesus blesses the children.

The Rich Young Man
(Mk 10.17–31; Lk 18.18–30)

16 Once a man came to Jesus. "Teacher," he
asked, "what good thing must I do to
receive eternal life?"
17 "Why do you ask me concerning what is
good?" answered Jesus. "There is only One
who is good. Keep the commandments if
you want to enter life."
18 "What commandments?" he asked.
Jesus answered, "Do not commit murder;
do not commit adultery; do not steal; do
not accuse anyone falsely; [19]respect your
father and your mother; and love your
neighbour as you love yourself."
20 "I have obeyed all these commandments,"
the young man replied. "What else do I need
to do?"
21 Jesus said to him, "If you want to be
perfect, go and sell all you have and give the
money to the poor, and you will have riches
in heaven; then come and follow me."
22 When the young man heard this, he
went away sad, because he was very rich.
23 Jesus then said to his disciples, "I assure
you: it will be very hard for rich people to
enter the Kingdom of heaven. [24]I repeat: it is
much harder for a rich person to enter the
Kingdom of God than for a camel to go
through the eye of a needle."
25 When the disciples heard this, they were
completely amazed. "Who, then, can be
saved?" they asked.
26 Jesus looked straight at them and
answered, "This is impossible for human
beings, but for God everything is possible."
27 Then Peter spoke up. "Look," he said,
"we have left everything and followed you.
What will we have?"
28 Jesus said to them, "You can be sure that
when the Son of Man sits on his glorious
throne in the New Age, then you twelve
followers of mine will also sit on thrones, to
rule the twelve tribes of Israel. [29]And
everyone who has left houses or brothers or
sisters or father or mother or children or
fields for my sake, will receive a hundred
times more and will be given eternal life.
[30]But many who now are first will be last,
and many who now are last will be first.

The Workers in the Vineyard

20 "The Kingdom of heaven is like this.
Once there was a man who went out
early in the morning to hire some men
to work in his vineyard. 2He agreed to pay
them the regular wage, a silver coin a day,
and sent them to work in his vineyard. 3He
went out again to the market place at nine
o'clock and saw some men standing there
doing nothing, 4so he told them, 'You also
go and work in the vineyard, and I will pay
you a fair wage.' 5So they went. Then at
twelve o'clock and again at three o'clock he
did the same thing. 6It was nearly five
o'clock when he went to the market place
and saw some other men still standing there.
'Why are you wasting the whole day here
doing nothing?' he asked them. 7'No one
hired us,' they answered. 'Well, then, you
also go and work in the vineyard,' he told
them.

8 "When evening came, the owner told his
foreman, 'Call the workers and pay them
their wages, starting with those who were
hired last and ending with those who were
hired first.' 9The men who had begun to
work at five o'clock were paid a silver coin
each. 10So when the men who were the first
to be hired came to be paid, they thought
they would get more; but they too were
given a silver coin each. 11They took their
money and started grumbling against the
employer. 12'These men who were hired last
worked only one hour,' they said, 'while we
put up with a whole day's work in the hot
sun – yet you paid them the same as you
paid us!'

13 " 'Listen, friend,' the owner answered
one of them, 'I have not cheated you. After
all, you agreed to do a day's work for one
silver coin. 14Now take your pay and go
home. I want to give this man who was
hired last as much as I have given you.
15Don't I have the right to do as I wish with
my own money? Or are you jealous because
I am generous?' "

16 And Jesus concluded, "So those who are
last will be first, and those who are first will
be last."

Jesus Speaks a Third Time about his Death

(Mk 10.32–34; Lk 18.31–34)

17 As Jesus was going up to Jerusalem, he
took the twelve disciples aside and spoke to
them privately, as they walked along.
18"Listen," he told them, "we are going up
to Jerusalem, where the Son of Man will be
handed over to the chief priests and the
teachers of the Law. They will condemn
him to death 19and then hand him over to
the Gentiles, who will mock him, whip
him, and crucify him; but three days later
he will be raised to life."

Jesus warns the disciples that he will be put to death.

A Mother's Request

(Mk 10.35–45)

20 Then the wife of Zebedee came to Jesus
with her two sons, bowed before him, and
asked him a favour.

21 "What do you want?" Jesus asked her.

She answered, "Promise me that these
two sons of mine will sit at your right and
your left when you are King."

22 "You don't know what you are asking

for," Jesus answered the sons. "Can you
drink the cup of suffering that I am about
to drink?"
"We can," they answered.
23 "You will indeed drink from my cup,"
Jesus told them, "but I do not have the
right to choose who will sit at my right and
my left. These places belong to those for
whom my Father has prepared them."
24 When the other ten disciples heard
about this, they became angry with the
two brothers. 25So Jesus called them all
together and said, "You know that the
rulers of the heathen have power over
them, and the leaders have complete
authority. 26This, however, is not the way
it shall be among you. If one of you wants
to be great, he must be the servant of the
rest; 27and if one of you wants to be first,
he must be your slave – 28like the Son of
Man, who did not come to be served, but
to serve and to give his life to redeem
many people."

Jesus Heals Two Blind Men

(Mk 10.46–52; Lk 18.35–43)

29 As Jesus and his disciples were leaving
Jericho, a large crowd was following.
30Two blind men who were sitting by the
road heard that Jesus was passing by, so
they began to shout, "Son of David! Take
pity on us, sir!"
31 The crowd scolded them and told them
to be quiet. But they shouted even more
loudly, "Son of David! Take pity on us, sir!"
32 Jesus stopped and called them. "What
do you want me to do for you?" he asked
them.
33 "Sir," they answered, "we want you to
give us our sight!"
34 Jesus had pity on them and touched
their eyes; at once they were able to see,
and they followed him.

The Triumphant Entry into Jerusalem

(Mk 11.1–11; Lk 19.28–40; Jn 12.12–19)

21 As Jesus and his disciples approached
Jerusalem, they came to Bethphage at
the Mount of Olives. There Jesus sent
two of the disciples on ahead 2with these
instructions: "Go to the village there ahead
of you, and at once you will find a donkey
tied up with her colt beside her. Untie
them and bring them to me. 3And if
anyone says anything, tell him, 'The
Master[a] needs them'; and then he will let
them go at once."
4 This happened in order to make what
the prophet had said come true:

5 "Tell the city of Zion,
Look, your king is coming to you!
He is humble and rides on a donkey
and on a colt, the foal of a donkey."

6 So the disciples went and did what Jesus
had told them to do: 7they brought the
donkey and the colt, threw their cloaks
over them, and Jesus got on. 8A large
crowd of people spread their cloaks on the
road while others cut branches from the
trees and spread them on the road. 9The
crowds walking in front of Jesus and those
walking behind began to shout, "Praise to
David's Son! God bless him who comes in
the name of the Lord! Praise God!"
10 When Jesus entered Jerusalem, the
whole city was thrown into an uproar.
"Who is he?" the people asked.
11 "This is the prophet Jesus, from
Nazareth in Galilee," the crowds answered.

A modern-day Palm Sunday procession reminds us of Jesus coming to Jerusalem.

[a] **21.3** The Master; *or* Their owner.

Jesus Goes to the Temple
(Mk 11.15–19; Lk 19.45–48; Jn 2.13–22)

12 Jesus went into the Temple and drove out
all those who were buying and selling there.
He overturned the tables of the
moneychangers and the stools of those who
sold pigeons, 13and said to them, "It is
written in the Scriptures that God said, 'My
Temple will be called a house of prayer.' But
you are making it a hideout for thieves!"
14 The blind and the crippled came to him
in the Temple, and he healed them. 15The
chief priests and the teachers of the Law
became angry when they saw the
wonderful things he was doing and the
children shouting in the Temple, "Praise to
David's Son!" 16So they asked Jesus, "Do
you hear what they are saying?"
"Indeed I do," answered Jesus. "Haven't
you ever read this scripture? 'You have
trained children and babies to offer perfect
praise.' "
17 Jesus left them and went out of the city
to Bethany, where he spent the night.

Jesus Curses the Fig Tree
(Mk 11.12–14, 20–24)

18 On his way back to the city early next
morning, Jesus was hungry. 19He saw a fig
tree by the side of the road and went to it,
but found nothing on it except leaves. So
he said to the tree, "You will never again
bear fruit!" At once the fig tree dried up.
20 The disciples saw this and were
astounded. "How did the fig tree dry up so
quickly?" they asked.
21 Jesus answered, "I assure you that if you
believe and do not doubt, you will be able
to do what I have done to this fig tree. And
not only this, but you will even be able to
say to this hill, 'Get up and throw yourself
in the sea,' and it will. 22If you believe, you
will receive whatever you ask for in prayer."

The Question about Jesus' Authority
(Mk 11.27–33; Lk 20.1–8)

23 Jesus came back to the Temple; and as he
taught, the chief priests and the elders came
to him and asked, "What right have you to
do these things? Who gave you this
right?"
24 Jesus answered them, "I will ask you just
one question, and if you give me an
answer, I will tell you what right I have to
do these things. 25Where did John's right
to baptize come from: was it from God or
from human beings?"
They started to argue among
themselves, "What shall we say? If we
answer, 'From God,' he will say to us,
'Why, then, did you not believe John?'
26But if we say, 'From human beings,' we
are afraid of what the people might do,
because they are all convinced that John
was a prophet." 27So they answered Jesus,
"We don't know."
And he said to them, "Neither will I tell
you, then, by what right I do these things.

The Parable of the Two Sons

28 "Now, what do you think? There was
once a man who had two sons. He went to
the elder one and said, 'Son, go and work
in the vineyard today.' 29'I don't want to,'
he answered, but later he changed his
mind and went. 30Then the father went to
the other son and said the same thing.
'Yes, sir,' he answered, but he did not go.
31Which one of the two did what his
father wanted?"
"The elder one," they answered.
So Jesus said to them, "I tell you: the tax
collectors and the prostitutes are going
into the Kingdom of God ahead of you.
32For John the Baptist came to you
showing you the right path to take, and
you would not believe him; but the tax
collectors and the prostitutes believed
him. Even when you saw this, you did not
later change your minds and believe him.

The Parable of the Tenants in the Vineyard
(Mk 12.1–12; Lk 20.9–19)

33 "Listen to another parable," Jesus said.
"There was once a landowner who planted
a vineyard, put a fence around it, dug a hole

for the winepress, and built a watchtower.
Then he let out the vineyard to tenants and
went on a journey. 34When the time came
to gather the grapes, he sent his slaves to the
tenants to receive his share of the harvest.
35The tenants seized his slaves, beat one,
killed another, and stoned another. 36Again
the man sent other slaves, more than the
first time, and the tenants treated them the
same way. 37Last of all he sent his son to
them. 'Surely they will respect my son,' he
said. 38But when the tenants saw the son,
they said to themselves, 'This is the owner's
son. Come on, let's kill him, and we will get
his property!' 39So they seized him, threw
him out of the vineyard, and killed him.

40 "Now, when the owner of the vineyard
comes, what will he do to those tenants?"
Jesus asked.

41 "He will certainly kill those evil men,"
they answered, "and let the vineyard out to
other tenants, who will give him his share
of the harvest at the right time."

42 Jesus said to them, "Haven't you ever
read what the Scriptures say?

> 'The stone which the builders rejected
> as worthless
> turned out to be the most important
> of all.
> This was done by the Lord;
> what a wonderful sight it is!'

43 "And so I tell you," added Jesus, "the
Kingdom of God will be taken away from
you and given to a people who will produce
the proper fruits."[a]

45 The chief priests and the Pharisees heard
Jesus' parables and knew that he was
talking about them, 46so they tried to
arrest him. But they were afraid of the
crowds, who considered Jesus to be a
prophet.

The Parable of the Wedding Feast
(Lk 14.15–24)

22 Jesus again used parables in talking to
the people. 2"The Kingdom of heaven
is like this. Once there was a king who
prepared a wedding feast for his son. 3He
sent his servants to tell the invited guests
to come to the feast, but they did not want
to come. 4So he sent other servants with
this message for the guests: 'My feast is
ready now; my bullocks and prize calves
have been butchered, and everything is
ready. Come to the wedding feast!' 5But
the invited guests paid no attention and
went about their business: one went to his
farm, another to his shop, 6while others
grabbed the servants, beat them, and killed
them. 7The king was very angry; so he sent
his soldiers, who killed those murderers
and burnt down their city. 8Then he called
his servants and said to them, 'My wedding
feast is ready, but the people I invited did
not deserve it. 9Now go to the main streets
and invite to the feast as many people as
you find.' 10So the servants went out into
the streets and gathered all the people they
could find, good and bad alike; and the
wedding hall was filled with people.

11 "The king went in to look at the guests
and saw a man who was not wearing
wedding clothes. 12'Friend, how did you
get in here without wedding clothes?' the
king asked him. But the man said nothing.
13Then the king told the servants, 'Tie him
up hand and foot, and throw him outside
in the dark. There he will cry and grind his
teeth.' "

14 And Jesus concluded, "Many are invited,
but few are chosen."

The Question about Paying Taxes
(Mk 12.13–17; Lk 20.20–26)

15 The Pharisees went off and made a plan
to trap Jesus with questions. 16Then they
sent to him some of their disciples and
some members of Herod's party. "Teacher,"
they said, "we know that you tell the truth.
You teach the truth about God's will for
people, without worrying about what
others think, because you pay no attention
to anyone's status. 17Tell us, then, what do
you think? Is it against our Law to pay
taxes to the Roman Emperor, or not?"

18 Jesus, however, was aware of their evil
plan, and so he said, "You hypocrites! Why

[a] **21.43** *Some manuscripts add verse 44:* Whoever falls on this stone will be cut to pieces; and if the stone falls on someone, it will crush him to dust *(see Lk 20.18).*

are you trying to trap me? [19]Show me the
coin for paying the tax!"
They brought him the coin, [20]and he
asked them, "Whose face and name are
these?"
21 "The Emperor's," they answered.
So Jesus said to them, "Well, then, pay
the Emperor what belongs to the Emperor,
and pay God what belongs to God."
22 When they heard this, they were
amazed; and they left him and went away.

The Question about Rising from Death

(Mk 12.18–27; Lk 20.27–40)

23 That same day some Sadducees came to
Jesus and claimed that people will not rise
from death. [24]"Teacher," they said, "Moses
said that if a man who has no children dies,
his brother must marry the widow so that
they can have children who will be
considered the dead man's children.
[25]Now, there were seven brothers who used
to live here. The eldest got married and
died without having children, so he left his
widow to his brother. [26]The same thing
happened to the second brother, to the
third, and finally to all seven. [27]Last of all,
the woman died. [28]Now, on the day when
the dead rise to life, whose wife will she be?
All of them had married her."
29 Jesus answered them, "How wrong you
are! It is because you don't know the
Scriptures or God's power. [30]For when the
dead rise to life, they will be like the angels
in heaven and will not marry. [31]Now, as for
the dead rising to life: haven't you ever read
what God has told you? He said, [32]'I am the
God of Abraham, the God of Isaac, and the
God of Jacob.' He is the God of the living,
not of the dead."
33 When the crowds heard this, they were
amazed at his teaching.

The Great Commandment

(Mk 12.28–34; Lk 10.25–28)

34 When the Pharisees heard that Jesus had
silenced the Sadducees, they came together,
[35]and one of them, a teacher of the Law,
tried to trap him with a question.
[36]"Teacher," he asked, "which is the
greatest commandment in the Law?"
37 Jesus answered, " 'Love the Lord your God
with all your heart, with all your soul, and
with all your mind.' [38]This is the greatest
and the most important commandment.
[39]The second most important
commandment is like it: 'Love your
neighbour as you love yourself.' [40]The
whole Law of Moses and the teachings of the
prophets depend on these two
commandments."

The Question about the Messiah

(Mk 12.35–37; Lk 20.41–44)

41 When some Pharisees gathered together,
Jesus asked them, [42]"What do you think
about the Messiah? Whose descendant is
he?"
"He is David's descendant," they
answered.
43 "Why, then," Jesus asked, "did the Spirit
inspire David to call him 'Lord'? David said,

44 'The Lord said to my Lord:
Sit here on my right
until I put your enemies under your
feet.'

45 If, then, David called him 'Lord', how
can the Messiah be David's descendant?"
46 No one was able to give Jesus any answer,
and from that day on no one dared to ask
him any more questions.

Jesus Warns against the Teachers of the Law and the Pharisees

(Mk 12.38–39; Lk 11.43, 46; 20.45–46)

23 Then Jesus spoke to the crowds and to
his disciples. [2]"The teachers of the Law
and the Pharisees are the authorized
interpreters of Moses' Law. [3]So you must
obey and follow everything they tell you to
do; do not, however, imitate their actions,
because they don't practise what they
preach. [4]They tie on to people's backs loads
that are heavy and hard to carry, yet they
aren't willing even to lift a finger to help
them carry those loads. [5]They do everything
so that people will see them. Look at the

straps with scripture verses on them which
they wear on their foreheads and arms, and
notice how large they are! Notice also how
long are the tassels on their cloaks![a] 6They
love the best places at feasts and the
reserved seats in the synagogues; 7they love
to be greeted with respect in the market
places and to be called 'Teacher'. 8You must
not be called 'Teacher', because you are all
members of one family and have only one
Teacher. 9And you must not call anyone
here on earth 'Father', because you have
only the one Father in heaven. 10Nor
should you be called 'Leader', because your
one and only leader is the Messiah. 11The
greatest one among you must be your
servant. 12Whoever makes himself great
will be humbled, and whoever humbles
himself will be made great.

Jesus Condemns their Hypocrisy
(Mk 12.40; Lk 11.39–42, 44, 52; 20.47)

13 "How terrible for you, teachers of the
Law and Pharisees! You hypocrites! You
lock the door to the Kingdom of heaven in
people's faces, and you yourselves don't go
in, nor do you allow in those who are
trying to enter![b]

15 "How terrible for you, teachers of the
Law and Pharisees! You hypocrites! You sail
the seas and cross whole countries to win
one convert; and when you succeed, you
make him twice as deserving of going to
hell as you yourselves are!

16 "How terrible for you, blind guides! You
teach, 'If someone swears by the Temple,
he isn't bound by his vow; but if he swears
by the gold in the Temple, he is bound.'
17Blind fools! Which is more important,
the gold or the Temple which makes the
gold holy? 18You also teach, 'If someone
swears by the altar, he isn't bound by his
vow; but if he swears by the gift on the
altar, he is bound.' 19How blind you are!
Which is the more important, the gift or
the altar which makes the gift holy? 20So
then, when a person swears by the altar, he
is swearing by it and by all the gifts on it;
21and when he swears by the Temple, he is
swearing by it and by God, who lives there;
22and when someone swears by heaven, he
is swearing by God's throne and by him
who sits on it.

23 "How terrible for you, teachers of the
Law and Pharisees! You hypocrites! You
give to God a tenth even of the seasoning
herbs, such as mint, dill, and cumin, but
you neglect to obey the really important
teachings of the Law, such as justice and
mercy and honesty. These you should
practise, without neglecting the others.
24Blind guides! You strain a fly out of your
drink, but swallow a camel!

25 "How terrible for you, teachers of the
Law and Pharisees! You hypocrites! You
clean the outside of your cup and plate,
while the inside is full of what you have
obtained by violence and selfishness.
26Blind Pharisee! Clean what is inside the
cup first, and then the outside will be clean
too!

27 "How terrible for you, teachers of the
Law and Pharisees! You hypocrites! You are
like whitewashed tombs, which look fine
on the outside but are full of bones and
decaying corpses on the inside. 28In the
same way, on the outside you appear good
to everybody, but inside you are full of
hypocrisy and sins.

Jesus Predicts their Punishment
(Lk 11.47–51)

29 "How terrible for you, teachers of the Law
and Pharisees! You hypocrites! You make
fine tombs for the prophets and decorate
the monuments of those who lived good
lives; 30and you claim that if you had lived
during the time of your ancestors, you
would not have done what they did and
killed the prophets. 31So you actually admit
that you are the descendants of those who
murdered the prophets! 32Go on, then, and
finish what your ancestors started! 33You
snakes and children of snakes! How do you
expect to escape from being condemned to

[a] **23.5** TASSELS ON THEIR CLOAKS: *These tassels were worn as a sign of devotion to God (see Num 15.37–41).*

[b] **23.13** *Some manuscripts add verse 14:* How terrible for you, teachers of the Law and Pharisees! You hypocrites! You take advantage of widows and rob them of their homes, and then make a show of saying long prayers! Because of this your punishment will be all the worse! *(see Mk 12.40).*

hell? 34And so I tell you that I will send you
prophets and wise men and teachers; you
will kill some of them, crucify others, and
whip others in the synagogues and chase
them from town to town. 35As a result, the
punishment for the murder of all innocent
people will fall on you, from the murder of
innocent Abel to the murder of Zachariah
son of Berachiah, whom you murdered
between the Temple and the altar. 36I tell you
indeed: the punishment for all these murders
will fall on the people of this day!

Jesus' Love for Jerusalem
(Lk 13.34–35)

37 "Jerusalem, Jerusalem! You kill the
prophets and stone the messengers God has
sent you! How many times have I wanted to
put my arms round all your people, just as a
hen gathers her chicks under her wings, but
you would not let me! 38And so your
Temple will be abandoned and empty.
39From now on, I tell you, you will never
see me again until you say, 'God bless him
who comes in the name of the Lord.' "

Jesus Speaks of the Destruction of the Temple
(Mk 13.1–2; Lk 21.5–6)

24 Jesus left and was going away from the
Temple when his disciples came to him
to call his attention to its buildings.
2"Yes," he said, "you may well look at all
these. I tell you this: not a single stone here
will be left in its place; every one of them
will be thrown down."

Troubles and Persecutions
(Mk 13.3–13; Lk 21.7–19)

3 As Jesus sat on the Mount of Olives, the
disciples came to him in private. "Tell us
when all this will be," they asked, "and
what will happen to show that it is the time
for your coming and the end of the age."
4 Jesus answered, "Be on your guard, and
do not let anyone deceive you. 5Many men,
claiming to speak for me, will come and say,
'I am the Messiah!' and they will deceive
many people. 6You are going to hear the
noise of battles close by and the news of
battles far away; but do not be troubled.
Such things must happen, but they do not
mean that the end has come. 7Countries
will fight each other, kingdoms will attack
one another. There will be famines and
earthquakes everywhere. 8All these things
are like the first pains of childbirth.
9 "Then you will be arrested and handed
over to be punished and be put to death. All
nations will hate you because of me.
10Many will give up their faith at that time;
they will betray one another and hate one
another. 11Then many false prophets will
appear and deceive many people. 12Such
will be the spread of evil that many people's
love will grow cold. 13But whoever holds
out to the end will be saved. 14And this
Good News about the Kingdom will be
preached through all the world for a witness
to all nations; and then the end will come.

The Awful Horror
(Mk 13.14–23; Lk 21.20–24)

15 "You will see 'The Awful Horror' of which
the prophet Daniel spoke. It will be
standing in the holy place." (Note to the
reader: be sure to understand what this
means!) 16"Then those who are in Judea
must run away to the hills. 17Someone who
is on the roof of his house must not take the
time to go down and get his belongings
from the house. 18Someone who is in the
field must not go back to get his cloak.
19How terrible it will be in those days for
women who are pregnant and for mothers
with little babies! 20Pray to God that you
will not have to run away during the winter
or on a Sabbath! 21For the trouble at that
time will be far more terrible than any there
has ever been, from the beginning of the
world to this very day. Nor will there ever be
anything like it again. 22But God has
already reduced the number of days; had he
not done so, nobody would survive. For the
sake of his chosen people, however, God
will reduce the days.
23 "Then, if anyone says to you, 'Look, here
is the Messiah!' or 'There he is!' – do not
believe it. 24For false Messiahs and false
prophets will appear; they will perform

great miracles and wonders in order to
deceive even God's chosen people, if
possible. [25]Listen! I have told you this
before the time comes.
26 "Or, if people should tell you, 'Look, he is
out in the desert!' – don't go there; or if
they say, 'Look, he is hiding here!' – don't
believe it. [27]For the Son of Man will come
like the lightning which flashes across the
whole sky from the east to the west.
28 "Wherever there is a dead body, the
vultures will gather.

The Coming of the Son of Man

(Mk 13.24–27; Lk 21.25–28)

29 "Soon after the trouble of those days, the
sun will grow dark, the moon will no longer
shine, the stars will fall from heaven, and
the powers in space will be driven from
their courses. [30]Then the sign of the Son of
Man will appear in the sky; and all the
peoples of earth will weep as they see the
Son of Man coming on the clouds of
heaven with power and great glory. [31]The
great trumpet will sound, and he will send
out his angels to the four corners of the
earth, and they will gather his chosen
people from one end of the world to the
other.

The Lesson of the Fig Tree

(Mk 13.28–31; Lk 21.29–33)

32 "Let the fig tree teach you a lesson. When
its branches become green and tender and
it starts putting out leaves, you know that
summer is near. [33]In the same way, when
you see all these things, you will know that
the time is near, ready to begin.[a]
[34]Remember that all these things will
happen before the people now living have
all died. [35]Heaven and earth will pass away,
but my words will never pass away.

No One Knows the Day and Hour

(Mk 13.32–37; Lk 17.26–30, 34–36)

36 "No one knows, however, when that day
and hour will come – neither the angels in
heaven nor the Son;[b] the Father alone
knows. [37]The coming of the Son of Man
will be like what happened in the time of
Noah. [38]In the days before the flood people
ate and drank, men and women married,
up to the very day Noah went into the boat;
[39]yet they did not realize what was
happening until the flood came and swept
them all away. That is how it will be when
the Son of Man comes. [40]At that time two
men will be working in a field: one will be
taken away, the other will be left behind.
[41]Two women will be at a mill grinding
meal: one will be taken away, the other will
be left behind.
42 "Be on your guard, then, because you do
not know what day your Lord will come.
[43]If the owner of a house knew the time
when the thief would come, you can be
sure that he would stay awake and not let
the thief break into his house. [44]So then,
you also must always be ready, because the
Son of Man will come at an hour when you
are not expecting him.

The Faithful or the Unfaithful Servant

(Lk 12.41–48)

45 "Who, then, is a faithful and wise
servant? It is the one that his master has
placed in charge of the other servants to
give them their food at the proper time.
[46]How happy that servant is if his master
finds him doing this when he comes home!
[47]Indeed, I tell you, the master will put that
servant in charge of all his property. [48]But if
he is a bad servant, he will tell himself that
his master will not come back for a long
time, [49]and he will begin to beat his fellow-
servants and to eat and drink with
drunkards. [50]Then that servant's master
will come back one day when the servant
does not expect him and at a time he does
not know. [51]The master will cut him in
pieces[c] and make him share the fate of the
hypocrites. There he will cry and grind his
teeth.

[a] **24.33** the time is near, ready to begin; *or* he is near, ready to come.

[b] **24.36** *Some manuscripts do not have* nor the Son.

[c] **24.51** cut him in pieces; *or* throw him out.

The Parable of the Ten Young Women

25 "At that time the Kingdom of heaven
will be like this. Once there were ten
young women who took their oil lamps
and went out to meet the bridegroom. [2]Five
of them were foolish, and the other five
were wise. [3]The foolish ones took their
lamps but did not take any extra oil with
them, [4]while the wise ones took containers
full of oil for their lamps. [5]The bridegroom
was late in coming, so the women began to
nod and fall asleep.
6 "It was already midnight when the cry
rang out, 'Here is the bridegroom! Come
and meet him!' [7]The ten women woke up
and trimmed their lamps. [8]Then the
foolish ones said to the wise ones, 'Let us
have some of your oil, because our lamps
are going out.' [9]'No, indeed,' the wise ones
answered, 'there is not enough for you and
for us. Go to the shop and buy some for
yourselves.' [10]So the foolish women went
off to buy some oil; and while they were
gone, the bridegroom arrived. The five who
were ready went in with him to the
wedding feast, and the door was closed.
11 "Later the other women arrived. 'Sir, sir!
Let us in!' they cried out. [12]'Certainly not!
I don't know you,' the bridegroom
answered."
13 And Jesus concluded, "Be on your guard,
then, because you do not know the day or
the hour.

The Parable of the Three Servants

(Lk 19.11–27)

14 "At that time the Kingdom of heaven
will be like this. Once there was a man who
was about to go on a journey; he called his
servants and put them in charge of his
property. [15]He gave to each one according
to his ability: to one he gave five thousand
gold coins, to another he gave two
thousand, and to another he gave one
thousand. Then he left on his journey.
[16]The servant who had received five
thousand coins went at once and invested
his money and earned another five
thousand. [17]In the same way the servant
who had received two thousand coins
earned another two thousand. [18]But the
servant who had received one thousand
coins went off, dug a hole in the ground,
and hid his master's money.
19 "After a long time the master of those
servants came back and settled accounts
with them. [20]The servant who had received
five thousand coins came in and handed
over the other five thousand. 'You gave me
five thousand coins, sir,' he said. 'Look!
Here are another five thousand that I have
earned.' [21]'Well done, you good and
faithful servant!' said his master. 'You have
been faithful in managing small amounts,
so I will put you in charge of large
amounts. Come on in and share my
happiness!'
22 "Then the servant who had been given
two thousand coins came in and said, 'You
gave me two thousand coins, sir. Look!
Here are another two thousand that I have
earned.' [23]'Well done, you good and
faithful servant!' said his master. 'You have
been faithful in managing small amounts,
so I will put you in charge of large
amounts. Come on in and share my
happiness!'
24 "Then the servant who had received one
thousand coins came in and said, 'Sir, I
know you are a hard man; you reap
harvests where you did not sow, and you
gather crops where you did not scatter seed.
[25]I was afraid, so I went off and hid your
money in the ground. Look! Here is what
belongs to you.'
26 " 'You bad and lazy servant!' his master
said. 'You knew, did you, that I reap
harvests where I did not sow, and gather
crops where I did not scatter seed? [27]Well,
then, you should have deposited my
money in the bank, and I would have
received it all back with interest when I
returned. [28]Now, take the money away
from him and give it to the one who has
ten thousand coins. [29]For to every person
who has something, even more will be
given, and he will have more than enough;
but the person who has nothing, even the
little that he has will be taken away from

him. 30As for this useless servant – throw
him outside in the darkness; there he will
cry and grind his teeth.'

The Final Judgement

31 "When the Son of Man comes as King
and all the angels with him, he will sit on
his royal throne, 32and the people of all the
nations will be gathered before him. Then
he will divide them into two groups, just as
a shepherd separates the sheep from the
goats. 33He will put the righteous people
on his right and the others on his left.
34Then the King will say to the people on
his right, 'Come, you that are blessed by
my Father! Come and possess the kingdom
which has been prepared for you ever since
the creation of the world. 35I was hungry
and you fed me, thirsty and you gave me a
drink; I was a stranger and you received me
in your homes, 36naked and you clothed
me; I was sick and you took care of me, in
prison and you visited me.'
37 "The righteous will then answer him,
'When, Lord, did we ever see you hungry
and feed you, or thirsty and give you a
drink? 38When did we ever see you a
stranger and welcome you in our homes, or
naked and clothe you? 39When did we ever
see you sick or in prison, and visit you?'
40The King will reply, 'I tell you, whenever
you did this for one of the least important
of these members of my family, you did it
for me!'
41 "Then he will say to those on
his left, 'Away from me, you
that are under God's curse!
Away to the eternal fire which
has been prepared for the Devil
and his angels! 42I was hungry
but you would not feed me,
thirsty but you would not give
me a drink; 43I was a stranger
but you would not welcome me
in your homes, naked but you
would not clothe me; I was sick
and in prison but you would
not take care of me.'
44 "Then they will answer him,
'When, Lord, did we ever see
you hungry or thirsty or a stranger or naked
or sick or in prison, and would not help
you?' 45The King will reply, 'I tell you,
whenever you refused to help one of these
least important ones, you refused to help
me.' 46These, then, will be sent off to
eternal punishment, but the righteous will
go to eternal life."

The Plot against Jesus
(Mk 14.1–2; Lk 22.1–2; Jn 11.45–53)

26 When Jesus had finished teaching all
these things, he said to his disciples,
2"In two days, as you know, it will be
the Passover Festival, and the Son of Man
will be handed over to be crucified."
3 Then the chief priests and the elders met
together in the palace of Caiaphas, the High
Priest, 4and made plans to arrest Jesus
secretly and put him to death. 5"We must
not do it during the festival," they said, "or
the people will riot."

Jesus is Anointed at Bethany
(Mk 14.3–9; Jn 12.1–8)

6 Jesus was in Bethany at the house of
Simon, a man who had suffered from a
dreaded skin disease. 7While Jesus was
eating, a woman came to him with an
alabaster jar filled with an expensive
perfume, which she poured on his head.
8The disciples saw this and became angry.
"Why all this waste?" they asked. 9"This

Mary anoints the feet of Jesus in this modern-day street play.

perfume could have been sold for a large amount and the money given to the poor!"

10 Jesus knew what they were saying, so he said to them, "Why are you bothering this woman? It is a fine and beautiful thing that she has done for me. 11You will always have poor people with you, but you will not always have me. 12What she did was to pour this perfume on my body to get me ready for burial. 13Now, I assure you that wherever this gospel is preached all over the world, what she has done will be told in memory of her."

Judas Agrees to Betray Jesus

(Mk 14.10–11; Lk 22.3–6)

14 Then one of the twelve disciples – the one named Judas Iscariot – went to the chief priests 15and asked, "What will you give me if I betray Jesus to you?" They counted out 30 silver coins and gave them to him. 16From then on Judas was looking for a good chance to hand Jesus over to them.

Jesus Eats the Passover Meal with his Disciples

(Mk 14.12–21; Lk 22.7–13, 21–23; Jn 13.21–30)

17 On the first day of the Festival of Unleavened Bread the disciples came to Jesus and asked him, "Where do you want us to get the Passover meal ready for you?"

18 "Go to a certain man in the city," he said to them, "and tell him: 'The Teacher says, My hour has come; my disciples and I will celebrate the Passover at your house.' "

19 The disciples did as Jesus had told them and prepared the Passover meal.

20 When it was evening, Jesus and the twelve disciples sat down to eat. 21During the meal Jesus said, "I tell you, one of you will betray me."

22 The disciples were very upset and began to ask him, one after the other, "Surely, Lord, you don't mean me?"

23 Jesus answered, "One who dips his bread in the dish with me will betray me. 24The Son of Man will die as the Scriptures say he will, but how terrible for that man who betrays the Son of Man! It would have been better for that man if he had never been born!"

25 Judas, the traitor, spoke up. "Surely, Teacher, you don't mean me?" he asked.

Jesus answered, "So you say."

The Lord's Supper

(Mk 14.22–26; Lk 22.14–20; 1 Cor. 11.23–25)

26 While they were eating, Jesus took a piece of bread, gave a prayer of thanks, broke it, and gave it to his disciples. "Take and eat it," he said; "this is my body."

27 Then he took a cup, gave thanks to God, and gave it to them. "Drink it, all of you," he said; 28"this is my blood, which seals God's covenant, my blood poured out for many for the forgiveness of sins. 29I tell you, I will never again drink this wine until the day I drink the new wine with you in my Father's Kingdom."

30 Then they sang a hymn and went out to the Mount of Olives.

Jesus Predicts Peter's Denial

(Mk 14.27–31; Lk 22.31–34; Jn 13.36–38)

31 Then Jesus said to them, "This very night all of you will run away and leave me, for the scripture says, 'God will kill the shepherd, and the sheep of the flock will be scattered.' 32But after I am raised to life, I will go to Galilee ahead of you."

33 Peter spoke up and said to Jesus, "I will never leave you, even though all the rest do!"

34 Jesus said to Peter, "I tell you that before the cock crows tonight, you will say three times that you do not know me."

35 Peter answered, "I will never say that, even if I have to die with you!"

And all the other disciples said the same thing.

Jesus Prays in Gethsemane

(Mk 14.32–42; Lk 22.39–46)

36 Then Jesus went with his disciples to a place called Gethsemane, and he said to them, "Sit here while I go over there and pray." 37He took with him Peter and the two sons of Zebedee. Grief and anguish came over him, 38and he said to them,

"The sorrow in my heart is so great that it
almost crushes me. Stay here and keep
watch with me."
39 He went a little farther on, threw himself
face downwards on the ground, and
prayed, "My Father, if it is possible, take
this cup of suffering from me! Yet not what
I want, but what you want."
40 Then he returned to the three disciples
and found them asleep; and he said to
Peter, "How is it that you three were not
able to keep watch with me even for one
hour? 41Keep watch and pray that you will
not fall into temptation. The spirit is
willing, but the flesh is weak."
42 Once more Jesus went away and prayed,
"My Father, if this cup of suffering cannot
be taken away unless I drink it, your will be
done." 43He returned once more and found
the disciples asleep; they could not keep
their eyes open.
44 Again Jesus left them, went away, and
prayed the third time, saying the same
words. 45Then he returned to the disciples
and said, "Are you still sleeping and
resting? Look! The hour has come for the
Son of Man to be handed over to the power
of sinners. 46Get up, let us go. Look, here is
the man who is betraying me!"

The Arrest of Jesus

(Mk 14.43–50; Lk 22.47–53; Jn 18.3–12)

47 Jesus was still speaking when Judas, one
of the twelve disciples, arrived. With him
was a large crowd armed with swords and
clubs and sent by the chief priests and the
elders. 48The traitor had given the crowd a
signal: "The man I kiss is the one you want.
Arrest him!"
49 Judas went straight to Jesus and said,
"Peace be with you, Teacher," and kissed
him.
50 Jesus answered, "Be quick about it,
friend!"[a]

Then they came up, arrested Jesus, and
held him tight. 51One of those who were
with Jesus drew his sword and struck at the
High Priest's slave, cutting off his ear.
52"Put your sword back in its place," Jesus
said to him. "All who take the sword will
die by the sword. 53Don't you know that I
could call on my Father for help, and at
once he would send me more than twelve
armies of angels? 54But in that case, how
could the Scriptures come true which say
that this is what must happen?"
55 Then Jesus spoke to the crowd, "Did you
have to come with swords and clubs to
capture me, as though I were an outlaw?
Every day I sat down and taught in the
Temple, and you did not arrest me. 56But
all this has happened in order to make
what the prophets wrote in the Scriptures
come true."

Then all the disciples left him and ran
away.

Jesus Before the Council

(Mk 14.53–65; Lk 22.54–55, 63–71; Jn 18.13–14, 19–24)

57 Those who had arrested Jesus took him
to the house of Caiaphas, the High Priest,
where the teachers of the Law and the
elders had gathered together. 58Peter
followed from a distance, as far as the
courtyard of the High Priest's house. He
went into the courtyard and sat down
with the guards to see how it would all
come out. 59The chief priests and the
whole Council tried to find some false
evidence against Jesus to put him to
death; 60but they could not find any, even
though many people came forward and
told lies about him. Finally two men
stepped up 61and said, "This man said, 'I
am able to tear down God's Temple and
three days later build it up again.' "
62 The High Priest stood up and said to
Jesus, "Have you no answer to give to this
accusation against you?" 63But Jesus kept
quiet. Again the High Priest spoke to him,
"In the name of the living God I now put
you on oath: tell us if you are the Messiah,
the Son of God."
64 Jesus answered him, "So you say. But I
tell all of you: from this time on you will
see the Son of Man sitting on the right of
the Almighty and coming on the clouds of
heaven!"

[a] **26.50** Be quick about it, friend!; *or* Why are you here, friend?

65 At this the High Priest tore his clothes
and said, "Blasphemy! We don't need any
more witnesses! You have just heard his
blasphemy! [66]What do you think?"
They answered, "He is guilty and must
die."
67 Then they spat in his face and beat him;
and those who slapped him [68]said,
"Prophesy for us, Messiah! Guess who hit
you!"

Peter Denies Jesus

(Mk 14.66–72; Lk 22.56–62; Jn 18.15–18, 25–27)

69 Peter was sitting outside in the courtyard
when one of the High Priest's servant
women came to him and said, "You, too,
were with Jesus of Galilee."
70 But he denied it in front of them all. "I
don't know what you are talking about," he
answered, [71]and went on out to the
entrance of the courtyard. Another servant
woman saw him and said to the men there,
"He was with Jesus of Nazareth."
72 Again Peter denied it and answered, "I
swear that I don't know that man!"
73 After a little while the men standing
there came to Peter. "Of course you are one
of them," they said. "After all, the way you
speak gives you away!"
74 Then Peter said, "I swear that I am telling
the truth! May God punish me if I am not!
I do not know that man!"
Just then a cock crowed, [75]and Peter
remembered what Jesus had told him:
"Before the cock crows, you will say three
times that you do not know me." He went
out and wept bitterly.

Jesus is Taken to Pilate

(Mk 15.1; Lk 23.1–2; Jn 18.28–32)

27 Early in the morning all the chief
priests and the elders made their plans
against Jesus to put him to death.
[2]They put him in chains, led him off, and
handed him over to Pilate, the Roman
governor.

The Death of Judas

(Acts 1.18–19)

3 When Judas, the traitor, learnt that Jesus
had been condemned, he repented and
took back the 30 silver coins to the chief
priests and the elders. [4]"I have sinned by
betraying an innocent man to death!" he
said.
"What do we care about that?" they
answered. "That is your business!"
5 Judas threw the coins down in the
Temple and left; then he went off and
hanged himself.
6 The chief priests picked up the coins and
said, "This is blood money, and it is against
our Law to put it in the temple treasury."
[7]After reaching an agreement about it, they
used the money to buy Potter's Field, as a
cemetery for foreigners. [8]That is why that
field is called "Field of Blood" to this very
day.
9 Then what the prophet Jeremiah had
said came true: "They took the thirty silver
coins, the amount the people of Israel had
agreed to pay for him, [10]and used the
money to buy the potter's field, as the Lord
had commanded me."

Pilate Questions Jesus

(Mk 15.2–5; Lk 23.3–5; Jn 18.33–38)

11 Jesus stood before the Roman governor,
who questioned him. "Are you the king of
the Jews?" he asked.

Jesus is questioned by Pontius Pilate, the Roman governor.

"So you say," answered Jesus. 12But he
said nothing in response to the accusations
of the chief priests and elders.
13 So Pilate said to him, "Don't you hear all
these things they accuse you of?"
14 But Jesus refused to answer a single word,
with the result that the Governor was
greatly surprised.

Jesus is Sentenced to Death

(Mk 15.6–15; Lk 23.13–25; Jn 18.39—19.16)

15 At every Passover Festival the Roman
governor was in the habit of setting free
any one prisoner the crowd asked for. 16At
that time there was a well-known prisoner
named Jesus Barabbas. 17So when the
crowd gathered, Pilate asked them, "Which
one do you want me to set free for you?
Jesus Barabbas or Jesus called the
Messiah?" 18He knew very well that the
Jewish authorities had handed Jesus over
to him because they were jealous.
19 While Pilate was sitting in the judgement
hall, his wife sent him a message: "Have
nothing to do with that innocent man,
because in a dream last night I suffered
much on account of him."
20 The chief priests and the elders
persuaded the crowd to ask Pilate to set
Barabbas free and have Jesus put to death.
21But Pilate asked the crowd, "Which one
of these two do you want me to set free for
you?"

"Barabbas!" they answered.
22 "What, then, shall I do with Jesus called
the Messiah?" Pilate asked them.

"Crucify him!" they all answered.
23 But Pilate asked, "What crime has he
committed?"

Then they started shouting at the top of
their voices: "Crucify him!"
24 When Pilate saw that it was no use to go
on, but that a riot might break out, he took
some water, washed his hands in front of
the crowd, and said, "I am not responsible
for the death of this man! This is your
doing!"
25 The whole crowd answered, "Let the
responsibility for his death fall on us and
our children!"
26 Then Pilate set Barabbas free for them;
and after he had Jesus whipped, he handed
him over to be crucified.

The Soldiers Mock Jesus

(Mk 15.16–20; Jn 19.2–3)

27 Then Pilate's soldiers took Jesus into the
governor's palace, and the whole company
gathered round him. 28They stripped off
his clothes and put a scarlet robe on him.
29Then they made a crown out of thorny
branches and placed it on his head, and
put a stick in his right hand; then they
knelt before him and mocked him. "Long
live the King of the Jews!" they said.
30They spat on him, and took the stick and
hit him over the head. 31When they had
finished mocking him, they took the robe
off and put his own clothes back on him.
Then they led him out to crucify him.

Jesus is Crucified

(Mk 15.21–32; Lk 23.26–43; Jn 19.17–27)

32 As they were going out, they met a man
from Cyrene named Simon, and the
soldiers forced him to carry Jesus' cross.
33They came to a place called Golgotha,
which means, "The Place of the Skull".
34There they offered Jesus wine mixed
with a bitter substance; but after tasting it,
he would not drink it.
35 They crucified him and then divided his
clothes among them by throwing dice.
36After that they sat there and watched
him. 37Above his head they put the
written notice of the accusation against
him: "This is Jesus, the King of the Jews."
38Then they crucified two bandits with
Jesus, one on his right and the other on his
left.
39 People passing by shook their heads and
hurled insults at Jesus: 40"You were going
to tear down the Temple and build it up
again in three days! Save yourself if you are
God's Son! Come on down from the cross!"
41 In the same way the chief priests and
the teachers of the Law and the elders
jeered at him: 42"He saved others, but he
cannot save himself! Isn't he the king of
Israel? If he comes down off the cross

now, we will believe in him! 43He trusts in
God and claims to be God's Son. Well,
then, let us see if God wants to save him
now!"
44 Even the bandits who had been crucified
with him insulted him in the same way.

The Death of Jesus

(Mk 15.33–41; Lk 23.44–49; Jn 19.28–30)

45 At noon the whole country was covered
with darkness, which lasted for three hours.
46At about three o'clock Jesus cried out
with a loud shout, *"Eli, Eli, lema sabachthani?"*
which means, "My God, my God, why did
you abandon me?"
47 Some of the people standing there heard
him and said, "He is calling for Elijah!"
48One of them ran up at once, took a
sponge, soaked it in cheap wine, put it on
the end of a stick, and tried to make him
drink it.
49 But the others said, "Wait, let us see if
Elijah is coming to save him!"
50 Jesus again gave a loud cry and breathed
his last.
51 Then the curtain hanging in the Temple
was torn in two from top to bottom. The
earth shook, the rocks split apart, 52the
graves broke open, and many of God's
people who had died were raised to
life. 53They left the graves, and
after Jesus rose from death,
they went into the Holy
City, where many people
saw them.
54 When the army
officer and the soldiers
with him who were
watching Jesus saw
the earthquake and
everything else that
happened, they were
terrified and said, "He
really was the Son of
God!"
55 There were many women
there, looking on from a
distance, who had followed
Jesus from Galilee and helped him.
56Among them were Mary Magdalene,
Mary the mother of James and Joseph, and
the wife of Zebedee.

The Burial of Jesus

(Mk 15.42–47; Lk 23.50–56; Jn 19.38–42)

57 When it was evening, a rich man from
Arimathea arrived; his name was Joseph,
and he also was a disciple of Jesus. 58He
went into the presence of Pilate and asked
for the body of Jesus. Pilate gave orders for
the body to be given to Joseph. 59So
Joseph took it, wrapped it in a new linen
sheet, 60and placed it in his own tomb,
which he had just recently dug out of
solid rock. Then he rolled a large stone
across the entrance to the tomb and went
away. 61Mary Magdalene and the other
Mary were sitting there, facing the tomb.

The Guard at the Tomb

62 The next day, which was a Sabbath, the
chief priests and the Pharisees met with
Pilate 63and said, "Sir, we remember that
while that liar was still alive he said, 'I will
be raised to life three days later.' 64Give
orders, then, for his tomb to be carefully
guarded until the third day, so that his
disciples will not be able to go
and steal the body, and
then tell the people
that he was raised
from death.
This last lie
would be
even worse
than the
first one."

Jesus died on the cross.

65 "Take a guard," Pilate told them; "go and
make the tomb as secure as you can."
66 So they left and made the tomb secure by
putting a seal on the stone and leaving the
guard on watch.

The Resurrection

(Mk 16.1–10; Lk 24.1–12; Jn 20.1–10)

28 After the Sabbath, as Sunday morning
was dawning, Mary Magdalene and
the other Mary went to look at the
tomb. [2]Suddenly there was a violent
earthquake; an angel of the Lord came
down from heaven, rolled
the stone away, and sat on
it. [3]His appearance was like
lightning, and his clothes
were white as snow. [4]The
guards were so afraid that
they trembled and became
like dead men.
5 The angel spoke to the
women. "You must not be
afraid," he said. "I know you
are looking for Jesus, who
was crucified. [6]He is not
here; he has been raised, just
as he said. Come here and
see the place where he was
lying. [7]Go quickly now, and
tell his disciples, 'He has been raised from
death, and now he is going to Galilee ahead
of you; there you will see him!' Remember
what I have told you."
8 So they left the tomb in a hurry, afraid
and yet filled with joy, and ran to tell his
disciples.
9 Suddenly Jesus met them and said, "Peace
be with you." They came up to him, took
hold of his feet, and worshipped him. [10]"Do
not be afraid," Jesus said to them. "Go and
tell my brothers to go to Galilee, and there
they will see me."

The Report of the Guard

11 While the women went on their way,
some of the soldiers guarding the tomb
went back to the city and told the chief
priests everything that had happened.
[12]The chief priests met with the elders and
made their plan; they gave a large sum of
money to the soldiers [13]and said, "You are
to say that his disciples came during the
night and stole his body while you were
asleep. [14]And if the Governor should hear
of this, we will convince him that you are
innocent, and you will have nothing to
worry about."
15 The guards took the money and did what
they were told to do. And so that is the
report spread round by the Jews to this very
day.

A church Easter garden showing three crosses and a tomb.

Jesus Appears to his Disciples

(Mk 16.14–18; Lk 24.36–49; Jn 20.19–23; Acts 1.6–8)

16 The eleven disciples went to the hill in
Galilee where Jesus had told them to go.
[17]When they saw him, they worshipped
him, even though some of them doubted.
[18]Jesus drew near and said to them, "I have
been given all authority in heaven and on
earth. [19]Go, then, to all peoples
everywhere and make them my disciples:
baptize them in the name of the Father, the
Son, and the Holy Spirit, [20]and teach them
to obey everything I have commanded you.
And I will be with you always, to the end of
the age."

The Gospel According to Mark

This is the shortest of the four Gospels. Mark was not a disciple of Jesus but it is thought that he was the first to write an account of the life of Jesus. When he starts his story Jesus is already grown up.

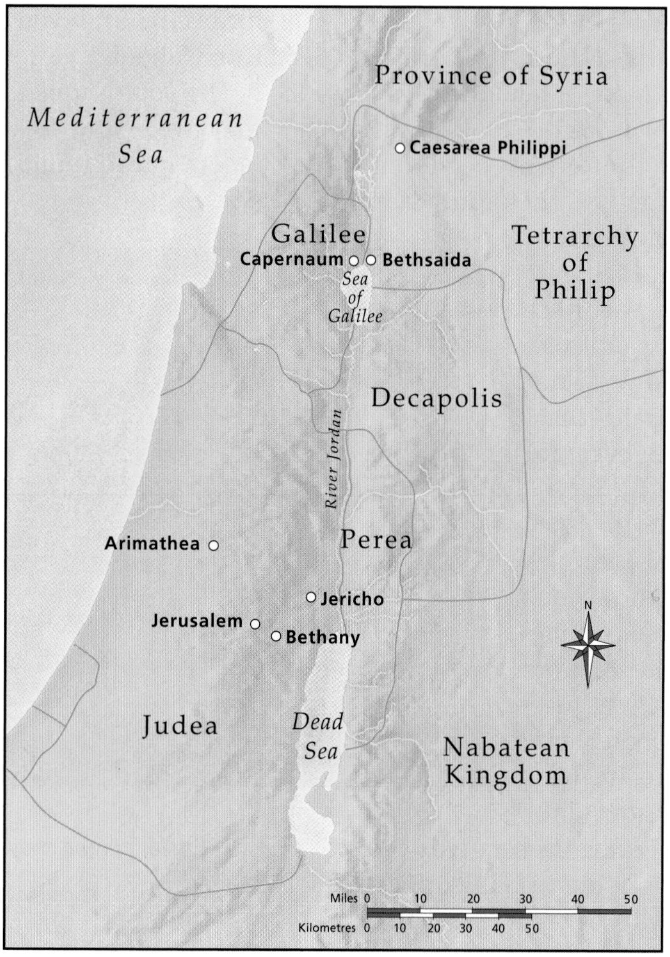

The Life of Jesus

(All dates are approximate)

10 | 0 | 10 | 20 | 30

5/4 BCE
Jesus is born in Bethlehem

7/8 CE
Jesus visits the Temple with his parents

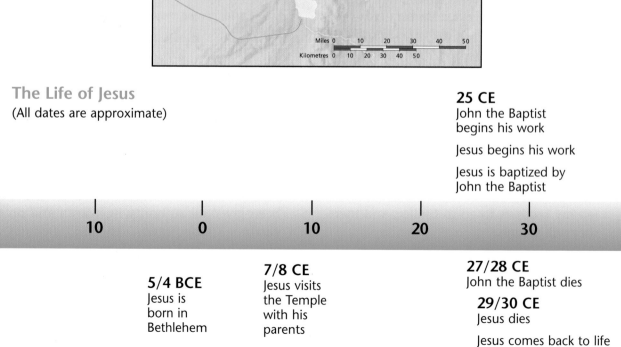

25 CE
John the Baptist begins his work

Jesus begins his work

Jesus is baptized by John the Baptist

27/28 CE
John the Baptist dies

29/30 CE
Jesus dies

Jesus comes back to life

The Preaching of John the Baptist
(Mt 3.1–12; Lk 3.1–18; Jn 1.19–28)

1 This is the Good News about Jesus
Christ, the Son of God.[a] [2]It began as
the prophet Isaiah had written:

"God said, 'I will send my messenger
ahead of you
to clear the way for you.'
3 Someone is shouting in the desert,
'Get the road ready for the Lord;
make a straight path for him to
travel!' "

4 So John appeared in the desert, baptizing
and preaching.[b] "Turn away from your sins
and be baptized," he told the people, "and
God will forgive your sins." [5]Many people
from the province of Judea and the city of
Jerusalem went out to hear John. They
confessed their sins, and he baptized them
in the River Jordan.
6 John wore clothes made of camel's hair,
with a leather belt round his waist, and his
food was locusts and wild honey. [7]He
announced to the people, "The man who
will come after me is much greater than I
am. I am not good enough even to bend
down and untie his sandals. [8]I baptize you
with water, but he will baptize you with the
Holy Spirit."

The Baptism and Temptation of Jesus
(Mt 3.13—4.11; Lk 3.21–22; 4.1–13)

9 Not long afterwards Jesus came from
Nazareth in the province of Galilee, and
was baptized by John in the Jordan. [10]As
soon as Jesus came up out of the water, he
saw heaven opening and the Spirit coming
down on him like a dove. [11]And a voice
came from heaven, "You are my own dear
Son. I am pleased with you."
12 At once the Spirit made him go into the
desert, [13]where he stayed 40 days, being
tempted by Satan. Wild animals were there
also, but angels came and helped him.

[a] **1.1** *Some manuscripts do not have* the Son of God.
[b] **1.4** John appeared in the desert, baptizing and preaching; *some manuscripts have* John the Baptist appeared in the desert, preaching.

Jesus Calls Four Fishermen
(Mt 4.12–22; Lk 4.14–15; 5.1–11)

14 After John had been put in prison, Jesus
went to Galilee and preached the Good
News from God. [15]"The right time has
come," he said, "and the Kingdom of God
is near! Turn away from your sins and
believe the Good News!"
16 As Jesus walked along the shore of Lake
Galilee, he saw two fishermen, Simon and
his brother Andrew, catching fish with a
net. [17]Jesus said to them, "Come with me,
and I will teach you to catch people." [18]At
once they left their nets and went with
him.
19 He went a little farther on and saw two
other brothers, James and John, the sons of
Zebedee. They were in their boat getting
their nets ready. [20]As soon as Jesus saw
them, he called them; they left their father
Zebedee in the boat with the hired men
and went with Jesus.

A Man with an Evil Spirit
(Lk 4.31–37)

21 Jesus and his disciples came to the town
of Capernaum, and on the next Sabbath
Jesus went to the synagogue and began to
teach. [22]The people who heard him were
amazed at the way he taught, for he wasn't
like the teachers of the Law; instead, he
taught with authority.
23 Just then a man with an evil spirit in him
came into the synagogue and screamed,
[24]"What do you want with us, Jesus of
Nazareth? Are you here to destroy us? I
know who you are – you are God's holy
messenger!"
25 Jesus ordered the spirit, "Be quiet, and
come out of the man!"
26 The evil spirit shook the man hard, gave
a loud scream, and came out of him. [27]The
people were all so amazed that they started
saying to one another, "What is this? Is it
some kind of new teaching? This man has
authority to give orders to the evil spirits,
and they obey him!"
28 And so the news about Jesus spread
quickly everywhere in the province of
Galilee.

Jesus Heals Many People
(Mt 8.14–17; Lk 4.38–41)

29 Jesus and his disciples, including James
and John, left the synagogue and went
straight to the home of Simon and Andrew.
30 Simon's mother-in-law was sick in bed
with a fever, and as soon as Jesus arrived,
he was told about her. 31 He went to her,
took her by the hand, and helped her up.
The fever left her, and she began to wait on
them.
32 After the sun had set and evening had
come, people brought to Jesus all the sick
and those who had demons. 33 All the
people of the town gathered in front of the
house. 34 Jesus healed many who were sick
with all kinds of diseases and drove out
many demons. He would not let the
demons say anything, because they knew
who he was.

Jesus Preaches in Galilee
(Lk 4.42–44)

35 Very early the next morning, long before
daylight, Jesus got up and left the house.
He went out of the town to a lonely place,
where he prayed. 36 But Simon and his
companions went out searching for him,
37 and when they found him, they said,
"Everyone is looking for you."
38 But Jesus answered, "We must go on to
the other villages round here. I have to
preach in them also, because that is why I
came."
39 So he travelled all over Galilee,
preaching in the synagogues and driving
out demons.

Jesus Heals a Man
(Mt 8.1–4; Lk 5.12–16)

40 A man suffering from a dreaded skin
disease came to Jesus, knelt down, and
begged him for help. "If you want to," he
said, "you can make me clean."[a]
41 Jesus was filled with pity,[b] and stretched
out his hand and touched him. "I do want
to," he answered. "Be clean!" 42 At once the
disease left the man, and he was clean.
43 Then Jesus spoke sternly to him and sent
him away at once, 44 after saying to him,
"Listen, don't tell anyone about this. But go
straight to the priest and let him examine
you; then in order to prove to everyone
that you are cured, offer the sacrifice that
Moses ordered."
45 But the man went away and began to
spread the news everywhere. Indeed, he
talked so much that Jesus could not go into
a town publicly. Instead, he stayed out in
lonely places, and people came to him from
everywhere.

Jesus frightened the disciples when he calmed a storm.

Jesus Heals a Paralysed Man
(Mt 9.1–8; Lk 5.17–26)

2 A few days later Jesus went back to
Capernaum, and the news spread that
he was at home. 2 So many people
came together that there was no room left,
not even out in front of the door. Jesus was

[a] **1.40** MAKE ME CLEAN: *This disease was considered to make a person ritually unclean.*

[b] **1.41** pity; *some manuscripts have* anger.

preaching the message to them [3]when four
men arrived, carrying a paralysed man to
Jesus. [4]Because of the crowd, however, they
could not get the man to him. So they
made a hole in the roof right above the
place where Jesus was. When they had
made an opening, they let the man down,
lying on his mat. [5]Seeing how much faith
they had, Jesus said to the paralysed man,
"My son, your sins are forgiven."
6 Some teachers of the Law who were
sitting there thought to themselves, [7]"How
does he dare to talk like this? This is
blasphemy! God is the only one who can
forgive sins!"
8 At once Jesus knew what they were
thinking, so he said to them, "Why do you
think such things? [9]Is it easier to say to this
paralysed man, 'Your sins are forgiven', or to
say, 'Get up, pick up your mat, and walk'?
[10]I will prove to you, then, that the Son of
Man has authority on earth to forgive sins."
So he said to the paralysed man, [11]"I tell
you, get up, pick up your mat, and go
home!"
12 While they all watched, the man got up,
picked up his mat, and hurried away. They
were all completely amazed and praised
God, saying, "We have never seen anything
like this!"

Jesus Calls Levi

(Mt 9.9–13; Lk 5.27–32)

13 Jesus went back again to the shore of
Lake Galilee. A crowd came to him, and he
started teaching them. [14]As he walked
along, he saw a tax collector, Levi son of
Alphaeus, sitting in his office. Jesus said to
him, "Follow me." Levi got up and
followed him.
15 Later on Jesus was having a meal in Levi's
house.[a] A large number of tax collectors
and other outcasts were following Jesus,
and many of them joined him and his
disciples at the table. [16]Some teachers of
the Law, who were Pharisees, saw that Jesus
was eating with these outcasts and tax
collectors, so they asked his disciples, "Why
does he eat with such people?"
17 Jesus heard them and answered, "People
who are well do not need a doctor, but only
those who are sick. I have not come to call
respectable people, but outcasts."

The Question about Fasting

(Mt 9.14–17; Lk 5.33–39)

18 On one occasion the followers of John
the Baptist and the Pharisees were fasting.
Some people came to Jesus and asked him,
"Why is it that the disciples of John the
Baptist and the disciples of the Pharisees
fast, but yours do not?"
19 Jesus answered, "Do you expect the
guests at a wedding party to go without
food? Of course not! As long as the
bridegroom is with them, they will not do
that. [20]But the day will come when the
bridegroom will be taken away from them,
and then they will fast.
21 "No one uses a piece of new cloth to
patch up an old coat, because the new
patch will shrink and tear off some of the
old cloth, making an even bigger hole.
[22]Nor does anyone pour new wine into
used wineskins, because the wine will burst
the skins, and both the wine and the skins
will be ruined. Instead, new wine must be
poured into fresh wineskins."

The Question about the Sabbath

(Mt 12.1–8; Lk 6.1–5)

23 Jesus was walking through some
cornfields on the Sabbath. As his disciples
walked along with him, they began to pick
the ears of corn. [24]So the Pharisees said to
Jesus, "Look, it is against our Law for your
disciples to do that on the Sabbath!"
25 Jesus answered, "Have you never read
what David did that time when he needed
something to eat? He and his men were
hungry, [26]so he went into the house of God
and ate the bread offered to God. This
happened when Abiathar was the High
Priest. According to our Law only the
priests may eat this bread – but David ate it
and even gave it to his men."
27 And Jesus concluded, "The Sabbath was
made for the good of human beings; they
were not made for the Sabbath. [28]So the
Son of Man is Lord even of the Sabbath."

[a] **2.15** in Levi's house; *or* in his *(that is,* Jesus') house.

The Man with a Paralysed Hand
(Mt 12.9–14; Lk 6.6–11)

3 Then Jesus went back to the synagogue,
where there was a man who had a
paralysed hand. [2]Some people were
there who wanted to accuse Jesus of doing
wrong; so they watched him closely to see
whether he would heal the man on the
Sabbath. [3]Jesus said to the man, "Come up
here to the front." [4]Then he asked the
people, "What does our Law allow us to do
on the Sabbath? To help or to harm? To save
someone's life or to destroy it?"
But they did not say a thing. [5]Jesus was
angry as he looked round at them, but at
the same time he felt sorry for them,
because they were so stubborn and wrong.
Then he said to the man, "Stretch out your
hand." He stretched it out, and it became
well again. [6]So the Pharisees left the
synagogue and met at once with some
members of Herod's party, and they made
plans to kill Jesus.

A Crowd by the Lake

7 Jesus and his disciples went away to Lake
Galilee, and a large crowd followed him.
They had come from Galilee, from Judea,
[8]from Jerusalem, from the territory of
Idumea, from the territory on the east side
of the Jordan, and from the region round
the cities of Tyre and Sidon. All these
people came to Jesus because they had
heard of the things he was doing. [9]The
crowd was so large that Jesus told his
disciples to get a boat ready for him, so that
the people would not crush him. [10]He had
healed many people, and all those who
were ill kept pushing their way to him in
order to touch him. [11]And whenever the
people who had evil spirits in them saw
him, they would fall down before him and
scream, "You are the Son of God!"
12 Jesus sternly ordered the evil spirits not
to tell anyone who he was.

Jesus Chooses the Twelve Apostles
(Mt 10.1–4; Lk 6.12–16)

13 Then Jesus went up a hill and called to
himself the men he wanted. They came to
him, [14]and he chose twelve, whom he
named apostles. "I have chosen you to be
with me," he told them. "I will also send
you out to preach, [15]and you will have
authority to drive out demons."
16 These are the twelve he chose: Simon
(Jesus gave him the name Peter); [17]James
and his brother John, the sons of Zebedee
(Jesus gave them the name Boanerges,
which means "Men of Thunder");
[18]Andrew, Philip, Bartholomew, Matthew,
Thomas, James son of Alphaeus,
Thaddaeus, Simon the Patriot, [19]and Judas
Iscariot, who betrayed Jesus.

Jesus and Beelzebul
(Mt 12.22–32; Lk 11.14–23; 12.10)

20 Then Jesus went home. Again such a
large crowd gathered that Jesus and his
disciples had no time to eat. [21]When his
family heard about it, they set out to take
charge of him, because people were
saying, "He's gone mad!"
22 Some teachers of the Law who had come
from Jerusalem were saying, "He has
Beelzebul in him! It is the chief of the
demons who gives him the power to drive
them out."
23 So Jesus called them to him and spoke to
them in parables: "How can Satan drive out
Satan? [24]If a country divides itself into
groups which fight each other, that country
will fall apart. [25]If a family divides itself
into groups which fight each other, that
family will fall apart. [26]So if Satan's
kingdom divides into groups, it cannot last,
but will fall apart and come to an end.
27 "No one can break into a strong man's
house and take away his belongings unless
he first ties up the strong man; then he can
plunder his house.
28 "I assure you that people can be forgiven
all their sins and all the evil things they
may say.[a] [29]But whoever says evil things
against the Holy Spirit will never be
forgiven, because he has committed an
eternal sin." [30](Jesus said this because some
people were saying, "He has an evil spirit in
him.")

[a] **3.28** evil things they may say; *or* evil things they may say against God.

Jesus' Mother and Brothers
(Mt 12.46–50; Lk 8.19–21)

31 Then Jesus' mother and brothers arrived.
They stood outside the house and sent in a
message, asking for him. [32]A crowd was
sitting round Jesus, and they said to him,
"Look, your mother and your brothers and
sisters are outside, and they want you."
33 Jesus answered, "Who is my mother?
Who are my brothers?" [34]He looked at the
people sitting round him and said, "Look!
Here are my mother and my brothers!
[35]Whoever does what God wants him to do
is my brother, my sister, my mother."

The Parable of the Sower
(Mt 13.1–9; Lk 8.4–8)

4 Again Jesus began to teach beside Lake
Galilee. The crowd that gathered
round him was so large that he got
into a boat and sat in it. The boat was out
in the water, and the crowd stood on the
shore at the water's edge. [2]He used parables
to teach them many things, saying to
them:
3 "Listen! Once there was a man who went
out to sow corn. [4]As he scattered the seed
in the field, some of it fell along the path,
and the birds came and ate it up. [5]Some of
it fell on rocky ground, where there was
little soil. The seeds soon sprouted, because
the soil wasn't deep. [6]Then, when the sun
came up, it burnt the young plants; and
because the roots had not grown deep
enough, the plants soon dried up. [7]Some of
the seed fell among thorn bushes, which
grew up and choked the plants, and they
didn't produce any corn. [8]But some seeds
fell in good soil, and the plants sprouted,
grew, and produced corn: some had thirty
grains, others sixty, and others a hundred."
9 And Jesus concluded, "Listen, then, if
you have ears!"

The Purpose of the Parables
(Mt 13.10–17; Lk 8.9–10)

10 When Jesus was alone, some of those
who had heard him came to him with the
twelve disciples and asked him to explain
the parables. [11]"You have been given the
secret of the Kingdom of God," Jesus
answered. "But the others, who are on the
outside, hear all things by means of
parables, [12]so that,

'They may look and look,
yet not see;
they may listen and listen,
yet not understand.
For if they did, they would turn to God,
and he would forgive them.' "

Jesus Explains the Parable of the Sower
(Mt 13.18–23; Lk 8.11–15)

13 Then Jesus asked them, "Don't you
understand this parable? How, then, will
you ever understand any parable? [14]The
sower sows God's message. [15]Some people
are like the seeds that fall along the path; as
soon as they hear the message, Satan comes
and takes it away. [16]Other people are like
the seeds that fall on rocky ground. As soon
as they hear the message, they receive it
gladly. [17]But it does not sink deep into
them, and they don't last long. So when
trouble or persecution comes because of the
message, they give up at once. [18]Other
people are like the seeds sown among the
thorn bushes. These are the ones who hear
the message, [19]but the worries about this
life, the love for riches, and all other kinds
of desires crowd in and choke the message,
and they don't bear fruit. [20]But other
people are like the seeds sown in good soil.
They hear the message, accept it, and bear
fruit: some thirty, some sixty, and some a
hundred."

A Lamp under a Bowl
(Lk 8.16–18)

21 Jesus continued, "Does anyone ever
bring in a lamp and put it under a bowl or
under the bed? Doesn't he put it on the
lampstand? [22]Whatever is hidden away
will be brought out into the open, and
whatever is covered up will be uncovered.
[23]Listen, then, if you have ears!"
24 He also said to them, "Pay attention to
what you hear! The same rules you use to

judge others will be used by God to judge
you – but with even greater severity.
[25]Those who have something will be given
more, and those who have nothing will
have taken away from them even the little
they have."

The Parable of the Growing Seed

26 Jesus went on to say, "The Kingdom of
God is like this. A man scatters seed in his
field. [27]He sleeps at night, is up and about
during the day, and all the while the seeds
are sprouting and growing. Yet he does not
know how it happens. [28]The soil itself
makes the plants grow and bear fruit; first
the tender stalk appears, then the ear, and
finally the ear full of corn. [29]When the
corn is ripe, the man starts cutting it with
his sickle, because harvest time has come.

The Parable of the Mustard Seed

(Mt 13.31–32, 34; Lk 13.18–19)

30 "What shall we say the Kingdom of God
is like?" asked Jesus. "What parable shall we
use to explain it? [31]It is like this. A man
takes a mustard seed, the smallest seed in
the world, and plants it in the ground.
[32]After a while it grows up and becomes
the biggest of all plants. It puts out such
large branches that the birds come and
make their nests in its shade."

33 Jesus preached his message to the people,
using many other parables like these; he
told them as much as they could
understand. [34]He would not speak to them
without using parables, but when he was
alone with his disciples, he would explain
everything to them.

Jesus Calms a Storm

(Mt 8.23–27; Lk 8.22–25)

35 On the evening of that same day Jesus
said to his disciples, "Let us go across to
the other side of the lake." [36]So they left
the crowd; the disciples got into the boat
in which Jesus was already sitting, and
they took him with them. Other boats
were there too. [37]Suddenly a strong wind
blew up, and the waves began to spill over
into the boat, so that it was about to fill
with water. [38]Jesus was in the back of the
boat, sleeping with his head on a pillow.
The disciples woke him up and said,
"Teacher, don't you care that we are about
to die?"

39 Jesus stood up and commanded the
wind, "Be quiet!" and he said to the waves,
"Be still!" The wind died down, and there
was a great calm. [40]Then Jesus said to his
disciples, "Why are you frightened? Have
you still no faith?"

41 But they were terribly afraid and said to
one another, "Who is this man? Even the
wind and the waves obey him!"

Jesus Heals a Man with Evil Spirits

(Mt 8.28–34; Lk 8.26–39)

5 Jesus and his disciples arrived on the
other side of Lake Galilee, in the
territory of Gerasa. [2]As soon as Jesus
got out of the boat, he was met by a man
who came out of the burial caves there.
This man had an evil spirit in him [3]and
lived among the tombs. Nobody could
keep him chained up any more; [4]many
times his feet and hands had been
chained, but every time he broke the
chains and smashed the irons on his feet.
He was too strong for anyone to control
him. [5]Day and night he wandered among
the tombs and through the hills,
screaming and cutting himself with
stones.

6 He was some distance away when he saw
Jesus; so he ran, fell on his knees before
him, [7]and screamed in a loud voice, "Jesus,
Son of the Most High God! What do you
want with me? For God's sake, I beg you,
don't punish me!" [8](He said this because
Jesus was saying, "Evil spirit, come out of
this man!")

9 So Jesus asked him, "What is your
name?"

The man answered, "My name is 'Mob' –
there are so many of us!" [10]And he kept
begging Jesus not to send the evil spirits out
of that region.

11 There was a large herd of pigs near by,
feeding on a hillside. [12]So the spirits
begged Jesus, "Send us to the pigs, and let

us go into them." [13]He let them go, and the evil spirits went out of the man and entered the pigs. The whole herd – about 2,000 pigs in all – rushed down the side of the cliff into the lake and was drowned.

14 The men who had been taking care of the pigs ran away and spread the news in the town and among the farms. People went out to see what had happened, [15]and when they came to Jesus, they saw the man who used to have the mob of demons in him. He was sitting there, clothed and in his right mind; and they were all afraid. [16]Those who had seen it told the people what had happened to the man with the demons, and about the pigs.

17 So they asked Jesus to leave their territory.

18 As Jesus was getting into the boat, the man who had had the demons begged him, "Let me go with you!"

19 But Jesus would not let him. Instead, he told him, "Go back home to your family and tell them how much the Lord has done for you and how kind he has been to you."

20 So the man left and went all through the Ten Towns, telling what Jesus had done for him. And all who heard it were amazed.

Jairus' Daughter and the Woman who Touched Jesus' Cloak

(Mt 9.18–26; Lk 8.40–56)

21 Jesus went back across to the other side of the lake. There at the lakeside a large crowd gathered round him. [22]Jairus, an official of the local synagogue, arrived, and when he saw Jesus, he threw himself down at his feet [23]and begged him earnestly, "My little daughter is very ill. Please come and place your hands on her, so that she will get well and live!"

24 Then Jesus started off with him. So many people were going along with Jesus that they were crowding him from every side.

25 There was a woman who had suffered terribly from severe bleeding for twelve years, [26]even though she had been treated by many doctors. She had spent all her money, but instead of getting better she got worse all the time. [27]She had heard about Jesus, so she came in the crowd behind him, [28]saying to herself, "If I just touch his clothes, I will get well."

29 She touched his cloak, and her bleeding stopped at once; and she had the feeling inside herself that she was healed of her trouble. [30]At once Jesus knew that power had gone out of him, so he turned round in the crowd and asked, "Who touched my clothes?"

31 His disciples answered, "You see how the people are crowding you; why do you ask who touched you?"

32 But Jesus kept looking round to see who had done it. [33]The woman realized what had happened to her, so she came, trembling with fear, knelt at his feet, and told him the whole truth. [34]Jesus said to her, "My daughter, your faith has made you well. Go in peace, and be healed of your trouble."

35 While Jesus was saying this, some messengers came from Jairus' house and told him, "Your daughter has died. Why bother the Teacher any longer?"

36 Jesus paid no attention to[a] what they said, but told him, "Don't be afraid, only believe." [37]Then he did not let anyone else go on with him except Peter and James and his brother John. [38]They arrived at Jairus' house, where Jesus saw the confusion and heard all the loud crying and wailing. [39]He went in and said to them, "Why all this confusion? Why are you crying? The child is not dead – she is only sleeping!"

40 They laughed at him, so he put them all out, took the child's father and mother and his three disciples, and went into the room where the child was lying. [41]He took her by the hand and said to her, "*Talitha, koum,*" which means, "Little girl, I tell you to get up!"

42 She got up at once and started walking around. (She was twelve years old.) When this happened, they were completely amazed. [43]But Jesus gave them strict orders not to tell anyone, and he said, "Give her something to eat."

[a] **5.36** paid no attention to; *or* overheard.

Jesus is Rejected at Nazareth
(Mt 13.53–58; Lk 4.16–30)

6 Jesus left that place and went back to
his home town, followed by his
disciples. [2]On the Sabbath he began to
teach in the synagogue. Many people were
there; and when they heard him, they were
all amazed. "Where did he get all this?"
they asked. "What wisdom is this that has
been given him? How does he perform
miracles? [3]Isn't he the carpenter, the son of
Mary, and the brother of James, Joseph,
Judas, and Simon? Aren't his sisters living
here?" And so they rejected him.
4 Jesus said to them, "Prophets are
respected everywhere except in their own
home town and by their relatives and their
family."
5 He was not able to perform any miracles
there, except that he placed his hands on a
few sick people and healed them. [6]He was
greatly surprised, because the people did
not have faith.

Jesus Sends out the Twelve Disciples
(Mt 10.5–15; Lk 9.1–6)

Then Jesus went to the villages round
there, teaching the people. [7]He called the
twelve disciples together and sent
them out two by two. He gave them
authority over the evil spirits [8]and
ordered them, "Don't take anything
with you on your journey except a
stick – no bread, no beggar's bag, no
money in your pockets. [9]Wear
sandals, but don't carry an extra
shirt." [10]He also said, "Wherever
you are welcomed, stay in the same
house until you leave that place.
[11]If you come to a town where
people do not welcome you or will
not listen to you, leave it and shake
the dust off your feet. That will be a
warning to them!"
12 So they went out and preached
that people should turn away from
their sins. [13]They drove out many
demons, and rubbed olive oil on
many sick people and healed them.

The Death of John the Baptist
(Mt 14.1–12; Lk 9.7–9)

14 Now King Herod[a] heard about all this,
because Jesus' reputation had spread
everywhere. Some people were saying,
"John the Baptist has come back to life!
That is why he has this power to perform
miracles."
15 Others, however, said, "He is Elijah."
Others said, "He is a prophet, like one of
the prophets of long ago."
16 When Herod heard it, he said, "He is
John the Baptist! I had his head cut off, but
he has come back to life!" [17]Herod himself
had ordered John's arrest, and he had him
chained and put in prison. Herod did this
because of Herodias, whom he had
married, even though she was the wife of
his brother Philip. [18]John the Baptist kept
telling Herod, "It isn't right for you to be
married to your brother's wife!"
19 So Herodias held a grudge against John
and wanted to kill him, but she could not
because of Herod. [20]Herod was afraid of
John because he knew that John was a good
and holy man, and so he kept him safe. He
liked to listen to him, even though he
became greatly disturbed every time he
heard him.
21 Finally Herodias got her chance. It was on Herod's birthday, when he gave a feast for all the chief government officials, the military commanders, and the leading citizens of Galilee.

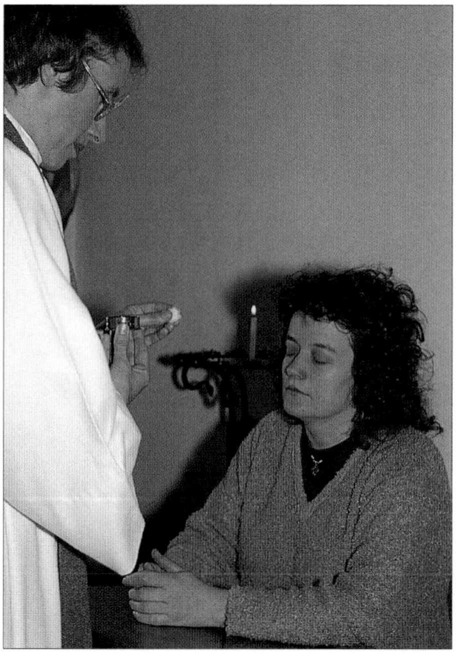

A priest anoints a sick person with oil to heal her.

[a] **6.14** KING HEROD: *Herod Antipas, ruler of Galilee.*

22 The daughter of Herodias[a] came in and
danced, and pleased Herod and his guests.
So the king said to the girl, "What would
you like to have? I will give you anything
you want." 23 With many vows he said to
her, "I swear that I will give you anything
you ask for, even as much as half my
kingdom!"
24 So the girl went out and asked her
mother, "What shall I ask for?"
"The head of John the Baptist," she
answered.
25 The girl hurried back at once to the king
and demanded, "I want you to give me
here and now the head of John the Baptist
on a dish!"
26 This made the king very sad, but he
could not refuse her because of the vows
he had made in front of all his guests. 27 So
he sent off a guard at once with orders to
bring John's head. The guard left, went to
the prison, and cut John's head off; 28 then
he brought it on a dish and gave it to the
girl, who gave it to her mother. 29 When
John's disciples heard about this, they came
and took away his body, and buried it.

Jesus Feeds a Great Crowd

(Mt 14.13–21; Lk 9.10–17; Jn 6.1–14)

30 The apostles returned and met with
Jesus, and told him all they had done and
taught. 31 There were so many people
coming and going that Jesus and his
disciples didn't even have time to eat. So he
said to them, "Let us go off by ourselves to
some place where we will be alone and you
can rest for a while." 32 So they started out
in a boat by themselves for a lonely place.
33 Many people, however, saw them leave
and knew at once who they were; so they
went from all the towns and ran ahead by
land and arrived at the place ahead of Jesus
and his disciples. 34 When Jesus got out of
the boat, he saw this large crowd, and his
heart was filled with pity for them, because
they were like sheep without a shepherd. So
he began to teach them many things.
35 When it was getting late, his disciples
came to him and said, "It is already very
late, and this is a lonely place. 36 Send the
people away, and let them go to the nearby
farms and villages in order to buy
themselves something to eat."
37 "You yourselves give them something to
eat," Jesus answered.
They asked, "Do you want us to go and
spend two hundred silver coins[b] on bread
in order to feed them?"
38 So Jesus asked them, "How much bread
have you got? Go and see."
When they found out, they told him,
"Five loaves and also two fish."
39 Jesus then told his disciples to make all
the people divide into groups and sit down
on the green grass. 40 So the people sat
down in rows, in groups of a hundred and
groups of fifty. 41 Then Jesus took the five
loaves and the two fish, looked up to
heaven, and gave thanks to God. He broke
the loaves and gave them to his disciples to
distribute to the people. He also divided
the two fish among them all. 42 Everyone
ate and had enough. 43 Then the disciples
took up twelve baskets full of what was left
of the bread and the fish. 44 The number of
men who were fed was 5,000.

Jesus Walks on the Water

(Mt 14.22–33; Jn 6.15–21)

45 At once Jesus made his disciples get into
the boat and go ahead of him to
Bethsaida, on the other side of the lake,
while he sent the crowd away. 46 After
saying goodbye to the people he went
away to a hill to pray. 47 When evening
came, the boat was in the middle of the
lake, while Jesus was alone on land. 48 He
saw that his disciples were straining at the
oars, because they were rowing against the
wind; so some time between three and six
o'clock in the morning he came to them,
walking on the water. He was going to pass
them by,[c] 49 but they saw him walking on
the water. "It's a ghost!" they thought, and
screamed. 50 They were all terrified when
they saw him.
Jesus spoke to them at once, "Courage!"
he said. "It is I. Don't be afraid!" 51 Then he

[a] **6.22** The daughter of Herodias; *some manuscripts have* His daughter Herodias.

[b] **6.37** SILVER COINS: *A silver coin was the daily wage of a rural worker (see Mt 20.2).*

[c] **6.48** pass them by; *or* join them.

got into the boat with them, and the wind died down. The disciples were completely amazed, [52]because they had not understood the real meaning of the feeding of the 5,000; their minds could not grasp it.

Jesus Heals the Sick in Gennesaret
(Mt 14.34–36)

53 They crossed the lake and came to land
at Gennesaret, where they tied up the boat.
[54]As they left the boat, people recognized
Jesus at once. [55]So they ran throughout the
whole region; and wherever they heard he was, they brought to him sick people lying
on their mats. [56]And everywhere Jesus
went, to villages, towns, or farms, people would take those who were ill to the market places and beg him to let them at least touch the edge of his cloak; and all who touched it were made well.

The Teaching of the Ancestors
(Mt 15.1–9)

7 Some Pharisees and teachers of the Law who had come from Jerusalem
gathered round Jesus. [2]They noticed
that some of his disciples were eating their food with hands that were ritually unclean – that is, they had not washed them in the way the Pharisees said people should.
3 (For the Pharisees, as well as the rest of the Jews, follow the teaching they received from their ancestors: they do not eat unless they wash their hands in the proper way;
[4]nor do they eat anything that comes from the market unless they wash it first.[a] And they follow many other rules which they have received, such as the proper way to wash cups, pots, copper bowls, and beds.[b])
5 So the Pharisees and the teachers of the Law asked Jesus, "Why is it that your disciples do not follow the teaching handed down by our ancestors, but instead eat with ritually unclean hands?"

6 Jesus answered them, "How right Isaiah was when he prophesied about you! You are hypocrites, just as he wrote:

'These people, says God, honour me
with their words,
but their heart is really far away from
me.
7 It is no use for them to worship me,
because they teach human rules
as though they were God's laws!'

8 "You put aside God's command and obey human teachings."
9 And Jesus continued, "You have a clever way of rejecting God's law in order to
uphold your own teaching. [10]For Moses
commanded, 'Respect your father and your mother,' and, 'Whoever curses his father or his mother is to be put to death.'
[11]But you teach that if a person has something he could use to help his father or mother, but says, 'This is Corban' (which means, it belongs to God), [12]he is
excused from helping his father or
mother. [13]In this way the teaching you
pass on to others cancels out the word of God. And there are many other things like this that you do."

Washing hands before eating was very important in the time of Jesus.

[a] **7.4** anything that comes from the market unless they wash it first; *or* anything after they come from the market unless they wash themselves first.
[b] **7.4** *Some manuscripts do not have* and beds.

The Things that Make a Person Unclean
(Mt 15.10–20)

14 Then Jesus called the crowd to him once
more and said to them, "Listen to me, all of
you, and understand. [15]There is nothing
that goes into a person from the outside
which can make him ritually unclean.
Rather, it is what comes out of a person
that makes him unclean."[a]
17 When he left the crowd and went into
the house, his disciples asked him to
explain this saying. [18]"You are no more
intelligent than the others," Jesus said to
them. "Don't you understand? Nothing
that goes into a person from the outside
can really make him unclean, [19]because it
does not go into his heart but into his
stomach and then goes on out of the
body." (In saying this, Jesus declared that
all foods are fit to be eaten.)
20 And he went on to say, "It is what comes
out of a person that makes him unclean.
[21]For from the inside, from a person's
heart, come the evil ideas which lead him
to do immoral things, to rob, kill,
[22]commit adultery, be greedy, and do all
sorts of evil things; deceit, indecency,
jealousy, slander, pride, and folly – [23]all
these evil things come from inside a person
and make him unclean."

A Woman's Faith
(Mt 15.21–28)

24 Then Jesus left and went away to the
territory near the city of Tyre. He went into
a house and did not want anyone to know
he was there, but he could not stay hidden.
[25]A woman, whose daughter had an evil
spirit in her, heard about Jesus and came to
him at once and fell at his feet. [26]The
woman was a Gentile, born in the region of
Phoenicia in Syria. She begged Jesus to
drive the demon out of her daughter. [27]But
Jesus answered, "Let us first feed the
children. It isn't right to take the children's
food and throw it to the dogs."
28 "Sir," she answered, "even the dogs
under the table eat the children's leftovers!"
29 So Jesus said to her, "Because of that
answer, go back home, where you will find
that the demon has gone out of your
daughter!"
30 She went home and found her child
lying on the bed; the demon had indeed
gone out of her.

Jesus Heals a Deaf-mute

31 Jesus then left the neighbourhood of
Tyre and went on through Sidon to Lake
Galilee, going by way of the territory of the
Ten Towns. [32]Some people brought him a
man who was deaf and could hardly speak,
and they begged Jesus to place his hands on
him. [33]So Jesus took him off alone, away
from the crowd, put his fingers in the
man's ears, spat, and touched the man's
tongue. [34]Then Jesus looked up to heaven,
gave a deep groan, and said to the man,
"*Ephphatha*," which means, "Open up!"
35 At once the man was able to hear, his
speech impediment was removed, and he
began to talk without any trouble. [36]Then
Jesus ordered the people not to speak of it
to anyone; but the more he ordered them
not to, the more they spoke. [37]And all who
heard were completely amazed. "How well
he does everything!" they exclaimed. "He
even causes the deaf to hear and the dumb
to speak!"

Jesus Feeds Four Thousand People
(Mt 15.32–39)

8 Not long afterwards another large
crowd came together. When the
people had nothing left to eat, Jesus
called the disciples to him and said, [2]"I feel
sorry for these people, because they have
been with me for three days and now have
nothing to eat. [3]If I send them home
without feeding them, they will faint as
they go, because some of them have come
a long way."
4 His disciples asked him, "Where in this
desert can anyone find enough food to feed
all these people?"
5 "How much bread have you got?" Jesus
asked.

[a] **7.15** *Some manuscripts add verse 16:* Listen, then, if you have ears! *(see 4.23).*

"Seven loaves," they answered.
6 He ordered the crowd to sit down on the
ground. Then he took the seven loaves, gave
thanks to God, broke them, and gave them
to his disciples to distribute to the crowd;
and the disciples did so. [7]They also had a
few small fish. Jesus gave thanks for these
and told the disciples to distribute them
too. [8–9]Everybody ate and had enough –
there were about 4,000 people. Then the
disciples took up seven baskets full of pieces
left over. Jesus sent the people away [10]and
at once got into a boat with his disciples
and went to the district of Dalmanutha.

The Pharisees Ask for a Miracle

(Mt 12.38–42; 16.1–4)

11 Some Pharisees came to Jesus and started
to argue with him. They wanted to trap
him, so they asked him to perform a miracle
to show that God approved of him. [12]But
Jesus gave a deep groan and said, "Why do
the people of this day ask for a miracle? No,
I tell you! No such proof will be given to
these people!"
13 He left them, got back into the boat, and
started across to the other side of the lake.

The Yeast of the Pharisees and of Herod

(Mt 16.5–12)

14 The disciples had forgotten to bring
enough bread and had only one loaf with
them in the boat. [15]"Take care," Jesus
warned them, "and be on your guard
against the yeast of the Pharisees and the
yeast of Herod."
16 They started discussing among
themselves: "He says this because we
haven't any bread."
17 Jesus knew what they were saying, so he
asked them, "Why are you discussing
about not having any bread? Don't you
know or understand yet? Are your minds
so dull? [18]You have eyes – can't you see?
You have ears – can't you hear? Don't you
remember [19]when I broke the five loaves
for the five thousand people? How many
baskets full of leftover pieces did you
take up?"
"Twelve," they answered.
20 "And when I broke the seven loaves for
the four thousand people," asked Jesus,
"how many baskets full of leftover pieces
did you take up?"
"Seven," they answered.
21 "And you still don't understand?" he
asked them.

Jesus Heals a Blind Man at Bethsaida

22 They came to Bethsaida, where some
people brought a blind man to Jesus and
begged him to touch him. [23]Jesus took
the blind man by the hand and led him
out of the village. After spitting on the
man's eyes, Jesus placed his hands on him
and asked him, "Can you see anything?"
24 The man looked up and said, "Yes, I
can see people, but they look like trees
walking about."
25 Jesus again placed his hands on the
man's eyes. This time the man looked
intently, his eyesight returned, and he
saw everything clearly. [26]Jesus then sent
him home with the order, "Don't go back
into the village."

Peter's Declaration about Jesus

(Mt 16.13–20; Lk 9.18–21)

27 Then Jesus and his disciples went away
to the villages near Caesarea Philippi. On
the way he asked them, "Tell me, who do
people say I am?"
28 "Some say that you are John the
Baptist," they answered; "others say that
you are Elijah, while others say that you
are one of the prophets."
29 "What about you?" he asked them.
"Who do you say I am?"
Peter answered, "You are the Messiah."
30 Then Jesus ordered them, "Do not tell
anyone about me."

Jesus Speaks about his Suffering and Death

(Mt 16.21–28; Lk 9.22–27)

31 Then Jesus began to teach his disciples:
"The Son of Man must suffer much and
be rejected by the elders, the chief priests,

and the teachers of the Law. He will be put
to death, but three days later he will rise to
life." [32]He made this very clear to them. So
Peter took him aside and began to rebuke
him. [33]But Jesus turned round, looked at
his disciples, and rebuked Peter. "Get away
from me, Satan," he said. "Your thoughts
don't come from God but from human
nature!"
34 Then Jesus called the crowd and his
disciples to him. "If anyone wants to come
with me," he told them, "he must forget
self, carry his cross, and follow me. [35]For
whoever wants to save his own life will lose
it; but whoever loses his life for me and for
the gospel will save it. [36]Do people gain
anything if they win the whole world but
lose their life? Of course not! [37]There is
nothing they can give to regain their life.
[38]If a person is ashamed of me and of my
teaching in this godless and wicked day,
then the Son of Man will be ashamed of
him when he comes in the glory of his
Father with the holy angels."

9 And he went on to say, "I tell you, there
are some here who will not die until
they have seen the Kingdom of God
come with power."

The Transfiguration
(Mt 17.1–13; Lk 9.28–36)

2 Six days later Jesus took with him Peter,
James, and John, and led them up a high
mountain, where they were alone. As they
looked on, a change came over Jesus, [3]and
his clothes became shining white – whiter
than anyone in the world could wash
them. [4]Then the three disciples saw Elijah
and Moses talking with Jesus. [5]Peter spoke
up and said to Jesus, "Teacher, how good it
is that we are here! We will make three
tents, one for you, one for Moses, and one
for Elijah." [6]He and the others were so
frightened that he did not know what to
say.
7 Then a cloud appeared and covered
them with its shadow, and a voice came
from the cloud, "This is my own dear Son
– listen to him!" [8]They took a quick look
round but did not see anyone else; only
Jesus was with them.
9 As they came down the mountain, Jesus
ordered them, "Don't tell anyone what you
have seen, until the Son of Man has risen
from death."
10 They obeyed his order, but among
themselves they started discussing the
matter, "What does this 'rising from death'
mean?" [11]And they asked Jesus, "Why do
the teachers of the Law say that Elijah has
to come first?"
12 His answer was, "Elijah is indeed coming
first in order to get everything ready. Yet
why do the Scriptures say that the Son of
Man will suffer much and be rejected? [13]I
tell you, however, that Elijah has already
come and that people treated him just as
they pleased, as the Scriptures say about
him."

Jesus Heals a Boy with an Evil Spirit
(Mt 17.14–21; Lk 9.37–43a)

14 When they joined the rest of the
disciples, they saw a large crowd round
them and some teachers of the Law
arguing with them. [15]When the people
saw Jesus, they were greatly surprised, and
ran to him and greeted him. [16]Jesus asked
his disciples, "What are you arguing with
them about?"
17 A man in the crowd answered, "Teacher,
I brought my son to you, because he has an
evil spirit in him and cannot talk.
[18]Whenever the spirit attacks him, it
throws him to the ground, and he foams at
the mouth, grits his teeth, and becomes
stiff all over. I asked your disciples to drive
the spirit out, but they could not."
19 Jesus said to them, "How unbelieving
you people are! How long must I stay with
you? How long do I have to put up with
you? Bring the boy to me!" [20]They brought
him to Jesus.

As soon as the spirit saw Jesus, it threw
the boy into a fit, so that he fell on the
ground and rolled round, foaming at the
mouth. [21]"How long has he been like
this?" Jesus asked the father.

"Ever since he was a child," he replied.

22“Many times the evil spirit has tried to kill him by throwing him in the fire and into water. Have pity on us and help us, if you possibly can!”

23 “Yes,” said Jesus, “if you yourself can! Everything is possible for the person who has faith.”

24 The father at once cried out, “I do have faith, but not enough. Help me to have more!”

25 Jesus noticed that the crowd was closing in on them, so he gave a command to the evil spirit. “Deaf and dumb spirit,” he said, “I order you to come out of the boy and never go into him again!”

26 The spirit screamed, threw the boy into a
bad fit, and came out. The boy looked like
a corpse, and everyone said, “He is dead!”
27But Jesus took the boy by the hand and
helped him to rise, and he stood up.

28 After Jesus had gone indoors, his disciples asked him privately, “Why couldn't we drive the spirit out?”

29 “Only prayer can drive this kind out,” answered Jesus; “nothing else can.”

Jesus Speaks Again about his Death
(Mt 17.22–23; Lk 9.43b–45)

30 Jesus and his disciples left that place and
went on through Galilee. Jesus did not
want anyone to know where he was,
31because he was teaching his disciples:
“The Son of Man will be handed over to
those who will kill him. Three days later,
however, he will rise to life.”

32 But they did not understand what this teaching meant, and they were afraid to ask him.

Who is the Greatest?
(Mt 18.1–5; Lk 9.46–48)

33 They came to Capernaum, and after going indoors Jesus asked his disciples, “What were you arguing about on the road?”

34 But they would not answer him, because
on the road they had been arguing among
themselves about who was the greatest.
35Jesus sat down, called the twelve
disciples, and said to them, “Whoever
wants to be first must place himself last of
all and be the servant of all.” 36Then he
took a child and made him stand in front
of them. He put his arms round him and
said to them, 37“Whoever welcomes in my
name one of these children, welcomes me;
and whoever welcomes me, welcomes not
only me but also the one who sent me.”

Jesus told his disciples that whoever welcomes a child welcomes God the Father.

Whoever is not Against Us is For Us
(Lk 9.49–50)

38 John said to him, “Teacher, we saw a man who was driving out demons in your name, and we told him to stop, because he doesn't belong to our group.”

39 “Do not try to stop him,” Jesus told
them, “because no one who performs a
miracle in my name will be able soon
afterwards to say evil things about me.
40For whoever is not against us is for us. 41I
assure you that anyone who gives you a
drink of water because you belong to me
will certainly receive his reward.

Temptations to Sin
(Mt 18.6–9; Lk 17.1–2)

42 “If anyone should cause one of these
little ones to lose his faith in me, it would
be better for that person to have a large
millstone tied round his neck and be
thrown into the sea. 43 So if your hand
makes you lose your faith, cut it off! It is
better for you to enter life without a hand
than to keep both hands and go off to
hell, to the fire that never goes out.[a]
45 And if your foot makes you lose your
faith, cut it off! It is better for you to enter
life without a foot than to keep both feet
and be thrown into hell.[b] 47 And if your
eye makes you lose your faith, take it out!
It is better for you to enter the Kingdom of
God with only one eye than to keep both
eyes and be thrown into hell. 48 There ‘the
worms that eat them never die, and the
fire that burns them is never put out.’
49 “Everyone will be purified by fire as a
sacrifice is purified by salt.
50 “Salt is good; but if it loses its saltiness,
how can you make it salty again?

“Have the salt of friendship among
yourselves, and live in peace with one
another.”

Jesus Teaches about Divorce
(Mt 19.1–12; Lk 16.18)

10 Then Jesus left that place, went to the
province of Judea, and crossed the
River Jordan. Crowds came flocking to
him again, and he taught them, as he
always did.
2 Some Pharisees came to him and tried to
trap him. “Tell us,” they asked, “does our
Law allow a man to divorce his wife?”
3 Jesus answered with a question, “What
law did Moses give you?”
4 Their answer was, “Moses gave
permission for a man to write a divorce
notice and send his wife away.”
5 Jesus said to them, “Moses wrote this law
for you because you are so hard to teach.
6 But in the beginning, at the time of
creation, ‘God made them male and
female,’ as the scripture says. 7 ‘And for this
reason a man will leave his father and
mother and unite with his wife,[c] 8 and the
two will become one.’ So they are no longer
two, but one. 9 No human being then must
separate what God has joined together.”
10 When they went back into the house,
the disciples asked Jesus about this matter.
11 He said to them, “A man who divorces
his wife and marries another woman
commits adultery against his wife. 12 In the
same way, a woman who divorces her
husband and marries another man
commits adultery.”

Jesus Blesses Little Children
(Mt 19.13–15; Lk 18.15–17)

13 Some people brought children to Jesus
for him to place his hands on them, but the
disciples scolded the people. 14 When Jesus
noticed this, he was angry and said to his
disciples, “Let the children come to me,
and do not stop them, because the
Kingdom of God belongs to such as these.
15 I assure you that whoever does not
receive the Kingdom of God like a child
will never enter it.” 16 Then he took the
children in his arms, placed his hands on
each of them, and blessed them.

The Rich Man
(Mt 19.16–30; Lk 18.18–30)

17 As Jesus was starting on his way again, a
man ran up, knelt before him, and asked
him, “Good Teacher, what must I do to
receive eternal life?”
18 “Why do you call me good?” Jesus asked
him. “No one is good except God alone.
19 You know the commandments: ‘Do not
commit murder; do not commit adultery;
do not steal; do not accuse anyone falsely;
do not cheat; respect your father and your
mother.’ ”
20 “Teacher,” the man said, “ever since I
was young, I have obeyed all these
commandments.”
21 Jesus looked straight at him with love

[a] **9.43** *Some manuscripts add verse 44:* There ‘the worms that eat them never die, and the fire that burns them is never put out’ *(see verse 48).*

[b] **9.45** *Some manuscripts add verse 46:* There ‘the worms that eat them never die, and the fire that burns them is never put out’ *(see verse 48).*

[c] **10.7** *Some manuscripts do not have* and unite with his wife.

and said, "You need only one thing. Go and
sell all you have and give the money to the
poor, and you will have riches in heaven;
then come and follow me." 22When the
man heard this, gloom spread over his face,
and he went away sad, because he was very
rich.

23 Jesus looked round at his disciples and
said to them, "How hard it will be for rich
people to enter the Kingdom of God!"

24 The disciples were shocked at these
words, but Jesus went on to say, "My
children, how hard it is to enter the
Kingdom of God! 25It is much harder for a
rich person to enter the Kingdom of God
than for a camel to go through the eye of a
needle."

26 At this the disciples were completely
amazed and asked one another, "Who,
then, can be saved?"

27 Jesus looked straight at them and
answered, "This is impossible for human
beings, but not for God; everything is
possible for God."

28 Then Peter spoke up, "Look, we have left
everything and followed you."

29 "Yes," Jesus said to them, "and I tell you
that anyone who leaves home or brothers
or sisters or mother or father or children or
fields for me and for the gospel, 30will
receive much more in this present age. He
will receive a hundred times more houses,
brothers, sisters, mothers, children and
fields – and persecutions as well; and in the
age to come he will receive eternal life.
31But many who now are first will be last,
and many who now are last will be first."

Jesus Speaks a Third Time about his Death

(Mt 20.17–19; Lk 18.31–34)

32 Jesus and his disciples were now on the
road going up to Jerusalem. Jesus was
going ahead of the disciples, who were
filled with alarm; the people who followed
behind were afraid. Once again Jesus took
the twelve disciples aside and spoke of the
things that were going to happen to him.
33"Listen," he told them, "we are going up
to Jerusalem where the Son of Man will be
handed over to the chief priests and the
teachers of the Law. They will condemn
him to death and then hand him over to
the Gentiles, 34who will mock him, spit
on him, whip him, and kill him; but three
days later he will rise to life."

The Request of James and John

(Mt 20.20–28)

35 Then James and John, the sons of
Zebedee, came to Jesus. "Teacher," they
said, "there is something we want you to do
for us."

36 "What is it?" Jesus asked them.

37 They answered, "When you sit on your
throne in your glorious Kingdom, we want
you to let us sit with you, one at your right
and one at your left."

38 Jesus said to them, "You don't know
what you are asking for. Can you drink the
cup of suffering that I must drink? Can you
be baptized in the way I must be baptized?"

39 "We can," they answered.

Jesus said to them, "You will indeed
drink the cup I must drink and be baptized
in the way I must be baptized. 40But I do
not have the right to choose who will sit at
my right and my left. It is God who will
give these places to those for whom he has
prepared them."

41 When the other ten disciples heard
about it, they became angry with James
and John. 42So Jesus called them all
together to him and said, "You know that
those who are considered rulers of the
heathen have power over them, and the
leaders have complete authority. 43This,
however, is not the way it is among you. If
one of you wants to be great, he must be
the servant of the rest; 44and if one of you
wants to be first, he must be the slave of
all. 45For even the Son of Man did not
come to be served; he came to serve and to
give his life to redeem many people."

Jesus Heals Blind Bartimaeus

(Mt 20.29–34; Lk 18.35–43)

46 They came to Jericho, and as Jesus was
leaving with his disciples and a large crowd,
a blind beggar named Bartimaeus son of

Timaeus was sitting by the road. [47]When he heard that it was Jesus of Nazareth, he began to shout, "Jesus! Son of David! Take pity on me!"

48 Many of the people scolded him and told him to be quiet. But he shouted even more loudly, "Son of David, take pity on me!"

49 Jesus stopped and said, "Call him."

So they called the blind man. "Cheer up!" they said. "Get up, he is calling you."

50 He threw off his cloak, jumped up, and came to Jesus.

51 "What do you want me to do for you?" Jesus asked him.

"Teacher," the blind man answered, "I want to see again."

52 "Go," Jesus told him, "your faith has made you well."

At once he was able to see and followed Jesus on the road.

The Triumphant Entry into Jerusalem
(Mt 21.1–11; Lk 19.28–40; Jn 12.12–19)

11 As they approached Jerusalem, near the towns of Bethphage and Bethany, they came to the Mount of Olives. Jesus sent two of his disciples on ahead
[2]with these instructions: "Go to the village there ahead of you. As soon as you get there, you will find a colt tied up that has never been ridden. Untie it and bring it
here. [3]And if someone asks you why you are doing that, tell him that the Master[a] needs it and will send it back at once."

4 So they went and found a colt out in the street, tied to the door of a house. As they
were untying it, [5]some of the bystanders asked them, "What are you doing, untying that colt?"

6 They answered just as Jesus had told them, and the bystanders let them go.
[7]They brought the colt to Jesus, threw their cloaks over the animal, and Jesus got on.
[8]Many people spread their cloaks on the road, while others cut branches in the fields
and spread them on the road. [9]The people
who were in front and those who followed behind began to shout, "Praise God! God bless him who comes in the name of the
Lord! [10]God bless the coming kingdom of King David, our father! Praise God!"

11 Jesus entered Jerusalem, went into the Temple, and looked round at everything. But since it was already late in the day, he went out to Bethany with the twelve disciples.

People carrying crosses in a Palm Sunday procession.

Jesus Curses the Fig Tree
(Mt 21.18–19)

12 The next day, as they were coming back
from Bethany, Jesus was hungry. [13]He saw in the distance a fig tree covered with leaves, so he went to see if he could find any figs on it. But when he came to it, he found only leaves, because it was not the
right time for figs. [14]Jesus said to the fig tree, "No one shall ever eat figs from you again!"

And his disciples heard him.

Jesus Goes to the Temple
(Mt 21.12–17; Lk 19.45–48; Jn 2.13–22)

15 When they arrived in Jerusalem, Jesus went to the Temple and began to drive out all those who were buying and selling. He overturned the tables of the money-changers and the stools of those who sold
pigeons, [16]and he would not let anyone

[a] **11.3** the Master; *or* its owner.

carry anything through the temple
courtyards. [17]He then taught the people:
"It is written in the Scriptures that God
said, 'My Temple will be called a house of
prayer for the people of all nations.' But
you have turned it into a hideout for
thieves!"
18 The chief priests and the teachers of the
Law heard of this, so they began looking for
some way to kill Jesus. They were afraid of
him, because the whole crowd was amazed
at his teaching.
19 When evening came, Jesus and his
disciples left the city.

The Lesson from the Fig Tree
(Mt 21.20–22)

20 Early next morning, as they walked
along the road, they saw the fig tree. It was
dead all the way down to its roots. [21]Peter
remembered what had happened and said
to Jesus, "Look, Teacher, the fig tree you
cursed has died!"
22 Jesus answered them, "Have faith in
God. [23]I assure you that whoever tells this
hill to get up and throw itself in the sea and
does not doubt in his heart, but believes
that what he says will happen, it will be
done for him. [24]For this reason I tell you:
when you pray and ask for something,
believe that you have received it, and you
will be given whatever you ask for. [25]And
when you stand and pray, forgive anything
you may have against anyone, so that your
Father in heaven will forgive the wrongs
you have done."[a]

The Question about Jesus' Authority
(Mt 21.23–27; Lk 20.1–8)

27 They arrived once again in Jerusalem. As
Jesus was walking in the Temple, the chief
priests, the teachers of the Law, and the
elders came to him [28]and asked him,
"What right have you to do these things?
Who gave you this right?"
29 Jesus answered them, "I will ask you just
one question, and if you give me an
answer, I will tell you what right I have to
do these things. [30]Tell me, where did John's
right to baptize come from: was it from
God or from human beings?"
31 They started to argue among themselves:
"What shall we say? If we answer, 'From
God,' he will say, 'Why, then, did you not
believe John?' [32]But if we say, 'From human
beings . . . ' "(They were afraid of the people,
because everyone was convinced that John
had been a prophet.) [33]So their answer to
Jesus was, "We don't know."

Jesus said to them, "Neither will I tell
you, then, by what right I do these things."

The Parable of the Tenants in the Vineyard
(Mt 21.33–46; Lk 20.9–19)

12 Then Jesus spoke to them in parables:
"Once there was a man who planted
a vineyard, put a fence round it, dug
a hole for the winepress, and built a
watchtower. Then he let out the vineyard to
tenants and left home on a journey. [2]When
the time came to gather the grapes, he sent
a slave to the tenants to receive from them
his share of the harvest. [3]The tenants seized
the slave, beat him, and sent him back
without a thing. [4]Then the owner sent
another slave; the tenants beat him over the
head and treated him shamefully. [5]The
owner sent another slave, and they killed
him; and they treated many others the same
way, beating some and killing others. [6]The
only one left to send was the man's own
dear son. Last of all, then, he sent his son to
the tenants. 'I am sure they will respect my
son,' he said. [7]But those tenants said to one
another, 'This is the owner's son. Come on,
let's kill him, and his property will be ours!'
[8]So they seized the son and killed him and
threw his body out of the vineyard.
9 "What, then, will the owner of the
vineyard do?" asked Jesus. "He will come
and kill those tenants and hand the
vineyard over to others. [10]Surely you have
read this scripture:

> 'The stone which the builders rejected as
> worthless

[a] **11.25** *Some manuscripts add verse 26:* If you do not forgive others, your Father in heaven will not forgive the wrongs you have done *(see Mt 6.15).*

turned out to be the most important
of all.
11 This was done by the Lord;
what a wonderful sight it is!' "

12 The Jewish leaders tried to arrest Jesus,
because they knew that he had told this
parable against them. But they were afraid
of the crowd, so they left him and went
away.

The Question about Paying Taxes
(Mt 22.15–22; Lk 20.20–26)

13 Some Pharisees and some members of
Herod's party were sent to Jesus to trap him
with questions. 14 They came to him and
said, "Teacher, we know that you tell the
truth, without worrying about what people
think. You pay no attention to anyone's
status, but teach the truth about God's will
for people. Tell us, is it against our Law to
pay taxes to the Roman Emperor? Should
we pay them or not?"
15 But Jesus saw through their trick and
answered, "Why are you trying to trap me?
Bring a silver coin, and let me see it."
16 They brought him one, and he asked,
"Whose face and name are these?"
"The Emperor's," they answered.
17 So Jesus said, "Well, then, pay the
Emperor what belongs to the Emperor, and
pay God what belongs to God."
And they were amazed at Jesus.

The Question about Rising from Death
(Mt 22.23–33; Lk 20.27–40)

18 Then some Sadducees, who say that
people will not rise from death, came to
Jesus and said, 19 "Teacher, Moses wrote this
law for us: 'If a man dies and leaves a wife
but no children, that man's brother must
marry the widow so that they can have
children who will be considered the dead
man's children.' 20 Once there were seven
brothers; the eldest got married and died
without having children. 21 Then the
second one married the woman, and he
also died without having children. The
same thing happened to the third brother,
22 and then to the rest: all seven brothers
married the woman and died without
having children. Last of all, the woman
died. 23 Now, when all the dead rise to life
on the day of resurrection, whose wife will
she be? All seven of them had married her."
24 Jesus answered them, "How wrong you
are! And do you know why? It is because
you don't know the Scriptures or God's
power. 25 For when the dead rise to life,
they will be like the angels in heaven and
will not marry. 26 Now, as for the dead
being raised: haven't you ever read in the
Book of Moses the passage about the
burning bush? There it is written that God
said to Moses, 'I am the God of Abraham,
the God of Isaac, and the God of Jacob.'
27 He is the God of the living, not of the
dead. You are completely wrong!"

The Great Commandment
(Mt 22.34–40; Lk 10.25–28)

28 A teacher of the Law was there who
heard the discussion. He saw that Jesus had
given the Sadducees a good answer, so he
came to him with a question: "Which
commandment is the most important of
all?"
29 Jesus replied, "The most important one is
this: 'Listen, Israel! The Lord our God is the
only Lord.[a] 30 Love the Lord your God
with all your heart, with all your soul,
with all your mind, and with all your
strength.' 31 The second most important
commandment is this: 'Love your neighbour
as you love yourself.' There is no other
commandment more important than these
two."
32 The teacher of the Law said to Jesus, "Well
done, Teacher! It is true, as you say, that only
the Lord is God and that there is no other
god but he. 33 And to love God with all your
heart and with all your mind and with all
your strength, and to love your neighbour as
yourself, is more important than to offer
animals and other sacrifices to God."
34 Jesus noticed how wise his answer was,
and so he told him, "You are not far from

[a] **12.29** The Lord our God is the only Lord; *or* The Lord is our God, the Lord alone.

the Kingdom of God."
After this nobody dared to ask Jesus any more questions.

The Question about the Messiah
(Mt 22.41–46; Lk 20.41–44)

35 As Jesus was teaching in the Temple, he
asked the question, "How can the teachers
of the Law say that the Messiah will be the
descendant of David? [36]The Holy Spirit
inspired David to say:

'The Lord said to my Lord:
Sit here on my right
until I put your enemies under your
feet.'

37 David himself called him 'Lord'; so how
can the Messiah be David's descendant?"

Jesus Warns against the Teachers of the Law
(Mt 23.1–36; Lk 20.45–47)

A large crowd was listening to Jesus gladly.
[38]As he taught them, he said, "Watch out for
the teachers of the Law, who like to walk
around in their long robes and be greeted
with respect in the market place, [39]who
choose the reserved seats in the synagogues
and the best places at feasts. [40]They take
advantage of widows and rob them of their
homes, and then make a show of saying long
prayers. Their punishment will be all the
worse!"

The Widow's Offering
(Lk 21.1–4)

41 As Jesus sat near the temple treasury, he
watched the people as they dropped in their
money. Many rich men dropped in a lot of
money; [42]then a poor widow came along
and dropped in two little copper coins,
worth about a penny. [43]He called his
disciples together and said to them, "I tell
you that this poor widow put more in the
offering box than all the others. [44]For the
others put in what they had to spare of their
riches; but she, poor as she is, put in all she
had – she gave all she had to live on."

Jesus Speaks of the Destruction of the Temple
(Mt 24.1–2; Lk 21.5–6)

13 As Jesus was leaving the Temple, one of
his disciples said, "Look, Teacher! What
wonderful stones and buildings!"

Jesus spoke to his disciples about his approaching death.

2 Jesus answered, "You see these great
buildings? Not a single stone here will be
left in its place; every one of them will be
thrown down."

Troubles and Persecutions
(Mt 24.3–14; Lk 21.7–19)

3 Jesus was sitting on the Mount of Olives,
across from the Temple, when Peter, James,
John, and Andrew came to him in private.
[4]"Tell us when this will be," they said, "and
tell us what will happen to show that the
time has come for all these things to take
place."
5 Jesus said to them, "Be on guard, and
don't let anyone deceive you. [6]Many men,
claiming to speak for me, will come and say,
'I am he!' and they will deceive many
people. [7]And don't be troubled when you

hear the noise of battles close by and news
of battles far away. Such things must
happen, but they do not mean that the end
has come. 8 Countries will fight each other;
kingdoms will attack one another. There
will be earthquakes everywhere, and there
will be famines. These things are like the
first pains of childbirth.
9 "You yourselves must be on guard. You
will be arrested and taken to court. You will
be beaten in the synagogues; you will stand
before rulers and kings for my sake to tell
them the Good News. 10 But before the end
comes, the gospel must be preached to all
peoples. 11 And when you are arrested and
taken to court, do not worry beforehand
about what you are going to say; when the
time comes, say whatever is then given to
you. For the words you speak will not be
yours; they will come from the Holy Spirit.
12 Men will hand over their own brothers to
be put to death, and fathers will do the
same to their children. Children will turn
against their parents and have them put to
death. 13 Everyone will hate you because of
me. But whoever holds out to the end will
be saved.

The Awful Horror

(Mt 24.15–28; Lk 21.20–24)

14 "You will see 'The Awful Horror'
standing in the place where he should not
be." (Note to the reader: be sure to
understand what this means!) "Then those
who are in Judea must run away to the
hills. 15 Someone who is on the roof of his
house must not lose time by going down
into the house to get anything to take with
him. 16 Someone who is in the field must
not go back to the house for his cloak.
17 How terrible it will be in those days for
women who are pregnant and for mothers
with little babies! 18 Pray to God that these
things will not happen in the winter! 19 For
the trouble of those days will be far worse
than any the world has ever known from
the very beginning when God created the
world until the present time. Nor will there
ever be anything like it again. 20 But the
Lord has reduced the number of those days;
if he had not, nobody would survive. For
the sake of his chosen people, however, he
has reduced those days.
21 "Then, if anyone says to you, 'Look, here
is the Messiah!' or, 'Look, there he is!' – do
not believe him. 22 For false Messiahs and
false prophets will appear. They will
perform miracles and wonders in order to
deceive even God's chosen people, if
possible. 23 Be on your guard! I have told
you everything before the time comes.

The Coming of the Son of Man

(Mt 24.29–31; Lk 21.25–28)

24 "In the days after that time of trouble the
sun will grow dark, the moon will no
longer shine, 25 the stars will fall from
heaven, and the powers in space will be
driven from their courses. 26 Then the Son
of Man will appear, coming in the clouds
with great power and glory. 27 He will send
the angels out to the four corners of the
earth to gather God's chosen people from
one end of the world to the other.

The Lesson of the Fig Tree

(Mt 24.32–35; Lk 21.29–33)

28 "Let the fig tree teach you a lesson.
When its branches become green and
tender and it starts putting out leaves, you
know that summer is near. 29 In the same
way, when you see these things happening,
you will know that the time is near, ready
to begin.[a] 30 Remember that all these things
will happen before the people now living
have all died. 31 Heaven and earth will pass
away, but my words will never pass away.

No one Knows the Day or Hour

(Mt 24.36–44)

32 "No one knows, however, when that day
or hour will come – neither the angels in
heaven, nor the Son; only the Father
knows. 33 Be on watch, be alert, for you do
not know when the time will come. 34 It
will be like a man who goes away from
home on a journey and leaves his servants
in charge, after giving to each one his own
work to do and after telling the doorkeeper
to keep watch. 35 Be on guard, then,

[a] **13.29** the time is near, ready to begin; *or* he is near, ready to come.

because you do not know when the master
of the house is coming – it might be in the
evening or at midnight or before dawn or
at sunrise. [36]If he comes suddenly, he must
not find you asleep. [37]What I say to you,
then, I say to all: watch!"

The Plot against Jesus

(Mt 26.1–5; Lk 22.1–2; Jn 11.45–53)

14 It was now two days before the Festival of Passover and Unleavened Bread. The chief priests and the teachers of the Law were looking for a way to arrest Jesus secretly and put him to death. [2]"We must not do it during the festival," they said, "or the people might riot."

Jesus is Anointed at Bethany

(Mt 26.6–13; Jn 12.1–8)

3 Jesus was in Bethany at the house of Simon, a man who had suffered from a dreaded skin disease. While Jesus was eating, a woman came in with an alabaster jar full of a very expensive perfume made of pure nard. She broke the jar and poured the perfume on Jesus' head. [4]Some of the people there became angry and said to one another, "What was the use of wasting the perfume? [5]It could have been sold for more than three hundred silver coins[a] and the money given to the poor!" And they criticized her harshly.

6 But Jesus said, "Leave her alone! Why are you bothering her? She has done a fine and beautiful thing for me. [7]You will always have poor people with you, and any time you want to, you can help them. But you will not always have me. [8]She did what she could; she poured perfume on my body to prepare it ahead of time for burial. [9]Now, I assure you that wherever the gospel is preached all over the world, what she has done will be told in memory of her."

Judas Agrees to Betray Jesus

(Mt 26.14–16; Lk 22.3–6)

10 Then Judas Iscariot, one of the twelve disciples, went off to the chief priests in order to betray Jesus to them. [11]They were pleased to hear what he had to say, and promised to give him money. So Judas started looking for a good chance to hand Jesus over to them.

Jesus Eats the Passover Meal with his Disciples

(Mt 26.17–25; Lk 22.7–14, 21–23; Jn 13.21–30)

12 On the first day of the Festival of Unleavened Bread, the day the lambs for the Passover meal were killed, Jesus' disciples asked him, "Where do you want us to go and get the Passover meal ready for you?"

13 Then Jesus sent two of them with these instructions: "Go into the city, and a man carrying a jar of water will meet you. Follow him [14]to the house he enters, and say to the owner of the house: 'The Teacher says, Where is the room where my disciples and I will eat the Passover meal?' [15]Then he will show you a large upstairs room, prepared and furnished, where you will get everything ready for us."

16 The disciples left, went to the city, and found everything just as Jesus had told them; and they prepared the Passover meal.

17 When it was evening, Jesus came with the twelve disciples. [18]While they were at the table eating, Jesus said, "I tell you that one of you will betray me – one who is eating with me."

19 The disciples were upset and began to ask him, one after the other, "Surely you don't mean me, do you?"

20 Jesus answered, "It will be one of you twelve, one who dips his bread in the dish with me. [21]The Son of Man will die as the Scriptures say he will; but how terrible for that man who betrays the Son of Man! It would have been better for that man if he had never been born!"

The Lord's Supper

(Mt 26.26–30; Lk 22.14–20; 1 Cor. 11.23–25)

22 While they were eating, Jesus took a piece of bread, gave a prayer of thanks, broke it, and gave it to his disciples. "Take it," he said, "this is my body."

[a] **14.5** SILVER COINS: *See 6.37.*

At the Last Supper Jesus gave bread and wine to his disciples.

23 Then he took a cup, gave thanks to God,
and handed it to them; and they all drank
from it. [24]Jesus said, "This is my blood
which is poured out for many, my blood
which seals God's covenant. [25]I tell you, I
will never again drink this wine until the
day I drink the new wine in the Kingdom of
God."

26 Then they sang a hymn and went out to
the Mount of Olives.

Jesus Predicts Peter's Denial

(Mt 26.31–35; Lk 22.31–34; Jn 13.36–38)

27 Jesus said to them, "All of you will run
away and leave me, for the scripture says,
'God will kill the shepherd, and the sheep
will all be scattered.' [28]But after I am raised
to life, I will go to Galilee ahead of you."

29 Peter answered, "I will never leave you,
even though all the rest do!"

30 Jesus said to Peter, "I tell you that before
the cock crows twice tonight, you will say
three times that you do not know me."

31 Peter answered even more strongly, "I
will never say that, even if I have to die
with you!"

And all the other disciples said the same
thing.

Jesus Prays in Gethsemane

(Mt 26.36–46; Lk 22.39–46)

32 They came to a place called Gethsemane,
and Jesus said to his disciples, "Sit here
while I pray." [33]He took Peter,
James, and John with him. Distress
and anguish came over him, [34]and
he said to them, "The sorrow in my
heart is so great that it almost
crushes me. Stay here and keep
watch."

35 He went a little farther on, threw
himself on the ground, and prayed
that, if possible, he might not have
to go through that time of suffering.
[36]"Father," he prayed, "my Father!
All things are possible for you. Take
this cup of suffering away from me.
Yet not what I want, but what you
want."

37 Then he returned and found the three
disciples asleep. He said to Peter, "Simon,
are you asleep? Weren't you able to stay
awake even for one hour?" [38]And he said to
them, "Keep watch, and pray that you will
not fall into temptation. The spirit is
willing, but the flesh is weak."

39 He went away once more and prayed,
saying the same words. [40]Then he came
back to the disciples and found them
asleep; they could not keep their eyes open.
And they did not know what to say to him.

41 When he came back the third time, he
said to them, "Are you still sleeping and
resting? Enough! The hour has come! Look,
the Son of Man is now being handed over
to the power of sinners. [42]Get up, let us go.
Look, here is the man who is betraying
me!"

The Arrest of Jesus

(Mt 26.47–56; Lk 22.47–53; Jn 18.3–12)

43 Jesus was still speaking when Judas, one
of the twelve disciples, arrived. With him
was a crowd armed with swords and clubs,
and sent by the chief priests, the teachers of
the Law, and the elders. [44]The traitor had
given the crowd a signal: "The man I kiss is
the one you want. Arrest him and take him
away under guard."

45 As soon as Judas arrived, he went up to
Jesus and said, "Teacher!" and kissed him.
[46]So they arrested Jesus and held him tight.
[47]But one of those standing there drew his

sword and struck at the High Priest's slave, cutting off his ear. 48Then Jesus spoke up and said to them, "Did you have to come with swords and clubs to capture me, as though I were an outlaw? 49Day after day I was with you teaching in the Temple, and you did not arrest me. But the Scriptures must come true."

50 Then all the disciples left him and ran away.

51 A certain young man, dressed only in a linen cloth, was following Jesus. They tried to arrest him, 52but he ran away naked, leaving the cloth behind.

Jesus before the Council

(Mt 26.57–68; Lk 22.54–55, 63–71; Jn 18.13–14, 19–24)

53 Then Jesus was taken to the High Priest's house, where all the chief priests, the elders, and the teachers of the Law were gathering. 54Peter followed from a distance and went into the courtyard of the High Priest's house. There he sat down with the guards, keeping himself warm by the fire. 55The chief priests and the whole Council tried to find some evidence against Jesus in order to put him to death, but they could not find any. 56Many witnesses told lies against Jesus, but their stories did not agree.

57 Then some men stood up and told this lie against Jesus: 58"We heard him say, 'I will tear down this Temple which men have made, and after three days I will build one that is not made by men.' "59Not even they, however, could make their stories agree.

60 The High Priest stood up in front of them all and questioned Jesus, "Have you no answer to the accusation they bring against you?"

61 But Jesus kept quiet and would not say a word. Again the High Priest questioned him, "Are you the Messiah, the Son of the Blessed God?"

62 "I am," answered Jesus, "and you will all see the Son of Man seated on the right of the Almighty and coming with the clouds of heaven!"

63 The High Priest tore his robes and said, "We don't need any more witnesses! 64You heard his blasphemy. What is your decision?"

They all voted against him: he was guilty and should be put to death.

65 Some of them began to spit on Jesus, and they blindfolded him and hit him. "Guess who hit you!" they said. And the guards took him and slapped him.

Peter Denies Jesus

(Mt 26.69–75; Lk 22.56–62; Jn 18.15–18, 25–27)

66 Peter was still down in the courtyard when one of the High Priest's servant women came by. 67When she saw Peter warming himself, she looked straight at him and said, "You, too, were with Jesus of Nazareth."

68 But he denied it. "I don't know . . . I don't understand what you are talking about," he answered, and went out into the passage. Just then a cock crowed.[a]

69 The servant woman saw him there and began to repeat to the bystanders, "He is one of them!" 70But Peter denied it again.

A little while later the bystanders accused Peter again, "You can't deny that you are one of them, because you, too, are from Galilee."

71 Then Peter said, "I swear that I am telling the truth! May God punish me if I am not! I do not know the man you are talking about!"

72 Just then a cock crowed a second time, and Peter remembered how Jesus had said to him, "Before the cock crows twice, you will say three times that you do not know me." And he broke down and cried.

Jesus is Brought before Pilate

(Mt 27.1–2, 11–14; Lk 23.1–5; Jn 18.28–38)

15 Early in the morning the chief priests met hurriedly with the elders, the teachers of the Law, and the whole Council, and made their plans. They put Jesus in chains, led him away, and handed him over to Pilate. 2Pilate questioned him, "Are you the king of the Jews?"

Jesus answered, "So you say."

[a] **14.68** *Some manuscripts do not have* Just then a cock crowed.

3 The chief priests were accusing Jesus of
many things, [4]so Pilate questioned him
again, "Aren't you going to answer? Listen
to all their accusations!"
5 Again Jesus refused to say a word, and
Pilate was amazed.

It was Pontius Pilate, the Roman Governor, who sent Jesus to his death.

Jesus is Sentenced to Death
(Mt 27.15–26; Lk 23.13–25; Jn 18.39—19.16)

6 At every Passover Festival Pilate was in
the habit of setting free any one prisoner
the people asked for. [7]At that time a man
named Barabbas was in prison with the
rebels who had committed murder in the
riot. [8]When the crowd gathered and began
to ask Pilate for the usual favour, [9]he asked
them, "Do you want me to set free for you
the king of the Jews?" [10]He knew very well
that the chief priests had handed Jesus over
to him because they were jealous.
11 But the chief priests stirred up the crowd
to ask, instead, for Pilate to set Barabbas
free for them. [12]Pilate spoke again to the
crowd, "What, then, do you want me to do
with the one you call the king of the Jews?"
13 They shouted back, "Crucify him!"
14 "But what crime has he committed?"
Pilate asked.

They shouted all the louder, "Crucify him!"
15 Pilate wanted to please the crowd, so he
set Barabbas free for them. Then he had
Jesus whipped and handed him over to be
crucified.

The Soldiers Mock Jesus
(Mt 27.27–31; Jn 19.2–3)

16 The soldiers took Jesus inside to the
courtyard of the governor's palace and
called together the rest of the company.
[17]They put a purple robe on Jesus, made a
crown out of thorny branches, and put it
on his head. [18]Then they began to salute
him: "Long live the King of the Jews!"
[19]They beat him over the head with a stick,
spat on him, fell on their knees, and bowed
down to him. [20]When they had finished
mocking him, they took off the purple robe
and put his own clothes back on him. Then
they led him out to crucify him.

Jesus is Crucified
(Mt 27.32–44; Lk 23.26–43; Jn 19.17–27)

21 On the way they met a man named
Simon, who was coming into the city from
the country, and the soldiers forced him to
carry Jesus' cross. (Simon was from Cyrene
and was the father of Alexander and Rufus.)
[22]They took Jesus to a place called
Golgotha, which means "The Place of the
Skull". [23]There they tried to give him wine
mixed with a drug called myrrh, but Jesus
would not drink it. [24]Then they crucified
him and divided his clothes among
themselves, throwing dice to see who
would get which piece of clothing. [25]It was
nine o'clock in the morning when they
crucified him. [26]The notice of the
accusation against him said: "The King of
the Jews". [27]They also crucified two bandits
with Jesus, one on his right and the other
on his left.[a]
29 People passing by shook their heads and
hurled insults at Jesus: "Aha! You were

[a] **15.27** *Some manuscripts add verse 28:* In this way the scripture came true which says, "He shared the fate of criminals" *(see Lk 22.37).*

going to tear down the Temple and build it
up again in three days! [30]Now come down
from the cross and save yourself!"
31 In the same way the chief priests and the
teachers of the Law jeered at Jesus, saying
to each other, "He saved others, but he
cannot save himself! [32]Let us see the
Messiah, the king of Israel, come down
from the cross now, and we will believe in
him!"
And the two who were crucified with
Jesus insulted him also.

Two thieves were crucified with Jesus, one on either side of him.

The Death of Jesus
(Mt 27.45–56; Lk 23.44–49; Jn 19.28–30)

33 At noon the whole country was covered
with darkness, which lasted for three hours.
[34]At three o'clock Jesus cried out with a
loud shout, *"Eloi, Eloi, lema sabachthani?"*
which means, "My God, my God, why did
you abandon me?"
35 Some of the people there heard him and
said, "Listen, he is calling for Elijah!" [36]One
of them ran up with a sponge, soaked it in
cheap wine, and put it on the end of a stick.
Then he held it up to Jesus' lips and said,
"Wait! Let us see if Elijah is coming to bring
him down from the cross!"
37 With a loud cry Jesus died.
38 The curtain hanging in the Temple was
torn in two, from top to bottom. [39]The
army officer who was standing there in
front of the cross saw how Jesus had died.[a]
"This man was really the Son of God!" he
said.
40 Some women were there, looking on
from a distance. Among them were Mary
Magdalene, Mary the mother of the
younger James and of Joseph, and Salome.
[41]They had followed Jesus while he was in
Galilee and had helped him. Many other
women who had come to Jerusalem with
him were there also.

The Burial of Jesus
(Mt 27.57–61; Lk 23.50–56; Jn 19.38–42)

42-43 It was towards evening
when Joseph of Arimathea
arrived. He was a respected
member of the Council, who
was waiting for the coming of
the Kingdom of God. It was
Preparation day (that is, the
day before the Sabbath), so
Joseph went boldly into
the presence of Pilate
and asked him for the body of
Jesus. [44]Pilate was surprised to
hear that Jesus was already
dead. He called the army officer and asked
him if Jesus had been dead a long time.
[45]After hearing the officer's report, Pilate
told Joseph he could have the body.
[46]Joseph bought a linen sheet, took the
body down, wrapped it in the sheet, and
placed it in a tomb which had been dug out
of solid rock. Then he rolled a large stone
across the entrance to the tomb. [47]Mary
Magdalene and Mary the mother of Joseph
were watching and saw where the body of
Jesus was placed.

The Resurrection
(Mt 28.1–8; Lk 24.1–12; Jn 20.1–10)

16 After the Sabbath was over, Mary
Magdalene, Mary the mother of James,
and Salome bought spices to go and
anoint the body of Jesus. [2]Very early on
Sunday morning, at sunrise, they went to
the tomb. [3–4]On the way they said to one
another, "Who will roll away the stone for

[a] **15.39** had died; *some manuscripts have* had cried out and died.

us from the entrance to the tomb?" (It was
a very large stone.) Then they looked up
and saw that the stone had already been
rolled back. [5]So they entered the tomb,
where they saw a young man sitting on the
right, wearing a white robe – and they were
alarmed.
6 "Don't be alarmed," he said. "I know you
are looking for Jesus of Nazareth, who was
crucified. He is not here – he has been
raised! Look, here is the place where they
put him. [7]Now go and give this message to
his disciples, including Peter: 'He is going
to Galilee ahead of you; there you will see
him, just as he told you.' "
8 So they went out and ran from the tomb,
distressed and terrified. They said nothing
to anyone, because they were afraid.

AN OLD ENDING TO THE GOSPEL[a]
16.9–20

Jesus Appears to Mary Magdalene
(Mt 28.9–10; Jn 20.11–18)

[[9]After Jesus rose from death early on
Sunday, he appeared first to Mary
Magdalene, from whom he had driven out
seven demons. [10]She went and told his
companions. They were mourning and
crying; [11]and when they heard her say that
Jesus was alive and that she had seen him,
they did not believe her.

Jesus Appears to Two Disciples
(Lk 24.13–35)

12 After this, Jesus appeared in a different
manner to two of them while they were on
their way to the country. [13]They returned
and told the others, but they would not
believe it.

Jesus Appears to the Eleven
(Mt 28.16–20; Lk 24.36–49; Jn 20.19–23; Acts 1.6–8)

14 Last of all, Jesus appeared to the eleven
disciples as they were eating. He scolded
them, because they did not have faith and
because they were too stubborn to believe
those who had seen him alive. [15]He said to
them, "Go throughout the whole world and
preach the gospel to the whole human race.
[16]Whoever believes and is baptized will be
saved; whoever does not believe will be
condemned. [17]Believers will be given the
power to perform miracles: they will drive
out demons in my name; they will speak in
strange tongues; [18]if they pick up snakes or
drink any poison, they will not be harmed;
they will place their hands on sick people,
who will get well."

Jesus is Taken Up to Heaven
(Lk 24.50–53; Acts 1.9–11)

19 After the Lord Jesus had talked with
them, he was taken up to heaven and sat at
the right side of God. [20]The disciples went
and preached everywhere, and the Lord
worked with them and proved that their
preaching was true by the miracles that
were performed.]

At the end of his life on earth, Jesus went to heaven.

ANOTHER OLD ENDING[b]
16.9–10

[[9]The women went to Peter and his
friends and gave them a brief account of all
they had been told. [10]After this, Jesus
himself sent out through his disciples from
the east to the west the sacred and ever-living message of eternal salvation.]

[a] **16.9–20 heading** *Some manuscripts and ancient translations do not have this ending to the Gospel (verses 9–20).*

[b] **16.9–10 heading** *Some manuscripts and ancient translations have this shorter ending to the Gospel in addition to the longer ending (verses 9–20).*

The Gospel According to Luke

Luke was a doctor and was not one of the disciples of Jesus. He wrote his Gospel at about the same time as Matthew. He begins his Gospel with the story of the birth of Jesus.

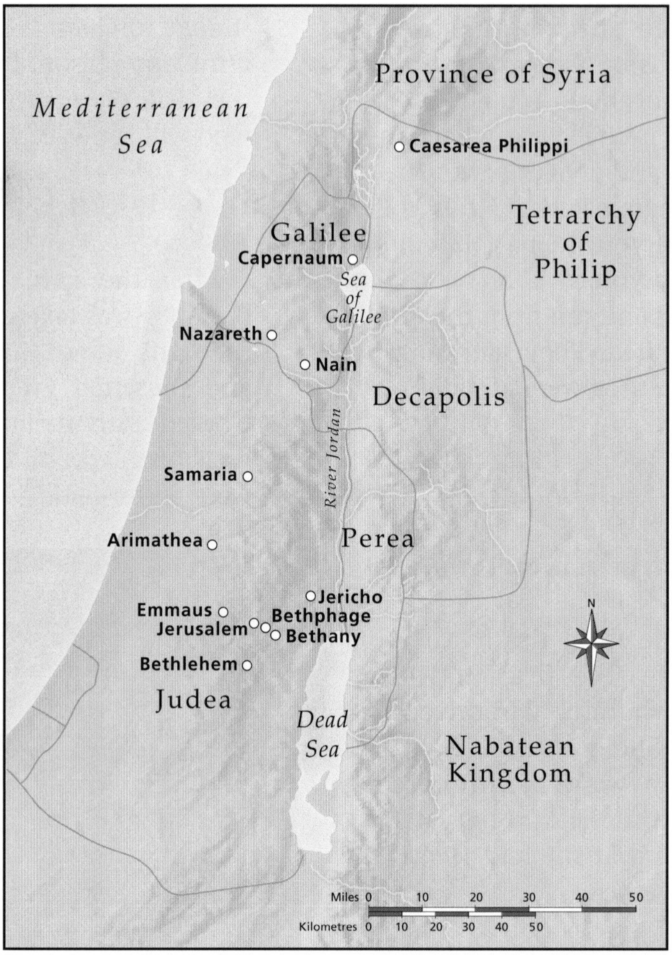

The Life of Jesus

(All dates are approximate)

10 | 0 | 10 | 20 | 30

5/4 BCE
Jesus is born in Bethlehem

7/8 CE
Jesus visits the Temple with his parents

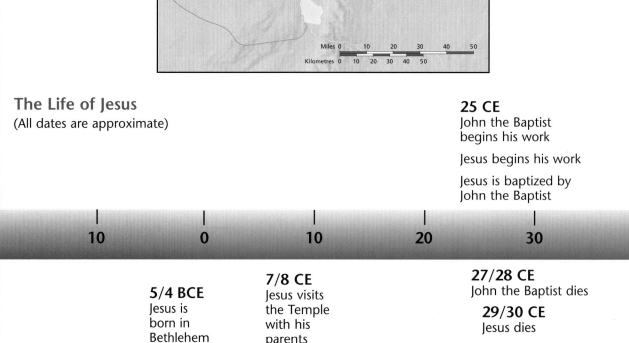

25 CE
John the Baptist begins his work

Jesus begins his work

Jesus is baptized by John the Baptist

27/28 CE
John the Baptist dies

29/30 CE
Jesus dies

Jesus comes back to life

1 Dear Theophilus:
Many people have done their best to
write a report of the things that have
taken place among us. 2They wrote what
we have been told by those who saw these
things from the beginning and who
proclaimed the message. 3And so, your
Excellency, because I have carefully studied
all these matters from their beginning, I
thought it would be good to write an
orderly account for you. 4I do this so that
you will know the full truth about
everything which you have been taught.

The Birth of John the Baptist is Announced

5 During the time when Herod was king of
Judea,[a] there was a priest named Zechariah,
who belonged to the priestly order of
Abijah. His wife's name was Elizabeth; she
also belonged to a priestly family. 6They
both lived good lives in God's sight and
obeyed fully all the Lord's laws and
commands. 7They had no children because
Elizabeth could not have any, and she and
Zechariah were both very old.
8 One day Zechariah was doing his work as
a priest in the Temple, taking his turn in
the daily service. 9According to the custom
followed by the priests, he was chosen by
lot to burn incense on the altar. So he went
into the Temple of the Lord, 10while the
crowd of people outside prayed during the
hour when the incense was burnt.
11 An angel of the Lord appeared to him,
standing on the right of the altar where the
incense was burnt. 12When Zechariah saw
him, he was alarmed and felt afraid. 13But
the angel said to him, "Don't be afraid,
Zechariah! God has heard your prayer, and
your wife Elizabeth will bear you a son. You
are to name him John. 14How glad and
happy you will be, and how happy many
others will be when he is born! 15He will be
a great man in the Lord's sight. He must
not drink any wine or strong drink. From
his very birth he will be filled with the Holy
Spirit, 16and he will bring back many of the
people of Israel to the Lord their God. 17He
will go ahead of the Lord, strong and
mighty like the prophet Elijah. He will
bring fathers and children together again;
he will turn disobedient people back to the
way of thinking of the righteous; he will get
the Lord's people ready for him."
18 Zechariah said to the angel, "How shall I
know if this is so? I am an old man, and my
wife is old also."
19 "I am Gabriel," the angel answered. "I
stand in the presence of God, who sent me
to speak to you and tell you this good news.
20But you have not believed my message,
which will come true at the right time.
Because you have not believed, you will be
unable to speak; you will remain silent
until the day my promise to you comes
true."
21 In the meantime the people were waiting
for Zechariah and wondering why he was
spending such a long time in the Temple.
22When he came out, he could not speak to
them, and so they knew that he had seen a
vision in the Temple. Unable to say a word,
he made signs to them with his hands.
23 When his period of service in the Temple
was over, Zechariah went back home.
24Some time later his wife Elizabeth
became pregnant and did not leave the
house for five months. 25"Now at last the
Lord has helped me," she said. "He has
taken away my public disgrace!"

The Birth of Jesus is Announced

26 In the sixth month of Elizabeth's
pregnancy God sent the angel Gabriel to a
town in Galilee named Nazareth. 27He had
a message for a young woman promised in
marriage to a man named Joseph, who was
a descendant of King David. Her name was
Mary. 28The angel came to her and said,
"Peace be with you! The Lord is with you
and has greatly blessed you!"
29 Mary was deeply troubled by the angel's
message, and she wondered what his words
meant. 30The angel said to her, "Don't be
afraid, Mary; God has been gracious to you.
31You will become pregnant and give birth
to a son, and you will name him Jesus.
32He will be great and will be called the Son
of the Most High God. The Lord God will

[a] **1.5** JUDEA: *The term here refers to the whole land of Palestine.*

make him a king, as his ancestor David was,
[33]and he will be the king of the
descendants of Jacob for ever; his kingdom
will never end!"
34 Mary said to the angel, "I am a virgin.
How, then, can this be?"
35 The angel answered, "The Holy Spirit
will come on you, and God's power will rest
upon you. For this reason the holy child
will be called the Son of God. [36]Remember
your relative Elizabeth. It is said that she
cannot have children, but she herself is
now six months pregnant, even though she
is very old. [37]For there is nothing that God
cannot do."
38 "I am the Lord's servant," said Mary;
"may it happen to me as you have said."
And the angel left her.

Mary Visits Elizabeth

39 Soon afterwards Mary got ready and
hurried off to a town in the hill country of
Judea. [40]She went into Zechariah's house
and greeted Elizabeth. [41]When Elizabeth
heard Mary's greeting, the baby moved
within her. Elizabeth was filled with the
Holy Spirit [42]and said in a loud voice, "You
are the most blessed
of all women, and
blessed is the child
you will bear!
[43]Why should this
great thing happen
to me, that my
Lord's mother
comes to visit me?
[44]For as soon
as I heard
your greeting,
the baby within
me jumped with
gladness. [45]How
happy you are to
believe that the
Lord's message to
you will come true!"

Mary visited Elizabeth after hearing that that Elizabeth, her relative, was to have a son.

Mary's Song of Praise

46 Mary said,

"My heart praises the Lord;
47 my soul is glad because of God my Saviour,
48 for he has remembered me, his lowly servant!
From now on all people will call me happy,
49 because of the great things the Mighty God has done for me.
His name is holy;
50 from one generation to another
he shows mercy to those who honour him.
51 He has stretched out his mighty arm
and scattered the proud with all their plans.
52 He has brought down mighty kings from their thrones,
and lifted up the lowly.
53 He has filled the hungry with good things,
and sent the rich away with empty hands.
54 He has kept the promise he made to our ancestors,
and has come to the help of his servant Israel.
55 He has remembered to show mercy to Abraham
and to all his descendants for ever!"

56 Mary stayed about
three months with
Elizabeth and then
went back home.

The Birth of John the Baptist

57 The time came for Elizabeth to have her
baby, and she gave birth to a son. 58Her
neighbours and relatives heard how
wonderfully good the Lord had been to her,
and they all rejoiced with her.
59 When the baby was a week old, they
came to circumcise him, and they were
going to name him Zechariah, after his
father. 60But his mother said, "No! His
name is to be John."
61 They said to her, "But you have no
relatives with that name!" 62Then they
made signs to his father, asking him what
name he would like the boy to have.
63 Zechariah asked for a writing tablet and
wrote, "His name is John." How surprised
they all were! 64At that moment Zechariah
was able to speak again, and he started
praising God. 65The neighbours were all
filled with fear, and the news about these
things spread through all the hill country
of Judea. 66Everyone who heard of it
thought about it and asked, "What is this
child going to be?" For it was plain that the
Lord's power was upon him.

Zechariah's Prophecy

67 John's father Zechariah was filled with
the Holy Spirit, and he spoke God's
message:

68 "Let us praise the Lord, the God of
Israel!
He has come to the help of his people
and has set them free.
69 He has provided for us a mighty Saviour,
a descendant of his servant David.
70 He promised through his holy prophets
long ago
71 that he would save us from our
enemies,
from the power of all those who hate
us.
72 He said he would show mercy to our
ancestors
and remember his sacred covenant.
73–74 With a solemn oath to our ancestor
Abraham
he promised to rescue us from our
enemies
and allow us to serve him without
fear,
75 so that we might be holy and righteous
before him
all the days of our life.

76 "You, my child, will be called a prophet
of the Most High God.
You will go ahead of the Lord
to prepare his road for him,
77 to tell his people that they will be saved
by having their sins forgiven.
78 Our God is merciful and tender.
He will cause the bright dawn of
salvation to rise on us
79 and to shine from heaven on all those
who live in the dark shadow of
death,
to guide our steps into the path of
peace."

80 The child grew and developed in body
and spirit. He lived in the desert until the
day when he appeared publicly to the
people of Israel.

The Birth of Jesus
(Mt 1.18–25)

2 At that time the Emperor Augustus
ordered a census to be taken
throughout the Roman Empire. 2When
this first census took place, Quirinius was
the governor of Syria. 3Everyone, then, went
to register himself, each to his own town.
4 Joseph went from the town of Nazareth
in Galilee to the town of Bethlehem in
Judea, the birthplace of King David. Joseph
went there because he was a descendant of
David. 5He went to register with Mary, who
was promised in marriage to him. She was
pregnant, 6and while they were in
Bethlehem, the time came for her to have
her baby. 7She gave birth to her first son,
wrapped him in strips of cloth and laid him
in a manger – there was no room for them
to stay in the inn.

Jesus was born in a manger in the town of Bethlehem.

The Shepherds and the Angels

8 There were some shepherds in that part
of the country who were spending the
night in the fields, taking care of their
flocks. [9]An angel of the Lord appeared to
them, and the glory of the Lord shone over
them. They were terribly afraid, [10]but the
angel said to them, "Don't be afraid! I am
here with good news for you, which will
bring great joy to all the people. [11]This very
day in David's town your Saviour was born
– Christ the Lord! [12]And this is what will
prove it to you: you will find a baby
wrapped in strips of cloth and lying in a
manger."

13 Suddenly a great army of heaven's angels
appeared with the angel, singing praises to
God:

14 "Glory to God in the highest heaven,
and peace on earth to those with
whom he is pleased!"

15 When the angels went away from them
back into heaven, the shepherds said to
one another, "Let's go to Bethlehem and
see this thing that has happened, which
the Lord has told us."

16 So they hurried off and found Mary and
Joseph and saw the baby lying in the
manger. [17]When the
shepherds saw him,
they told them what
the angel had said
about the child.
[18]All who heard it
were amazed at what
the shepherds said.
[19]Mary remembered
all these things
and thought deeply
about them. [20]The
shepherds went
back, singing praises
to God for all they
had heard and seen;
it had been just as
the angel had told
them.

Jesus is Named

21 A week later, when the time came for the
baby to be circumcised, he was named
Jesus, the name which the angel had given
him before he had been conceived.

Jesus is Presented in the Temple

22 The time came for Joseph and Mary to
perform the ceremony of purification, as
the Law of Moses commanded. So they
took the child to Jerusalem to present him
to the Lord, [23]as it is written in the law of
the Lord: "Every firstborn male is to be
dedicated to the Lord." [24]They also went to
offer a sacrifice of a pair of doves or two
young pigeons, as required by the law of
the Lord.

25 At that time there was a man named
Simeon living in Jerusalem. He was a good,
God-fearing man and was waiting for Israel
to be saved. The Holy Spirit was with him
[26]and had assured him that he would not
die before he had seen the Lord's promised
Messiah. [27]Led by the Spirit, Simeon went
into the Temple. When the parents brought
the child Jesus into the Temple to do for
him what the Law required, [28]Simeon took
the child in his arms and gave thanks to
God:

29 "Now, Lord, you have kept your promise,
and you may let your servant go in peace.
30 With my own eyes I have seen your salvation,
31 which you have prepared in the presence of all peoples:
32 A light to reveal your will to the Gentiles
and bring glory to your people Israel."

33 The child's father and mother were
amazed at the things Simeon said about
him. 34Simeon blessed them and said to
Mary, his mother, "This child is chosen by
God for the destruction and the salvation
of many in Israel. He will be a sign from
God which many people will speak against
35and so reveal their secret thoughts. And
sorrow, like a sharp sword, will break your
own heart."
36–37 There was a very old prophet, a widow
named Anna, daughter of Phanuel of the
tribe of Asher. She had been married for
only seven years and was now 84 years
old.[a] She never left the Temple; day and
night she worshipped God, fasting and
praying. 38That very same hour she arrived
and gave thanks to God and spoke about
the child to all who were waiting for God
to set Jerusalem free.

The Return to Nazareth

39 When Joseph and Mary had finished
doing all that was required by the law of
the Lord, they returned to their home town
of Nazareth in Galilee. 40The child grew
and became strong; he was full of wisdom,
and God's blessings were upon him.

The Boy Jesus in the Temple

41 Every year the parents of Jesus went to
Jerusalem for the Passover Festival.
42When Jesus was twelve years old, they
went to the festival as usual. 43When the
festival was over, they started back home,
but the boy Jesus stayed in Jerusalem. His
parents did not know this; 44they thought
that he was with the group, so they
travelled a whole day and then started
looking for him among their relatives and
friends. 45They did not find him, so they
went back to Jerusalem looking for him.
46On the third day they found him in the
Temple, sitting with the Jewish teachers,
listening to them and asking questions.
47All who heard him were amazed at his
intelligent answers. 48His parents were
astonished when they saw him, and his
mother said to him, "My son, why have
you done this to us? Your father and I have
been terribly worried trying to find you."
49 He answered them, "Why did you have
to look for me? Didn't you know that I had
to be in my Father's house?" 50But they did
not understand his answer.
51 So Jesus went back with them to
Nazareth, where he was obedient to them.
His mother treasured all these things in her
heart. 52Jesus grew both in body and in
wisdom, gaining favour with God and
people.

Jesus grew up in Nazareth with Mary and Joseph.

[a] **2.36–37** was now 84 years old; *or* had been a widow 84 years.

The Preaching of John the Baptist
(Mt 3.1–12; Mk 1.1–8; Jn 1.19–28)

3 It was the fifteenth year of the rule of
the Emperor Tiberius; Pontius Pilate
was governor of Judea, Herod was ruler
of Galilee, and his brother Philip was ruler
of the territory of Iturea and Trachonitis;
Lysanias was ruler of Abilene, [2]and Annas
and Caiaphas were high priests. At that
time the word of God came to John son of
Zechariah in the desert. [3]So John went
throughout the whole territory of the River
Jordan, preaching, "Turn away from your
sins and be baptized, and God will forgive
your sins." [4]As it is written in the book of
the prophet Isaiah:

"Someone is shouting in the desert:
'Get the road ready for the Lord;
make a straight path for him to travel!
5 Every valley must be filled up,
every hill and mountain levelled off.
The winding roads must be made straight,
and the rough paths made smooth.
6 The whole human race will see God's
salvation!' "

7 Crowds of people came out to John to be
baptized by him. "You snakes!" he said to
them. "Who told you that you could escape
from the punishment God is about to send?
[8]Do those things that will show that you
have turned from your sins. And don't start
saying among yourselves that Abraham is
your ancestor. I tell you that God can take
these stones and make descendants for
Abraham! [9]The axe is ready to cut down the
trees at the roots; every tree that does not
bear good fruit will be cut down and
thrown in the fire."
10 The people asked him, "What are we to
do, then?"
11 He answered, "Whoever has two shirts
must give one to the man who has none,
and whoever has food must share it."
12 Some tax collectors came to be baptized,
and they asked him, "Teacher, what are we
to do?"
13 "Don't collect more than is legal," he
told them.
14 Some soldiers also asked him, "What
about us? What are we to do?"

He said to them, "Don't take money
from anyone by force or accuse anyone
falsely. Be content with your pay."
15 People's hopes began to rise, and they
began to wonder whether John perhaps
might be the Messiah. [16]So John said to
all of them, "I baptize you with water, but
someone is coming who is much greater
than I am. I am not good enough even to
untie his sandals. He will baptize you with
the Holy Spirit and fire. [17]He has his
winnowing shovel with him, to thresh
out all the grain and gather the wheat
into his barn; but he will burn the chaff in
a fire that never goes out."
18 In many different ways John preached
the Good News to the people and urged
them to change their ways. [19]But John
reprimanded Herod, the governor,
because he had married Herodias, his
brother's wife, and had done many other
evil things. [20]Then Herod did an even
worse thing by putting John in prison.

The Baptism of Jesus
(Mt 3.13–17; Mk 1.9–11)

21 After all the people had been baptized,
Jesus also was baptized. While he was
praying, heaven was opened, [22]and the
Holy Spirit came down upon him in
bodily form like a dove. And a voice came
from heaven, "You are my own dear Son.
I am pleased with you."

The Ancestors of Jesus
(Mt 1.1–17)

23 When Jesus began his work, he was
about 30 years old. He was the son, so
people thought, of Joseph, who was the
son of Heli, [24]the son of Matthat, the son
of Levi, the son of Melchi, the son of
Jannai, the son of Joseph, [25]the son of
Mattathias, the son of Amos, the son of
Nahum, the son of Esli, the son of Naggai,
[26]the son of Maath, the son of
Mattathias, the son of Semein, the son
of Josech, the son of Joda, [27]the son of
Joanan, the son of Rhesa, the

son of Zerubbabel, the son of Shealtiel, the son of Neri, [28]the son of Melchi, the son of Addi, the son of Cosam, the son of Elmadam, the son of Er, [29]the son of Joshua, the son of Eliezer, the son of Jorim, the son of Matthat, the son of Levi, [30]the son of Simeon, the son of Judah, the son of Joseph, the son of Jonam, the son of Eliakim, [31]the son of Melea, the son of Menna, the son of Mattatha, the son of Nathan, the son of David, [32]the son of Jesse, the son of Obed, the son of Boaz, the son of Salmon, the son of Nahshon, [33]the son of Amminadab, the son of Admin, the son of Arni, the son of Hezron, the son of Perez, the son of Judah, [34]the son of Jacob, the son of Isaac, the son of Abraham, the son of Terah, the son of Nahor, [35]the son of Serug, the son of Reu, the son of Peleg, the son of Eber, the son of Shelah, [36]the son of Cainan, the son of Arphaxad, the son of Shem, the son of Noah, the son of Lamech, [37]the son of Methuselah, the son of Enoch, the son of Jared, the son of Mahalaleel, the son of Kenan, [38]the son of Enosh, the son of Seth, the son of Adam, the son of God.

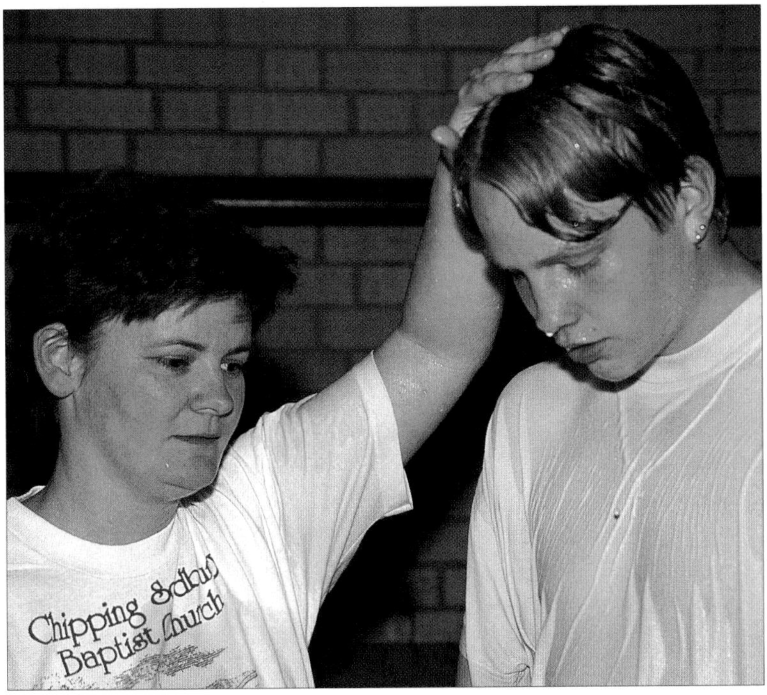

Following the example of Jesus, many Christians are baptized today.

The Temptation of Jesus
(Mt 4.1–11; Mk 1.12–13)

4 Jesus returned from the Jordan full of the Holy Spirit and was led by the Spirit into the desert, [2]where he was tempted by the Devil for 40 days. In all that time he ate nothing, so that he was hungry when it was over.
3 The Devil said to him, "If you are God's Son, order this stone to turn into bread."
4 But Jesus answered, "The scripture says, 'Human beings cannot live on bread alone.' "
5 Then the Devil took him up and showed him in a second all the kingdoms of the world. [6]"I will give you all this power and all this wealth," the Devil told him. "It has all been handed over to me, and I can give it to anyone I choose. [7]All this will be yours, then, if you worship me."
8 Jesus answered, "The scripture says, 'Worship the Lord your God and serve only him!' "
9 Then the Devil took him to Jerusalem and set him on the highest point of the Temple, and said to him, "If you are God's Son, throw yourself down from here. [10]For the scripture says, 'God will order his angels to take good care of you.' [11]It also says, 'They will hold you up with their hands so that not even your feet will be hurt on the stones.' "
12 But Jesus answered, "The scripture says, 'Do not put the Lord your God to the test.' "
13 When the Devil finished tempting Jesus in every way, he left him for a while.

Jesus Begins his Work in Galilee
(Mt 4.12–17; Mk 1.14–15)

14 Then Jesus returned to Galilee, and the power of the Holy Spirit was with him. The news about him spread throughout all that territory. [15]He taught in the synagogues and was praised by everyone.

Jesus is Rejected at Nazareth
(Mt 13.53–58; Mk 6.1–6)

16 Then Jesus went to Nazareth, where he
had been brought up, and on the Sabbath
he went as usual to the synagogue. He
stood up to read the Scriptures [17]and was
handed the book of the prophet Isaiah. He
unrolled the scroll and found the place
where it is written:

18 "The Spirit of the Lord is upon me,
because he has chosen me to bring
good news to the poor.
He has sent me to proclaim liberty to
the captives
and recovery of sight to the blind;
to set free the oppressed
19 and announce that the time has come
when the Lord will save his people."

20 Jesus rolled up the scroll, gave it back to
the attendant, and sat down. All the people
in the synagogue had their eyes fixed on
him, [21]as he said to them, "This passage of
scripture has come true today, as you heard
it being read."
22 They were all well impressed with him
and marvelled at the eloquent words that
he spoke. They said, "Isn't he the son of
Joseph?"
23 He said to them, "I am sure that you will
quote this proverb to me, 'Doctor, heal
yourself.' You will also tell me to do here in
my home town the same things you heard
were done in Capernaum. [24]I tell you this,"
Jesus added, "prophets are never welcomed
in their home town.
25 "Listen to me: it is true that there were
many widows in Israel during the time of
Elijah, when there was no rain for three
and a half years and a severe famine spread
throughout the whole land. [26]Yet Elijah
was not sent to anyone in Israel, but only
to a widow living in Zarephath in the
territory of Sidon. [27]And there were many
people suffering from a dreaded skin
disease who lived in Israel during the time
of the prophet Elisha; yet not one of them
was healed, but only Naaman the Syrian."
28 When the people in the synagogue heard
this, they were filled with anger. [29]They
rose up, dragged Jesus out of the town, and
took him to the top of the hill on which
their town was built. They meant to throw
him over the cliff, [30]but he walked through
the middle of the crowd and went his way.

In the synagogue in Nazareth, Jesus read the Scripture from a scroll.

A Man with an Evil Spirit
(Mk 1.21–28)

31 Then Jesus went to Capernaum, a town
in Galilee, where he taught the people on
the Sabbath. [32]They were all amazed at the
way he taught, because he spoke with
authority. [33]In the synagogue was a man
who had the spirit of an evil demon in him;
he screamed out in a loud voice, [34]"Ah!
What do you want with us, Jesus of
Nazareth? Are you here to destroy us? I
know who you are: you are God's holy
messenger!"
35 Jesus ordered the spirit, "Be quiet and
come out of the man!" The demon threw
the man down in front of them and went
out of him without doing him any harm.
36 The people were all amazed and said to
one another, "What kind of words are
these? With authority and power this man
gives orders to the evil spirits, and they
come out!" [37]And the report about Jesus
spread everywhere in that region.

Jesus Heals Many People

(Mt 8.14–17; Mk 1.29–34)

38 Jesus left the synagogue and went to Simon's house. Simon's mother-in-law was sick with a high fever, and they spoke to Jesus about her. [39]He went and stood at her bedside and ordered the fever to leave her. The fever left her, and she got up at once and began to wait on them.

40 After sunset all who had friends who were sick with various diseases brought them to Jesus; he placed his hands on every one of them and healed them all. [41]Demons also went out from many people, screaming, "You are the Son of God!"

Jesus gave the demons an order and would not let them speak, because they knew that he was the Messiah.

Jesus Preaches in the Synagogues

(Mk 1.35–39)

42 At daybreak Jesus left the town and went off to a lonely place. The people started looking for him, and when they found him, they tried to keep him from leaving. [43]But he said to them, "I must preach the Good News about the Kingdom of God in other towns also, because that is what God sent me to do."

44 So he preached in the synagogues throughout the country.

Jesus Calls the First Disciples

(Mt 4.18–22; Mk 1.16–20)

5 One day Jesus was standing on the shore of Lake Gennesaret while the people pushed their way up to him to listen to the word of God. [2]He saw two boats pulled up on the beach; the fishermen had left them and were washing the nets. [3]Jesus got into one of the boats – it belonged to Simon – and asked him to push off a little from the shore. Jesus sat in the boat and taught the crowd.

4 When he finished speaking, he said to Simon, "Push the boat out further to the deep water, and you and your partners let down your nets for a catch."

5 "Master," Simon answered, "we worked hard all night long and caught nothing. But if you say so, I will let down the nets." [6]They let them down and caught such a large number of fish that the nets were about to break. [7]So they motioned to their partners in the other boat to come and help them. They came and filled both boats so full of fish that the boats were about to sink. [8]When Simon Peter saw what had happened, he fell on his knees before Jesus and said, "Go away from me, Lord! I am a sinful man!"

9 He and the others with him were all amazed at the large number of fish they had caught. [10]The same was true of Simon's partners, James and John, the sons of Zebedee. Jesus said to Simon, "Don't be afraid; from now on you will be catching people."

11 They pulled the boats up on the beach, left everything, and followed Jesus.

Two of the first disciples of Jesus were fishermen.

Jesus Heals a Man
(Mt 8.1–4; Mk 1.40–45)

12 Once Jesus was in a town where there
was a man who was suffering from a
dreaded skin disease. When he saw Jesus, he
threw himself down and begged him, "Sir, if
you want to, you can make me clean!"[a]
13 Jesus stretched out his hand and touched
him. "I do want to," he answered. "Be
clean!" At once the disease left the man.
[14]Jesus ordered him, "Don't tell anyone,
but go straight to the priest and let him
examine you; then to prove to everyone
that you are cured, offer the sacrifice as
Moses ordered."
15 But the news about Jesus spread all the
more widely, and crowds of people came to
hear him and be healed from their diseases.
[16]But he would go away to lonely places,
where he prayed.

Jesus Heals a Paralysed Man
(Mt 9.1–8; Mk 2.1–12)

17 One day when Jesus was teaching, some
Pharisees and teachers of the Law were
sitting there who had come from every
town in Galilee and Judea and from
Jerusalem. The power of the Lord was
present for Jesus to heal the sick. [18]Some
men came carrying a paralysed man on a
bed, and they tried to take him into the
house and put him in front of Jesus.
[19]Because of the crowd, however, they
could find no way to take him in. So they
carried him up on the roof, made an
opening in the tiles, and let him down on
his bed into the middle of the group in
front of Jesus. [20]When Jesus saw how
much faith they had, he said to the man,
"Your sins are forgiven, my friend."
21 The teachers of the Law and the
Pharisees began to say to themselves, "Who
is this man who speaks such blasphemy!
God is the only one who can forgive sins!"
22 Jesus knew their thoughts and said to
them, "Why do you think such things?
[23]Is it easier to say, 'Your sins are forgiven
you,' or to say, 'Get up and walk'? [24]I will
prove to you, then, that the Son of Man
has authority on earth to forgive sins." So
he said to the paralysed man, "I tell you,
get up, pick up your bed, and go home!"
25 At once the man got up in front of them
all, took the bed he had been lying on,
and went home, praising God. [26]They
were all completely amazed! Full of fear,
they praised God, saying, "What
marvellous things we have seen today!"

Jesus Calls Levi
(Mt 9.9–13; Mk 2.13–17)

27 After this, Jesus went out and saw a tax
collector named Levi, sitting in his office.
Jesus said to him, "Follow me." [28]Levi got
up, left everything, and followed him.
29 Then Levi had a big feast in his house for
Jesus, and among the guests was a large
number of tax collectors and other people.
[30]Some Pharisees and some teachers of the
Law who belonged to their group
complained to Jesus' disciples. "Why do
you eat and drink with tax collectors and
other outcasts?" they asked.
31 Jesus answered them, "People who are
well do not need a doctor, but only those
who are sick. [32]I have not come to call
respectable people to repent, but outcasts."

The Question about Fasting
(Mt 9.14–17; Mk 2.18–22)

33 Some people said to Jesus, "The disciples
of John fast frequently and offer prayers,
and the disciples of the Pharisees do the
same; but your disciples eat and drink."
34 Jesus answered, "Do you think you can
make the guests at a wedding party go
without food as long as the bridegroom is
with them? Of course not! [35]But the day
will come when the bridegroom will be
taken away from them, and then they will
fast."
36 Jesus also told them this parable: "No
one tears a piece off a new coat to patch up
an old coat. If he does, he will have torn
the new coat, and the piece of new cloth
will not match the old. [37]Nor does anyone
pour new wine into used wine skins,
because the new wine will burst the skins,
the wine will pour out, and the skins will be
ruined. [38]Instead, new wine must be

[a] **5.12** MAKE ME CLEAN: *This disease was considered to make a person ritually unclean.*

poured into fresh wineskins! [39]And no one
wants new wine after drinking old wine.
'The old is better,' he says."

The Question about the Sabbath
(Mt 12.1–8; Mk 2.23–28)

6 Jesus was walking through some
cornfields on the Sabbath. His
disciples began to pick the ears of
corn, rub them in their hands, and eat the
grain. [2]Some Pharisees asked, "Why are you
doing what our Law says you cannot do on
the Sabbath?"
3 Jesus answered them, "Haven't you read
what David did when he and his men were
hungry? [4]He went into the house of God,
took the bread offered to God, ate it, and
gave it also to his men. Yet it is against our
Law for anyone except the priests to eat
that bread."
5 And Jesus concluded, "The Son of Man is
Lord of the Sabbath."

The Man with a Paralysed Hand
(Mt 12.9–14; Mk 3.1–6)

6 On another Sabbath Jesus went into a
synagogue and taught. A man was there
whose right hand was paralysed. [7]Some
teachers of the Law and some Pharisees
wanted a reason to accuse Jesus of doing
wrong, so they watched him closely to see
if he would heal on the Sabbath. [8]But Jesus
knew their thoughts and said to the man,
"Stand up and come here to the front." The
man got up and stood there. [9]Then Jesus
said to them, "I ask you: what does our Law
allow us to do on the Sabbath? To help or
to harm? To save someone's life or destroy
it?" [10]He looked around at them all; then
he said[a] to the man, "Stretch out your
hand." He did so, and his hand became
well again.
11 They were filled with rage and began to
discuss among themselves what they could
do to Jesus.

Jesus Chooses the Twelve Apostles
(Mt 10.1–4; Mk 3.13–19)

12 At that time Jesus went up a hill to pray
and spent the whole night there praying to
God. [13]When day came, he called his
disciples to him and chose twelve of them,
whom he named apostles: [14]Simon (whom
he named Peter) and his brother Andrew;
James and John, Philip and Bartholomew,
[15]Matthew and Thomas, James son of
Alphaeus, and Simon (who was called the
Patriot), [16]Judas son of James, and Judas
Iscariot, who became the traitor.

Jesus Teaches and Heals
(Mt 4.23–25)

17 When Jesus had come down from the hill
with the apostles, he stood on a level place
with a large number of his disciples. A large
crowd of people was there from all over
Judea and from Jerusalem and from the
coastal cities of Tyre and Sidon; [18]they had
come to hear him and to be healed of their
diseases. Those who were troubled by evil
spirits also came and were healed. [19]All the
people tried to touch him, for power was
going out from him and healing them all.

Happiness and Sorrow
(Mt 5.1–12)

20 Jesus looked at his disciples and said,

"Happy are you poor;
  the Kingdom of God is yours!
21 Happy are you who are hungry now;
  you will be filled!
Happy are you who weep now;
  you will laugh!

22 "Happy are you when people hate you,
reject you, insult you, and say that you are
evil, all because of the Son of Man! [23]Be
glad when that happens, and dance for joy,
because a great reward is kept for you in
heaven. For their ancestors did the very
same things to the prophets.

24 "But how terrible for you who are rich
    now;
  you have had your easy life!
25 How terrible for you who are full now;
  you will go hungry!
How terrible for you who laugh now;
  you will mourn and weep!

[a] **6.10** said; *some manuscripts have* said angrily.

26 "How terrible when all people speak well
of you; their ancestors said the very same
things about the false prophets.

Love for Enemies

(Mt 5.38–48; 7.12a)

27 "But I tell you who hear me: love your
enemies, do good to those who hate you,
28bless those who curse you, and pray for
those who ill-treat you. 29If anyone hits
you on one cheek, let him hit the other one
too; if someone takes your coat, let him
have your shirt as well. 30Give to everyone
who asks you for something, and when
someone takes what is yours, do not ask for
it back. 31Do for others just what you want
them to do for you.
32 "If you love only the people who love
you, why should you receive a blessing?
Even sinners love those who love them!
33And if you do good only to those who do
good to you, why should you receive a
blessing? Even sinners do that! 34And if
you lend only to those from whom you
hope to get it back, why should you receive
a blessing? Even sinners lend to sinners, to
get back the same amount! 35No! Love your
enemies and do good to them; lend and
expect nothing back. You will then have a
great reward, and you will be children of
the Most High God. For he is good to the
ungrateful and the wicked. 36Be merciful
just as your Father is merciful.

Judging Others

(Mt 7.1–5)

37 "Do not judge others, and God will not
judge you; do not condemn others, and
God will not condemn you; forgive others,
and God will forgive you. 38Give to
others, and God will give to you. Indeed,
you will receive a full measure, a generous
helping, poured into your hands – all that
you can hold. The measure you use for
others is the one that God will use for
you."
39 And Jesus told them this parable: "One
blind man cannot lead another one; if he
does, both will fall into a ditch. 40No
pupil is greater than his teacher; but every
pupil, when he has completed his
training, will be like his teacher.
41 "Why do you look at the speck in your
brother's eye, but pay no attention to the
log in your own eye? 42How can you say to
your brother, 'Please, brother, let me take
that speck out of your eye,' yet cannot even
see the log in your own eye? You hypocrite!
First take the log out of your own eye, and
then you will be able to see clearly to take
the speck out of your brother's eye.

A Tree and its Fruit

(Mt 7.16–20; 12.33–35)

43 "A healthy tree does not bear bad fruit,
nor does a poor tree bear good fruit.
44Every tree is known by the fruit it bears;
you do not pick figs from thorn bushes or
gather grapes from bramble bushes. 45A
good person brings good out of the treasure
of good things in his heart; a bad person
brings bad out of his treasure of bad things.
For the mouth speaks what the heart is full
of.

The Two House Builders

(Mt 7.24–27)

46 "Why do you call me, 'Lord, Lord,' and
yet don't do what I tell you? 47Anyone
who comes to me and listens to my words
and obeys them – I will show you what he
is like. 48He is like a man who, in building
his house, dug deep and laid the
foundation on rock. The river overflowed
and hit that house but could not shake it,
because it was well built. 49But anyone
who hears my words and does not obey
them is like a man who built his house
without laying a foundation; when the
flood hit that house it fell at once – and
what a terrible crash that was!"

Jesus Heals a Roman Officer's Servant

(Mt 8.5–13)

7 When Jesus had finished saying all
these things to the people, he went to
Capernaum. 2A Roman officer there
had a servant who was very dear to him; the
man was sick and about to die. 3When the

officer heard about Jesus, he sent some
Jewish elders to ask him to come and heal
his servant. [4]They came to Jesus and begged
him earnestly, "This man really deserves
your help. [5]He loves our people and he
himself built a synagogue for us."
6 So Jesus went with them. He was not far
from the house when the officer sent
friends to tell him, "Sir, don't trouble
yourself. I do not deserve to have you come
into my house, [7]neither do I consider
myself worthy to come to you in person.
Just give the order, and my servant will get
well. [8]I, too, am a man placed under the
authority of superior officers, and I have
soldiers under me. I order this one, 'Go!'
and he goes; I order that one, 'Come!' and
he comes; and I order my slave, 'Do this!'
and he does it."
9 Jesus was surprised when he heard this;
he turned round and said to the crowd
following him, "I tell you, I have never
found faith like this, not even in Israel!"
10 The messengers went back to the officer's
house and found his servant well.

Jesus Raises a Widow's Son

11 Soon afterwards[a] Jesus went to a town
called Nain, accompanied by his disciples
and a large crowd. [12]Just as he arrived at
the gate of the town, a funeral procession
was coming out. The dead man was the
only son of a woman who was a widow,
and a large crowd from the town was with
her. [13]When the Lord saw her, his heart
was filled with pity for her, and he said to
her, "Don't cry." [14]Then he walked over
and touched the coffin, and the men
carrying it stopped. Jesus said, "Young man!
Get up, I tell you!" [15]The dead man sat up
and began to talk, and Jesus gave him back
to his mother.
16 They all were filled with fear and praised
God. "A great prophet has appeared among
us!" they said; "God has come to save his
people!"
17 This news about Jesus went out through
all the country and the surrounding
territory.

[a] **7.11** Soon afterwards; *some manuscripts have* The next day.

The Messengers from John the Baptist

(Mt 11.2–19)

18 When John's disciples told him about all
these things, he called two of them [19]and
sent them to the Lord to ask him, "Are you
the one John said was going to come, or
should we expect someone else?"
20 When they came to Jesus, they said,
"John the Baptist sent us to ask if you are
the one he said was going to come, or if we
should expect someone else."
21 At that very time Jesus cured many
people of their sicknesses, diseases, and evil
spirits, and gave sight to many blind
people. [22]He answered John's messengers,
"Go back and tell John what you have seen
and heard: the blind can see, the lame can
walk, those who suffer from dreaded skin
diseases are made clean,[b] the deaf can hear,
the dead are raised to life, and the Good
News is preached to the poor. [23]How happy
are those who have no doubts about me!"
24 After John's messengers had left, Jesus
began to speak about him to the crowds:
"When you went out to John in the desert,
what did you expect to see? A blade of grass
bending in the wind? [25]What did you go
out to see? A man dressed up in fancy
clothes? People who dress like that and live
in luxury are found in palaces! [26]Tell me,
what did you go out to see? A prophet? Yes
indeed, but you saw much more than a
prophet. [27]For John is the one of whom the
scripture says: 'God said, I will send my
messenger ahead of you to open the way for
you.' [28]I tell you," Jesus added, "John is
greater than anyone who has ever lived. But
the one who is least in the Kingdom of God
is greater than John."
29 All the people heard him; they and
especially the tax collectors were the ones
who had obeyed God's righteous demands
and had been baptized by John. [30]But the
Pharisees and the teachers of the Law
rejected God's purpose for themselves and
refused to be baptized by John.
31 Jesus continued, "Now to what can I
compare the people of this day? What are
they like? [32]They are like children sitting in

[b] **7.22** MADE CLEAN: *See 5.12.*

the market place. One group shouts to the
other, 'We played wedding music for you,
but you wouldn't dance! We sang funeral
songs, but you wouldn't cry!' 33John the
Baptist came, and he fasted and drank no
wine, and you said, 'He has a demon in
him!' 34The Son of Man came, and he ate
and drank, and you said, 'Look at this man!
He is a glutton and a drinker, a friend of tax
collectors and other outcasts!' 35God's
wisdom, however, is shown to be true by all
who accept it."

A woman anoints the feet of Jesus at the house of Simon the Pharisee.

Jesus at the Home of Simon the Pharisee

36 A Pharisee invited Jesus to have dinner
with him, and Jesus went to his house and
sat down to eat. 37In that town was a
woman who lived a sinful life. She heard
that Jesus was eating in the Pharisee's
house, so she brought an alabaster jar full
of perfume 38and stood behind Jesus, by
his feet, crying and wetting his feet with
her tears. Then she dried his feet with her
hair, kissed them, and poured the perfume
on them. 39When the Pharisee saw this, he
said to himself, "If this man really were a
prophet, he would know who this woman
is who is touching him; he would know
what kind of sinful life she lives!"
40 Jesus spoke up and said to him, "Simon,
I have something to tell you."
"Yes, Teacher," he said, "tell me."
41 "There were two men who owed money
to a money-lender," Jesus began. "One
owed him five hundred silver coins, and
the other owed him fifty. 42Neither of them
could pay him back, so he cancelled the
debts of both. Which one, then, will love
him more?"
43 "I suppose," answered Simon, "that it
would be the one who was forgiven more."
"You are right," said Jesus. 44Then he
turned to the woman and said to Simon,
"Do you see this woman? I came into your
home, and you gave me no water for my
feet, but she has washed my feet with her
tears and dried them with her hair. 45You
did not welcome me with a kiss, but she has
not stopped kissing my feet since I came.
46You provided no olive oil for my head,
but she has covered my feet with perfume.
47I tell you, then, the great love she has
shown proves that her many sins have
been forgiven. But whoever has been
forgiven little shows only a little love."
48 Then Jesus said to the woman, "Your sins
are forgiven."
49 The others sitting at the table began to
say to themselves, "Who is this, who even
forgives sins?"
50 But Jesus said to the woman, "Your faith
has saved you; go in peace."

Women who Accompanied Jesus

8 Some time later Jesus travelled
through towns and villages, preaching
the Good News about the Kingdom of
God. The twelve disciples went with him,
2and so did some women who had been
healed of evil spirits and diseases: Mary
(who was called Magdalene), from whom
seven demons had been driven out;
3Joanna, whose husband Chuza was an
officer in Herod's court; and Susanna, and
many other women who used their own
resources to help Jesus and his disciples.

The Parable of the Sower
(Mt 13.1–9; Mk 4.1–9)

4 People kept coming to Jesus from one town after another; and when a great crowd gathered, Jesus told this parable:

5 "Once there was a man who went out to
sow corn. As he scattered the seed in the
field, some of it fell along the path, where
it was stepped on, and the birds ate it up.
6Some of it fell on rocky ground, and when
the plants sprouted, they dried up because
the soil had no moisture. 7Some of the seed
fell among thorn bushes, which grew up
with the plants and choked them. 8And
some seeds fell in good soil; the plants grew
and produced corn, a hundred grains
each."

And Jesus concluded, "Listen, then, if you have ears!"

The Purpose of the Parables
(Mt 13.10–17; Mk 4.10–12)

9 His disciples asked Jesus what this
parable meant, 10and he answered, "The
knowledge of the secrets of the Kingdom of
God has been given to you, but to the rest
it comes by means of parables, so that they
may look but not see, and listen but not
understand.

Jesus Explains the Parable of the Sower
(Mt 13.18–23; Mk 4.13–20)

11 "This is what the parable means: the seed
is the word of God. 12The seeds that fell
along the path stand for those who hear;
but the Devil comes and takes the message
away from their hearts in order to keep
them from believing and being saved.
13The seeds that fell on rocky ground stand
for those who hear the message and receive
it gladly. But it does not sink deep into
them; they believe only for a while but
when the time of testing comes, they fall
away. 14The seeds that fell among thorn
bushes stand for those who hear; but the
worries and riches and pleasures of this life
crowd in and choke them, and their fruit
never ripens. 15The seeds that fell in good
soil stand for those who hear the message
and retain it in a good and obedient heart,
and they persist until they bear fruit.

A Lamp under a Bowl
(Mk 4.21–25)

16 "People do not light a lamp and cover it with a bowl or put it under a bed. Instead, they put it on the lampstand, so that people will see the light as they come in.

17 "Whatever is hidden away will be brought out into the open, and whatever is covered up will be found and brought to light.

18 "Be careful, then, how you listen; because those who have something will be given more, but those who have nothing will have taken away from them even the little they think they have."

Jesus' Mother and Brothers
(Mt 12.46–50; Mk 3.31–35)

19 Jesus' mother and brothers came to him,
but were unable to join him because of the
crowd. 20Someone said to Jesus, "Your
mother and brothers are standing outside
and want to see you."

21 Jesus said to them all, "My mother and brothers are those who hear the word of God and obey it."

We do not know what Jesus' mother, Mary, looked like, but this is an artist's idea of her.

Jesus Calms a Storm
(Mt 8.23–27; Mk 4.35–41)

22 One day Jesus got into a boat with his
disciples and said to them, "Let us go across
to the other side of the lake." So they started
out. 23As they were sailing, Jesus fell asleep.
Suddenly a strong wind blew down on the
lake, and the boat began to fill with water,
so that they were all in great danger. 24The
disciples went to Jesus and woke him up,
saying, "Master, Master! We are about to
die!"

Jesus got up and gave an order to the
wind and the stormy water; they died
down, and there was a great calm. 25Then
he said to the disciples, "Where is your
faith?"

But they were amazed and afraid, and
said to one another, "Who is this man? He
gives orders to the winds and waves, and
they obey him!"

Jesus Heals a Man with Demons
(Mt 8.28–34; Mk 5.1–20)

26 Jesus and his disciples sailed on over to
the territory of Gerasa,[a] which is across the
lake from Galilee. 27As Jesus stepped ashore,
he was met by a man from the town who
had demons in him. For a long time this
man had gone without clothes and would
not stay at home, but spent his time in the
burial caves. 28When he saw Jesus, he gave
a loud cry, threw himself down at his feet,
and shouted, "Jesus, Son of the Most High
God! What do you want with me? I beg you,
don't punish me!" 29He said this because
Jesus had ordered the evil spirit to go out of
him. Many times it had seized him, and
even though he was kept a prisoner, his
hands and feet fastened with chains, he
would break the chains and be driven by the
demon out into the desert.

30 Jesus asked him, "What is your name?"

"My name is 'Mob'," he answered –
because many demons had gone into him.
31The demons begged Jesus not to send
them into the abyss.[b]

32 There was a large herd of pigs near by,
feeding on a hillside. So the demons begged
Jesus to let them go into the pigs, and he let
them. 33They went out of the man and into
the pigs. The whole herd rushed down the
side of the cliff into the lake and was
drowned.

34 The men who had been taking care of the
pigs saw what happened, so they ran off and
spread the news in the town and among the
farms. 35People went out to see what had
happened, and when they came to Jesus,
they found the man from whom the
demons had gone out sitting at the feet of
Jesus, clothed and in his right mind; and
they were all afraid. 36Those who had seen
it told the people how the man had been
cured. 37Then all the people from that
territory asked Jesus to go away, because
they were terribly afraid. So Jesus got into
the boat and left. 38The man from whom
the demons had gone out begged Jesus, "Let
me go with you."

But Jesus sent him away, saying, 39"Go
back home and tell what God has done for
you."

The man went through the town, telling
what Jesus had done for him.

Jairus' Daughter and the Woman who Touched Jesus' Cloak
(Mt 9.18–26; Mk 5.21–43)

40 When Jesus returned to the other side of
the lake, the people welcomed him, because
they had all been waiting for him. 41Then a
man named Jairus arrived; he was an official
in the local synagogue. He threw himself
down at Jesus' feet and begged him to go to
his home, 42because his only daughter, who
was twelve years old, was dying.

As Jesus went along, the people were
crowding him from every side. 43Among
them was a woman who had suffered from
severe bleeding for twelve years; she had
spent all she had on doctors,[c] but no one
had been able to cure her. 44She came up
in the crowd behind Jesus and touched the
edge of his cloak, and her bleeding stopped
at once. 45Jesus asked, "Who touched me?"

Everyone denied it, and Peter said,

[a] **8.26** Gerasa; *some manuscripts have* Gadara *(see Mt 8.28); others have* Gergesa.

[b] **8.31** ABYSS: *It was thought that the demons were to be imprisoned in the depths of the earth until their final punishment.*

[c] **8.43** *Some manuscripts do not have* she had spent all she had on doctors.

"Master, the people are all round you and
crowding in on you."
46 But Jesus said, "Someone touched me, for
I knew it when power went out of me."
47 The woman saw that she had been found
out, so she came trembling and threw
herself at Jesus' feet. There in front of
everybody, she told him why she had
touched him and how she had been healed
at once. 48 Jesus said to her, "My daughter,
your faith has made you well. Go in peace."
49 While Jesus was saying this, a messenger
came from the official's house. "Your
daughter has died," he told Jairus; "don't
bother the Teacher any longer."
50 But Jesus heard it and said to Jairus,
"Don't be afraid; only believe, and she will
be well."
51 When he arrived at the house, he would
not let anyone go in with him except Peter,
John, and James, and the child's father and
mother. 52 Everyone there was crying and
mourning for the child. Jesus said, "Don't
cry; the child is not dead – she is only
sleeping!"
53 They all laughed at him, because they
knew that she was dead. 54 But Jesus took
her by the hand and called out, "Get up,
my child!" 55 Her life returned, and she got
up at once, and Jesus ordered them to give
her something to eat. 56 Her parents were
astounded, but Jesus commanded them
not to tell anyone what had happened.

Jesus Sends Out the Twelve Disciples

(Mt 10.5–15; Mk 6.7–13)

9 Jesus called the twelve disciples
together and gave them power and
authority to drive out all demons and
to cure diseases. 2 Then he sent them out to
preach the Kingdom of God and to heal the
sick, 3 after saying to them, "Take nothing
with you for the journey: no stick, no
beggar's bag, no food, no money, not even
an extra shirt. 4 Wherever you are
welcomed, stay in the same house until you
leave that town; 5 wherever people don't
welcome you, leave that town and shake
the dust off your feet as a warning to them."

The disciples left and travelled through
all the villages, preaching the Good News
and healing people everywhere.

Herod's Confusion

(Mt 14.1–12; Mk 6.14–29)

7 When Herod, the ruler of Galilee, heard
about all the things that were happening,
he was very confused, because some people
were saying that John the Baptist had
come back to life. 8 Others were saying that
Elijah had appeared, and still others that
one of the prophets of long ago had come
back to life. 9 Herod said, "I had John's
head cut off; but who is this man I hear
these things about?" And he kept trying to
see Jesus.

Jesus Feeds a Great Crowd

(Mt 14.13–21; Mk 6.30–44; Jn 6.1–14)

10 The apostles came back and told Jesus
everything they had done. He took them
with him, and they went off by themselves
to a town called Bethsaida. 11 When the
crowds heard about it, they followed him. He
welcomed them, spoke to them about the
Kingdom of God, and healed those who
needed it.
12 When the sun was beginning to set, the
twelve disciples came to him and said,
"Send the people away so that they can go
to the villages and farms round here and
find food and lodging, because this is a
lonely place."
13 But Jesus said to them, "You yourselves
give them something to eat."

They answered, "All we have are five
loaves and two fish. Do you want us to go
and buy food for this whole crowd?"
14 (There were about 5,000 men there.)

Jesus said to his disciples, "Make the
people sit down in groups of about fifty
each."
15 After the disciples had done so, 16 Jesus
took the five loaves and two fish, looked up
to heaven, thanked God for them, broke
them, and gave them to the disciples to
distribute to the people. 17 They all ate and
had enough, and the disciples took up twelve
baskets of what was left over.

Peter's Declaration about Jesus
(Mt 16.13–19; Mk 8.27–29)

18 One day when Jesus was praying alone,
the disciples came to him. "Who do the
crowds say I am?" he asked them.
19 "Some say that you are John the
Baptist," they answered. "Others say that
you are Elijah, while others say that one of
the prophets of long ago has come back to
life."
20 "What about you?" he asked them.
"Who do you say I am?"
Peter answered, "You are God's
Messiah."

Jesus Speaks about his Suffering and Death
(Mt 16.20–28; Mk 8.30—9.1)

21 Then Jesus gave them strict orders not to
tell this to anyone. 22He also said to them,
"The Son of Man must suffer much and be
rejected by the elders, the chief priests, and
the teachers of the Law. He will be put to
death, but three days later he will be raised
to life."
23 And he said to them all, "Anyone who
wants to come with me must forget self,
take up their cross every day, and follow
me. 24For whoever wants
to save their own life will
lose it, but whoever loses
their life for my sake
will save it. 25Will people
gain anything if they win
the whole world but
are themselves lost or
defeated? Of course not!
26If people are ashamed of
me and of my teaching,
then the Son of Man will
be ashamed of them when
he comes in his glory and
in the glory of the Father
and of the holy angels. 27I
assure you that there are
some here who will not die
until they have seen the
Kingdom of God."

Jesus told his disciples that many of them would die because of him.

The Transfiguration
(Mt 17.1–8; Mk 9.2–8)

28 About a week after he had said these
things, Jesus took Peter, John, and James
with him and went up a hill to pray.
29While he was praying, his face changed
its appearance, and his clothes became
dazzling white. 30Suddenly two men were
there talking with him. They were Moses
and Elijah, 31who appeared in heavenly
glory and talked with Jesus about the way
in which he would soon fulfil God's
purpose by dying in Jerusalem. 32Peter and
his companions were sound asleep, but
they woke up and saw Jesus' glory and the
two men who were standing with him.
33As the men were leaving Jesus, Peter said
to him, "Master, how good it is that we are
here! We will make three tents, one for
you, one for Moses, and one for Elijah."
(He did not really know what he was
saying.)
34 While he was still speaking, a cloud
appeared and covered them with its
shadow; and the disciples were afraid as
the cloud came over them. 35A voice said
from the cloud, "This is my Son, whom I
have chosen – listen to him!"
36 When the voice
stopped, there
was Jesus all
alone. The
disciples kept
quiet about all
this, and told no
one at that time
anything they
had seen.

Jesus Heals a Boy with an Evil Spirit
(Mt 17.14–18; Mk 9.14–27)

37 The next day
Jesus and the
three disciples
went down
from the hill,

and a large crowd met Jesus. [38]A man
shouted from the crowd, "Teacher! I beg
you, look at my son – my only son! [39]A
spirit attacks him with a sudden shout and
throws him into a fit, so that he foams at
the mouth; it keeps on hurting him and
will hardly let him go! [40]I begged your
disciples to drive it out, but they couldn't."
41 Jesus answered, "How unbelieving and
wrong you people are! How long must I stay
with you? How long do I have to put up
with you?" Then he said to the man, "Bring
your son here."
42 As the boy was coming, the demon
knocked him to the ground and threw him
into a fit. Jesus gave a command to the evil
spirit, healed the boy, and gave him back to
his father. [43]All the people were amazed at
the mighty power of God.

Jesus Speaks Again about his Death

(Mt 17.22–23; Mk 9.30–32)

The people were still marvelling at
everything Jesus was doing, when he said
to his disciples, [44]"Don't forget what I am
about to tell you! The Son of Man is going
to be handed over to the power of human
beings." [45]But the disciples did not know
what this meant. It had been hidden from
them so that they could not understand it,
and they were afraid to ask him about the
matter.

Who is the Greatest?

(Mt 18.1–5; Mk 9.33–37)

46 An argument broke out among the
disciples as to which one of them was the
greatest. [47]Jesus knew what they were
thinking, so he took a child, stood him by
his side, [48]and said to them, "Whoever
welcomes this child in my name, welcomes
me; and whoever welcomes me, also
welcomes the one who sent me. For the one
who is least among you all is the greatest."

Whoever is not Against You is For You

(Mk 9.38–40)

49 John spoke up, "Master, we saw a man
driving out demons in your name, and we
told him to stop, because he doesn't belong
to our group."
50 "Do not try to stop him," Jesus said to
him and to the other disciples, "because
whoever is not against you is for you."

A Samaritan Village Refuses to Receive Jesus

51 As the time drew near when Jesus would
be taken up to heaven, he made up his
mind and set out on his way to Jerusalem.
[52]He sent messengers ahead of him, who
went into a village in Samaria to get
everything ready for him. [53]But the people
there would not receive him, because it was
clear that he was on his way to Jerusalem.
[54]When the disciples James and John saw
this, they said, "Lord, do you want us to call
fire down from heaven to destroy them?"[a]
55 Jesus turned and rebuked them.[b] [56]Then
Jesus and his disciples went on to another
village.

The Would-be Followers of Jesus

(Mt 8.19–22)

57 As they went on their way, a man said to
Jesus, "I will follow you wherever you go."
58 Jesus said to him, "Foxes have holes, and
birds have nests, but the Son of Man has
nowhere to lie down and rest."
59 He said to another man, "Follow me."
But that man said, "Sir, first let me go
back and bury my father."
60 Jesus answered, "Let the dead bury their
own dead. You go and proclaim the
Kingdom of God."
61 Someone else said, "I will follow you, sir;
but first let me go and say goodbye to my
family."
62 Jesus said to him, "Anyone who starts to
plough and then keeps looking back is of
no use to the Kingdom of God."

[a] **9.54** *Some manuscripts add* as Elijah did.
[b] **9.55** *Some manuscripts add* and said, "You don't know what kind of a Spirit you belong to; for the Son of Man did not come to destroy people's lives, but to save them."

Jesus Sends Out the Seventy-two

10 After this the Lord chose another 72[a] men and sent them out two by two, to go ahead of him to every town and place where he himself was about to go. [2]He said to them, "There is a large harvest, but few workers to gather it in. Pray to the owner of the harvest that he will send out workers to gather in his harvest. [3]Go! I am sending you like lambs among wolves. [4]Don't take a purse or a beggar's bag or shoes; don't stop to greet anyone on the road. [5]Whenever you go into a house, first say, 'Peace be with this house.' [6]If a peace-loving person lives there, let your greeting of peace remain on him; if not, take back your greeting of peace. [7]Stay in that same house, eating and drinking whatever they offer you, for workers should be given their pay. Don't move round from one house to another. [8]Whenever you go into a town and are made welcome, eat what is set before you, [9]heal the sick in that town, and say to the people there, 'The Kingdom of God has come near you.' [10]But whenever you go into a town and are not welcomed, go out in the streets and say, [11]'Even the dust from your town that sticks to our feet we wipe off against you. But remember that the Kingdom of God has come near you!' [12]I assure you that on Judgement Day God will show more mercy to Sodom than to that town!

The Unbelieving Towns
(Mt 11.20–24)

13 "How terrible it will be for you, Chorazin! How terrible for you too, Bethsaida! If the miracles which were performed in you had been performed in Tyre and Sidon, the people there would long ago have sat down, put on sackcloth, and sprinkled ashes on themselves, to show that they had turned from their sins! [14]God will show more mercy on Judgement Day to Tyre and Sidon than to you. [15]And as for you, Capernaum! Did you want to lift yourself up to heaven? You will be thrown down to hell!"

16 Jesus said to his disciples, "Whoever listens to you listens to me; whoever rejects you rejects me; and whoever rejects me rejects the one who sent me."

The Return of the Seventy-two

17 The 72[b] men came back in great joy. "Lord," they said, "even the demons obeyed us when we gave them a command in your name!"

18 Jesus answered them, "I saw Satan fall like lightning from heaven. [19]Listen! I have given you authority, so that you can walk on snakes and scorpions and overcome all the power of the Enemy, and nothing will hurt you. [20]But don't be glad because the evil spirits obey you; rather be glad because your names are written in heaven."

Jesus Rejoices
(Mt 11.25–27; 13.16–17)

21 At that time Jesus was filled with joy by the Holy Spirit[c] and said, "Father, Lord of heaven and earth! I thank you because you have shown to the unlearned what you have hidden from the wise and learned. Yes, Father, this was how you wanted it to happen.

22 "My Father has given me all things. No one knows who the Son is except the Father, and no one knows who the Father is except the Son and those to whom the Son chooses to reveal him."

23 Then Jesus turned to the disciples and said to them privately, "How fortunate you are to see the things you see! [24]I tell you that many prophets and kings wanted to see what you see, but they could not, and to hear what you hear, but they did not."

The Parable of the Good Samaritan

25 A teacher of the Law came up and tried to trap Jesus. "Teacher," he asked, "what must I do to receive eternal life?"

26 Jesus answered him, "What do the Scriptures say? How do you interpret them?"

27 The man answered, " 'Love the Lord your God with all your heart, with all your soul,

[a] **10.1** 72; *some manuscripts have* 70.

[b] **10.17** 72; *some manuscripts have* 70 *(see verse 1).*
[c] **10.21** by the Holy Spirit; *some manuscripts have* by the Spirit; *others have* in his spirit.

with all your strength, and with all your mind'; and 'Love your neighbour as you love yourself.' "

28 "You are right," Jesus replied; "do this and you will live."

29 But the teacher of the Law wanted to justify himself, so he asked Jesus, "Who is my neighbour?"

30 Jesus answered, "There was once a man who was going down from Jerusalem to Jericho when robbers attacked him, stripped him, and beat him up, leaving him half dead.
31It so happened that a priest was going down that road; but when he saw the man, he walked on by, on the other side.
32In the same way a Levite also came along, went over and looked at the man, and then walked on by, on the other side.
33But a Samaritan who was travelling that way came upon the man, and when he saw him, his heart was filled with pity.
34He went over to him, poured oil and wine on his wounds and bandaged them; then he put the man on his own animal and took him to an inn, where he took care of him.
35The next day he took out two silver coins and gave them to the innkeeper. 'Take care of him,' he told the innkeeper, 'and when I come back this way, I will pay you whatever else you spend on him.' "

36 And Jesus concluded, "In your opinion, which one of these three acted like a neighbour towards the man attacked by the robbers?"

37 The teacher of the Law answered, "The one who was kind to him."

Jesus replied, "You go, then, and do the same."

Jesus told the parable of the good Samaritan.

Jesus Visits Martha and Mary

38 As Jesus and his disciples went on their way, he came to a village where a woman named Martha welcomed him in her home.
39She had a sister named Mary, who sat down at the feet of the Lord and listened to his teaching.
40Martha was upset over all the work she had to do, so she came and said, "Lord, don't you care that my sister has left me to do all the work by myself? Tell her to come and help me!"

41 The Lord answered her, "Martha, Martha! You are worried and troubled over so many things,
42but just one is needed. Mary has chosen the right thing, and it will not be taken away from her."

Jesus' Teaching on Prayer

(Mt 6.9–13; 7.7–11)

11 One day Jesus was praying in a certain place. When he had finished, one of his disciples said to him, "Lord, teach us to pray, just as John taught his disciples."

2 Jesus said to them, "When you pray, say this:

'Father:
May your holy name be honoured;
may your Kingdom come.
3 Give us day by day the food we need.[a]
4 Forgive us our sins,
for we forgive everyone who does us wrong.
And do not bring us to hard testing.' "

[a] **11.3** the food we need; *or* food for the next day.

5 And Jesus said to his disciples, "Suppose
one of you should go to a friend's house at
midnight and say, 'Friend, let me borrow
three loaves of bread. 6A friend of mine
who is on a journey has just come to my
house, and I haven't got any food for
him!' 7And suppose your friend should
answer from inside, 'Don't bother me! The
door is already locked, and my children
and I are in bed. I can't get up and give
you anything.' 8Well, what then? I tell

Jesus taught his followers how to pray.

you that even if he will not get up and
give you the bread because you are his
friend, yet he will get up and give you
everything you need because you are not
ashamed to keep on asking.
9 "And so I say to you: ask, and you will
receive; seek, and you will find; knock, and
the door will be opened to you. 10For all
those who ask will receive, and those who
seek will find, and the door will be opened
to anyone who knocks. 11Would any of
you who are fathers give your son a snake
when he asks for fish? 12Or would you give
him a scorpion when he asks for an egg?
13Bad as you are, you know how to give
good things to your children. How much
more, then, will the Father in heaven give
the Holy Spirit to those who ask him!"

Jesus and Beelzebul

(Mt 12.22–30; Mk 3.20–27)

14 Jesus was driving out a demon that could
not talk; and when the demon went out,
the man began to talk. The crowds were
amazed, 15but some of the people said, "It
is Beelzebul, the chief of the demons, who
gives him the power to drive them out."
16 Others wanted to trap Jesus, so they asked
him to perform a miracle to show that God
approved of him. 17But Jesus knew what
they were thinking, so he
said to them, "Any
country that divides itself
into groups which fight
each other will not last
very long; a family
divided against itself falls
apart. 18So if Satan's
kingdom has groups
fighting each other, how
can it last? You say that I
drive out demons because
Beelzebul gives me the
power to do so. 19If this is
how I drive them out,
how do your followers
drive them out? Your own
followers prove that you
are wrong! 20No, it is
rather by means of God's power that I drive
out demons, and this proves that the
Kingdom of God has already come to you.
21 "When a strong man, with all his
weapons ready, guards his own house, all
his belongings are safe. 22But when a
stronger man attacks him and defeats him,
he carries away all the weapons the owner
was depending on and divides up what he
stole.
23 "Anyone who is not for me is really
against me; anyone who does not help me
gather is really scattering.

The Return of the Evil Spirit

(Mt 12.43–45)

24 "When an evil spirit goes out of a person,
it travels over dry country looking for a
place to rest. If it can't find one, it says to
itself, 'I will go back to my house.' 25So it

goes back and finds the house clean and tidy. [26]Then it goes out and brings seven other spirits even worse than itself, and they come and live there. So when it is all over, that person is in a worse state than he was at the beginning."

True Happiness

27 When Jesus had said this, a woman spoke up from the crowd and said to him, "How happy is the woman who bore you and nursed you!"

28 But Jesus answered, "Rather, how happy are those who hear the word of God and obey it!"

The Demand for a Miracle

(Mt 12.38–42)

29 As the people crowded round Jesus, he
went on to say, "How evil are the people of
this day! They ask for a miracle, but none
will be given them except the miracle of
Jonah. [30]In the same way that the prophet
Jonah was a sign for the people of Nineveh,
so the Son of Man will be a sign for the
people of this day. [31]On Judgement Day
the Queen of Sheba will stand up and
accuse the people of today, because she
travelled all the way from her country to
listen to King Solomon's wise teaching; and
I tell you there is something here greater
than Solomon. [32]On Judgement Day the
people of Nineveh will stand up and accuse
you, because they turned from their sins
when they heard Jonah preach; and I assure
you that there is something here greater
than Jonah!

The Light of the Body

(Mt 5.15; 6.22–23)

33 "No one lights a lamp and then hides it
or puts it under a bowl;[a] instead, he puts it
on the lampstand, so that people may see
the light as they come in. [34]Your eyes are
like a lamp for the body. When your eyes
are sound, your whole body is full of light;
but when your eyes are no good, your
whole body will be in darkness. [35]Make
certain, then, that the light in you is not
darkness. [36]If your whole body is full of
light, with no part of it in darkness, it will
be bright all over, as when a lamp shines on
you with its brightness."

Jesus Accuses the Pharisees and the Teachers of the Law

(Mt 23.1–36; Mk 12.38–40)

37 When Jesus finished speaking, a Pharisee
invited him to eat with him; so he went in
and sat down to eat. [38]The Pharisee was
surprised when he noticed that Jesus had
not washed before eating. [39]So the Lord
said to him, "Now then, you Pharisees
clean the outside of your cup and plate, but
inside you are full of violence and evil.
[40]Fools! Did not God, who made the
outside, also make the inside? [41]But give
what is in your cups and plates to the poor,
and everything will be ritually clean for
you.

42 "How terrible for you Pharisees! You give God a tenth of the seasoning herbs, such as mint and rue and all the other herbs, but you neglect justice and love for God. These you should practise, without neglecting the others.

43 "How terrible for you Pharisees! You love
the reserved seats in the synagogues and to
be greeted with respect in the market
places. [44]How terrible for you! You are like
unmarked graves which people walk on
without knowing it."

45 One of the teachers of the Law said to him, "Teacher, when you say this, you insult us too!"

46 Jesus answered, "How terrible also for
you teachers of the Law! You put loads on
people's backs which are hard to carry, but
you yourselves will not stretch out a finger
to help them carry those loads. [47]How
terrible for you! You make fine tombs for
the prophets – the very prophets your
ancestors murdered. [48]You yourselves
admit, then, that you approve of what your
ancestors did; they murdered the prophets,
and you build their tombs. [49]For this
reason the Wisdom of God said, 'I will send
them prophets and messengers; they will
kill some of them and persecute others.'
[50]So the people of this time will be

[a] **11.33** *Some manuscripts do not have* or puts it under a bowl.

punished for the murder of all the prophets
killed since the creation of the world,
[51]from the murder of Abel to the murder of
Zechariah, who was killed between the altar
and the Holy Place. Yes, I tell you, the
people of this time will be punished for
them all!
52 "How terrible for you teachers of the Law!
You have kept the key that opens the door
to the house of knowledge; you yourselves
will not go in, and you stop those who are
trying to go in!"
53 When Jesus left that place, the teachers of
the Law and the Pharisees began to criticize
him bitterly and ask him questions about
many things, [54]trying to lay traps for him
and catch him saying something wrong.

A Warning against Hypocrisy
(Mt 10.26–27)

12 As thousands of people crowded
together, so that they were stepping on
each other, Jesus said first to his
disciples, "Be on guard against the yeast of
the Pharisees – I mean their hypocrisy.
[2]Whatever is covered up will be uncovered,
and every secret will be made known. [3]So
then, whatever you have said in the dark
will be heard in broad daylight, and
whatever you have whispered in private in a
closed room will be shouted from the
housetops.

Whom to Fear
(Mt 10.28–31)

4 "I tell you, my friends, do not be afraid of
those who kill the body but cannot
afterwards do anything worse. [5]I will show
you whom to fear: fear God, who, after
killing, has the authority to throw into hell.
Believe me, he is the one you must fear!
6 "Aren't five sparrows sold for two
pennies? Yet not one sparrow is forgotten by
God. [7]Even the hairs of your head have all
been counted. So do not be afraid; you are
worth much more than many sparrows!

Confessing and Rejecting Christ
(Mt 10.32–33; 12.32; 10.19–20)

8 "I assure you that for those who declare
publicly that they belong to me, the Son of
Man will do the same before the angels of
God. [9]But those who reject me publicly, the
Son of Man will also reject before the angels
of God.
10 "Whoever says a word against the Son of
Man can be forgiven; but those who say evil
things against the Holy Spirit will not be
forgiven.
11 "When they bring you to be tried in the
synagogues or before governors or rulers, do
not be worried about how you will defend
yourself or what you will say. [12]For the Holy
Spirit will teach you at that time what you
should say."

The Parable of the Rich Fool

13 A man in the crowd said to Jesus,
"Teacher, tell my brother to divide with me
the property our father left us."
14 Jesus answered him, "My friend, who
gave me the right to judge or to divide the
property between you two?" [15]And he went
on to say to them all, "Watch out and guard
yourselves from every kind of greed;
because a person's true life is not made up of
the things he owns, no matter how rich he
may be."
16 Then Jesus told them this parable: "There
was once a rich man who had land which
bore good crops. [17]He began to think to
himself, 'I haven't anywhere to keep all my
crops. What can I do? [18]This is what I will
do,' he told himself; 'I will tear down my
barns and build bigger ones, where I will
store my corn and all my other goods.
[19]Then I will say to myself, Lucky man! You
have all the good things you need for many
years. Take life easy, eat, drink, and enjoy
yourself!' [20]But God said to him, 'You fool!
This very night you will have to give up
your life; then who will get all these things
you have kept for yourself?'"
21 And Jesus concluded, "This is how it is
with those who pile up riches for
themselves but are not rich in God's sight."

Trust in God
(Mt 6.25–34)

22 Then Jesus said to the disciples, "And so

I tell you not to worry about the food you
need to stay alive or about the clothes you
need for your body. 23Life is much more
important than food, and the body much
more important than clothes. 24Look at
the crows: they don't sow seeds or gather
a harvest; they don't have store-rooms or
barns; God feeds them! You are worth so
much more than birds! 25Can any of you
live a bit longer[a] by worrying about it? 26If
you can't manage even such a small thing,
why worry about the other things? 27Look
how the wild flowers grow: they don't
work or make clothes for themselves. But I
tell you that not even King Solomon with
all his wealth had clothes as beautiful as
one of these flowers. 28It is God who
clothes the wild grass – grass that is here
today and gone tomorrow, burnt up in the
oven. Won't he be all the more sure to
clothe you? How little faith you have!
29 "So don't be all upset, always concerned
about what you will eat and drink. 30(For
the pagans of this world are always
concerned about all these things.) Your
Father knows that you need these things.
31Instead, be concerned with his Kingdom,
and he will provide you with these things.

Riches in Heaven
(Mt 6.19–21)

32 "Do not be afraid, little flock, for your
Father is pleased to give you the Kingdom.
33Sell all your belongings and give the
money to the poor. Provide for yourselves
purses that don't wear out, and save your
riches in heaven, where they will never
decrease, because no thief can get to them,
and no moth can destroy them. 34For your
heart will always be where your riches are.

Watchful Servants

35 "Be ready for whatever comes, dressed for
action and with your lamps lit, 36like
servants who are waiting for their master to
come back from a wedding feast. When he
comes and knocks, they will open the door
for him at once. 37How happy are those
servants whose master finds them awake
and ready when he returns! I tell you, he will
take off his coat, ask them to sit down, and
will wait on them. 38How happy they are if
he finds them ready, even if he should come
at midnight or even later! 39And you can be
sure that if the owner of a house knew the
time when the thief would come, he would
not let the thief break into his house. 40And
you, too, must be ready, because the Son of
Man will come at an hour when you are not
expecting him."

The Faithful or the Unfaithful Servant
(Mt 24.45–51)

41 Peter said, "Lord, does this parable apply
to us, or do you mean it for everyone?"
42 The Lord answered, "Who, then, is the
faithful and wise servant? He is the one
that his master will put in charge, to run
the household and give the other servants
their share of the food at the proper time.
43How happy that servant is if his master
finds him doing this when he comes home!
44Indeed, I tell you, the master will put that
servant in charge of all his property. 45But
if that servant says to himself that his
master is taking a long time to come back
and if he begins to beat the other servants,
both the men and the women, and eats and
drinks and gets drunk, 46then the master
will come back one day when the servant
does not expect him and at a time he does
not know. The master will cut him in
pieces[a] and make him share the fate of the
disobedient.
47 "The servant who knows what his master
wants him to do, but does not get himself
ready and do it, will be punished with a
heavy whipping. 48But the servant who
does not know what his master wants, and
yet does something for which he deserves a
whipping, will be punished with a light
whipping. Much is required from the
person to whom much is given; much more
is required from the person to whom much
more is given.

Jesus the Cause of Division
(Mt 10.34–36)

49 "I came to set the earth on fire, and how

[a] **12.25** live a bit longer; *or* grow a bit taller.

[b] **12.46** cut him in pieces; *or* throw him out.

I wish it were already kindled! 50I have a
baptism to receive, and how distressed I am
until it is over! 51Do you suppose that I
came to bring peace to the world? No, not
peace, but division. 52From now on a
family of five will be divided, three against
two and two against three. 53Fathers will be
against their sons, and sons against
their fathers; mothers will be against
their daughters, and daughters against their
mothers; mothers-in-law will be against
their daughters-in-law, and daughters-in-
law against their mothers-in-law."

Understanding the Time

(Mt 16.2–3)

54 Jesus said also to the people, "When you
see a cloud coming up in the west, at once
you say that it is going to rain – and it does.
55And when you feel the south wind
blowing, you say that it is going to get hot
– and it does. 56Hypocrites! You can look at
the earth and the sky and predict the
weather; why, then, don't you know the
meaning of this present time?

Settle with your Opponent

(Mt 5.25–26)

57 "Why do you not judge for yourselves
the right thing to do? 58If someone brings
a lawsuit against you and takes you to
court, do your best to settle the dispute
with them before you get to court. If you
don't, they will drag you before the judge,
who will hand you over to the police, and
you will be put in jail. 59There you will
stay, I tell you, until you pay the last
penny of your fine."

Turn from your Sins or Die

13 At that time some people were there
who told Jesus about the Galileans
whom Pilate had killed while they
were offering sacrifices to God. 2Jesus
answered them, "Because those Galileans
were killed in that way, do you think it
proves that they were worse sinners than
all the other Galileans? 3No indeed! And I
tell you that if you do not turn from your
sins, you will all die as they did. 4What
about those eighteen people in Siloam who
were killed when the tower fell on them?
Do you suppose this proves that they were
worse than all the other people living in
Jerusalem? 5No indeed! And I tell you that
if you do not turn from your sins, you will
all die as they did."

The Parable of the Unfruitful Fig Tree

6 Then Jesus told them this parable:
"There was once a man who had a fig tree
growing in his vineyard. He went looking
for figs on it but found none. 7So he said
to his gardener, 'Look, for three years I
have been coming here looking for figs on
this fig tree, and I haven't found any. Cut
it down! Why should it go on using up the
soil?' 8But the gardener answered, 'Leave
it alone, sir, just one more year; I will dig
round it and put in some manure. 9Then if
the tree bears figs next year, so much the
better; if not, then you can have it cut
down.' "

Jesus Heals a Crippled Woman on the Sabbath

10 One Sabbath Jesus was teaching in a
synagogue. 11A woman there had an evil
spirit that had made her ill for eighteen
years; she was bent over and could not
straighten up at all. 12When Jesus saw her,
he called out to her, "Woman, you are free
from your illness!" 13He placed his hands
on her, and at once she straightened herself
up and praised God.

14 The official of the synagogue was angry
that Jesus had healed on the Sabbath, so
he spoke up and said to the people, "There
are six days in which we should work; so
come during those days and be healed, but
not on the Sabbath!"

15 The Lord answered him, "You
hypocrites! Any one of you would untie
your ox or your donkey from the stall and
take it out to give it water on the Sabbath.
16Now here is this descendant of Abraham
whom Satan has kept bound up for
eighteen years; should she not be released
on the Sabbath?" 17His answer made his

enemies ashamed of themselves, while the people rejoiced over all the wonderful things that he did.

The Parable of the Mustard Seed
(Mt 13.31–32; Mk 4.30–32)

18 Jesus asked, "What is the Kingdom of
God like? What shall I compare it with?
[19]It is like this. A man takes a mustard seed
and sows it in his field. The plant grows
and becomes a tree, and the birds make
their nests in its branches."

The Parable of the Yeast
(Mt 13.33)

20 Again Jesus asked, "What shall I compare
the Kingdom of God with? [21]It is like this.
A woman takes some yeast and mixes it
with forty litres of flour until the whole
batch of dough rises."

The Narrow Door
(Mt 7.13–14, 21–23)

22 Jesus went through towns and villages,
teaching the people and making his way
towards Jerusalem. [23]Someone asked him,
"Sir, will just a few people be saved?"
Jesus answered them, [24]"Do your best to
go in through the narrow door; because
many people will surely try to go in but will
not be able. [25]The master of the house will
get up and close the door; then when you
stand outside and begin to knock on the
door and say, 'Open the door for us, sir!' he
will answer you, 'I don't know where you
come from!' [26]Then you will answer, 'We
ate and drank with you; you taught in our
town!' [27]But he will say again, 'I don't
know where you come from. Get away
from me, all you wicked people!' [28]How
you will cry and grind your teeth when you
see Abraham, Isaac, and Jacob, and all the
prophets in the Kingdom of God, while you
are thrown out! [29]People will come from
the east and the west, from the north and
the south, and sit down at the feast in the
Kingdom of God. [30]Then those who are
now last will be first, and those who are
now first will be last."

Jesus' Love for Jerusalem
(Mt 23.37–39)

31 At that same time some Pharisees came
to Jesus and said to him, "You must get out
of here and go somewhere else, because
Herod wants to kill you."
32 Jesus answered them, "Go and tell that
fox: 'I am driving out demons and
performing cures today and tomorrow, and
on the third day I shall finish my work.'
[33]Yet I must be on my way today,
tomorrow, and the next day; it is not right
for a prophet to be killed anywhere except
in Jerusalem.
34 "Jerusalem, Jerusalem! You kill the
prophets, you stone the messengers God
has sent you! How many times have I
wanted to put my arms round all your
people, just as a hen gathers her chicks
under her wings, but you would not let me!
[35]And so your Temple will be abandoned. I
assure you that you will not see me until
the time comes when you say, 'God bless
him who comes in the name of the Lord.' "

Jesus Heals a Sick Man

14 One Sabbath Jesus went to eat a meal at
the home of one of the leading
Pharisees; and people were watching
Jesus closely. [2]A man whose legs and arms
were swollen came to Jesus, [3]and Jesus asked
the teachers of the Law and the Pharisees,
"Does our Law allow healing on the Sabbath
or not?"
4 But they would not say anything. Jesus
took the man, healed him, and sent him
away. [5]Then he said to them, "If any one of
you had a son or an ox that happened to
fall in a well on a Sabbath, would you not
pull them out at once on the Sabbath
itself?"
6 But they were not able to answer him
about this.

Humility and Hospitality

7 Jesus noticed how some of the guests
were choosing the best places, so he told
this parable to all of them: [8]"When
someone invites you to a wedding feast, do
not sit down in the best place. It could

happen that someone more important
than you has been invited, [9]and your host,
who invited both of you, would have to
come and say to you, 'Let him have this
place.' Then you would be embarrassed and
have to sit in the lowest place. [10]Instead,
when you are invited, go and sit in the
lowest place, so that your host will come to
you and say, 'Come on up, my friend, to a
better place.' This will bring you honour in
the presence of all the other guests. [11]For
all those who make themselves great will be
humbled, and those who humble
themselves will be made great."
12 Then Jesus said to his host, "When you
give a lunch or a dinner, do not invite your
friends or your brothers or your relatives or
your rich neighbours – for they will invite
you back, and in this way you will be paid
for what you did. [13]When you give a feast,
invite the poor, the crippled, the lame, and
the blind; [14]and you will be blessed,
because they are not able to pay you back.
God will repay you on the day the good
people rise from death."

The Parable of the Great Feast
(Mt 22.1–10)

15 When one of the men sitting at table
heard this, he said to Jesus, "How happy are
those who will sit down at the feast in the
Kingdom of God!"
16 Jesus said to him, "There was once a man
who was giving a great feast to which he
invited many people. [17]When it was time
for the feast, he sent his servant to tell his
guests, 'Come, everything is ready!' [18]But
they all began, one after another, to make
excuses. The first one told the servant, 'I
have bought a field and must go and look
at it; please accept my apologies.'
[19]Another one said, 'I have bought five
pairs of oxen and am on my way to try
them out; please accept my apologies.'
[20]Another one said, 'I have just got
married, and for that reason I cannot
come.'
21 "The servant went back and told all this
to his master. The master was furious and
said to his servant, 'Hurry out to the streets
and alleys of the town, and bring back the
poor, the crippled, the blind, and the lame.'
[22]Soon the servant said, 'Your order has
been carried out, sir, but there is room for
more.' [23]So the master said to the servant,
'Go out to the country roads and lanes and
make people come in, so that my house
will be full. [24]I tell you all that none of
those who were invited will taste my
dinner!'"

The Cost of Being a Disciple
(Mt 10.37–38)

25 Once when large crowds of people were
going along with Jesus, he turned and said
to them, [26]"Those who come to me cannot
be my disciples unless they love me more
than they love father and mother, wife
and children, brothers and sisters, and
themselves as well. [27]Those who do not
carry their own cross and come after me
cannot be my disciples.
28 "If one of you is planning to build a
tower, you sit down first and work out what
it will cost, to see if you have enough
money to finish the job. [29]If you don't, you
will not be able to finish the tower after
laying the foundation; and all who see
what happened will laugh at you. [30]'This
man began to build but can't finish the
job!' they will say.
31 "If a king goes out with ten thousand
men to fight another king who comes
against him with twenty thousand men, he
will sit down first and decide if he is strong
enough to face that other king. [32]If he isn't,
he will send messengers to meet the other
king, to ask for terms of peace while he is
still a long way off. [33]In the same way,"
concluded Jesus, "none of you can be my
disciple unless you give up everything you
have.

Worthless Salt
(Mt 5.13; Mk 9.50)

34 "Salt is good, but if it loses its saltiness,
there is no way to make it salty again. [35]It
is no good for the soil or for the manure
heap; it is thrown away. Listen, then, if you
have ears!"

The Lost Sheep
(Mt 18.12–14)

15 One day when many tax collectors
and other outcasts came to listen to
Jesus, [2]the Pharisees and the teachers
of the Law started grumbling, "This man
welcomes outcasts and even eats with
them!" [3]So Jesus told them this parable:
4 "Suppose one of you has a hundred
sheep and loses one of them – what do you
do? You leave the other ninety-nine sheep
in the pasture and go looking for the one
that got lost until you find it. [5]When you
find it, you are so happy that you put it on
your shoulders [6]and carry it back home.
Then you call your friends and neighbours
together and say to them, 'I am so happy I
found my lost sheep. Let us celebrate!' [7]In
the same way, I tell you, there will be more
joy in heaven over one sinner who repents
than over ninety-nine respectable people
who do not need to repent.

Jesus often used sheep as an example to teach important lessons.

The Lost Coin

8 "Or suppose a woman who has ten silver
coins loses one of them – what does she do?
She lights a lamp, sweeps her house, and
looks carefully everywhere until she finds
it. [9]When she finds it, she calls her friends
and neighbours together, and says to them,
'I am so happy I found the coin I lost. Let
us celebrate!' [10]In the same way, I tell you,
the angels of God rejoice over one sinner
who repents."

The Lost Son

11 Jesus went on to say, "There was once a
man who had two sons. [12]The younger one
said to him, 'Father, give me my share of
the property now.' So the man divided his
property between his two sons. [13]After a
few days the younger son sold his part of
the property and left home with the
money. He went to a country far away,
where he wasted his money in reckless
living. [14]He spent everything he had. Then
a severe famine spread over that country,
and he was left without a thing. [15]So he
went to work for one of the citizens of that
country, who sent him out to his farm to
take care of the pigs. [16]He wished he could
fill himself with the bean pods the pigs ate,
but no one gave him anything to eat. [17]At
last he came to his senses and said, 'All my
father's hired workers have more than they
can eat, and here I am about to starve! [18]I
will get up and go to my father and say,
Father, I have sinned against God and
against you. [19]I am no longer fit to be
called your son; treat me as one of your
hired workers.' [20]So he got up and started
back to his father.

"He was still a long way from home
when his father saw him; his heart was
filled with pity, and he ran, threw his arms
round his son, and kissed him. [21]'Father,'
the son said, 'I have sinned against God
and against you. I am no longer fit to be
called your son.' [22]But the father called his
servants. 'Hurry!' he said. 'Bring the best
robe and put it on him. Put a ring on his
finger and shoes on his feet. [23]Then go and
get the prize calf and kill it, and let us

celebrate with a feast! [24]For this son of
mine was dead, but now he is alive; he was
lost, but now he has been found.' And so
the feasting began.
25 "In the meantime the elder son was out
in the field. On his way back, when he
came close to the house, he heard the
music and dancing. [26]So he called one of
the servants and asked him, 'What's going
on?' [27]'Your brother has come back home,'
the servant answered, 'and your father has
killed the prize calf, because he got him
back safe and sound.'
28 "The elder brother was so angry that he
would not go into the house; so his father
came out and begged him to come in.
[29]But he answered his father, 'Look, all
these years I have worked for you like a
slave, and I have never disobeyed your
orders. What have you given me? Not even
a goat for me to have a feast with my
friends! [30]But this son of yours wasted all
your property on prostitutes, and when he
comes back home, you kill the prize calf for
him!' [31]'My son,' the father answered, 'you
are always here with me, and everything I
have is yours. [32]But we had to celebrate
and be happy, because your brother was
dead, but now he is alive; he was lost, but
now he has been found.' "

The Shrewd Manager

16 Jesus said to his disciples, "There was
once a rich man who had a servant
who managed his property. The rich
man was told that the manager was wasting
his master's money, [2]so he called him in
and said, 'What is this I hear about you?
Hand in a complete account of your
handling of my property, because you
cannot be my manager any longer.' [3]The
servant said to himself, 'My master is going
to dismiss me from my job. What shall I
do? I am not strong enough to dig ditches,
and I am ashamed to beg. [4]Now I know
what I will do! Then when my job is gone,
I shall have friends who will welcome me
in their homes.'
5 "So he called in all the people who were
in debt to his master. He asked the first one,
'How much do you owe my master?' [6]'One
hundred barrels of olive oil,' he answered.
'Here is your account,' the manager told
him; 'sit down and write fifty.' [7]Then he
asked another one, 'And you – how much
do you owe?' 'A thousand sacks of wheat,'
he answered. 'Here is your account,' the
manager told him; 'write eight hundred.'
8 "As a result the master of this dishonest
manager praised him for doing such a
shrewd thing; because the people of this
world are much more shrewd in handling
their affairs than the people who belong to
the light."
9 And Jesus went on to say, "And so I tell
you: make friends for yourselves with
worldly wealth, so that when it gives out,
you will be welcomed in the eternal home.
[10]Whoever is faithful in small matters will
be faithful in large ones; whoever is
dishonest in small matters will be
dishonest in large ones. [11]If, then, you
have not been faithful in handling worldly
wealth, how can you be trusted with true
wealth? [12]And if you have not been
faithful with what belongs to someone
else, who will give you what belongs to
you?
13 "No servant can be the slave of two
masters; such a servant will hate one and
love the other or will be loyal to one and
despise the other. You cannot serve both
God and money."

Some Sayings of Jesus

(Mt 11.12–13; 5.31–32; Mk 10.11–12)

14 When the Pharisees heard all this, they
sneered at Jesus, because they loved money.
[15]Jesus said to them, "You are the ones who
make yourselves look right in other
people's sight, but God knows your hearts.
For the things that are considered of great
value by human beings are worth nothing
in God's sight.
16 "The Law of Moses and the writings of
the prophets were in effect up to the time
of John the Baptist; since then the Good
News about the Kingdom of God is being
told, and everyone forces their way in.
[17]But it is easier for heaven and earth to

disappear than for the smallest detail of the Law to be done away with.

18 "Any man who divorces his wife and marries another woman commits adultery; and the man who marries a divorced woman commits adultery.

The Rich Man and Lazarus

19 "There was once a rich man who dressed in the most expensive clothes and lived in great luxury every day. [20]There was also a poor man named Lazarus, covered with sores, who used to be brought to the rich man's door, [21]hoping to eat the bits of food that fell from the rich man's table. Even the dogs would come and lick his sores.

22 "The poor man died and was carried by the angels to sit beside Abraham at the feast in heaven. The rich man died and was buried, [23]and in Hades,[a] where he was in great pain, he looked up and saw Abraham, far away, with Lazarus at his side. [24]So he called out, 'Father Abraham! Take pity on me, and send Lazarus to dip his finger in some water and cool my tongue, because I am in great pain in this fire!'

25 "But Abraham said, 'Remember, my son, that in your lifetime you were given all the good things, while Lazarus got all the bad things. But now he is enjoying himself here, while you are in pain. [26]Besides all that, there is a deep pit lying between us, so that those who want to cross over from here to you cannot do so, nor can anyone cross over to us from where you are.' [27]The rich man said, 'Then I beg you, father Abraham, send Lazarus to my father's house, [28]where I have five brothers. Let him go and warn them so that they, at least, will not come to this place of pain.'

29 "Abraham said, 'Your brothers have Moses and the prophets to warn them; your brothers should listen to what they say.' [30]The rich man answered, 'That is not enough, father Abraham! But if someone were to rise from death and go to them, then they would turn from their sins.' [31]But Abraham said, 'If they will not listen to Moses and the prophets, they will not be convinced even if someone were to rise from death.' "

[a] **16.23** HADES: *The world of the dead.*

Sin

(Mt 18.6–7, 21–22; Mk 9.42)

17 Jesus said to his disciples, "Things that make people fall into sin are bound to happen, but how terrible for the one who makes them happen! [2]It would be better for him if a large millstone were tied round his neck and he were thrown into the sea than for him to cause one of these little ones to sin. [3]So watch what you do!

"If your brother sins, rebuke him, and if he repents, forgive him. [4]If he sins against you seven times in one day, and each time he comes to you saying, 'I repent,' you must forgive him."

Faith

5 The apostles said to the Lord, "Make our faith greater."

6 The Lord answered, "If you had faith as big as a mustard seed, you could say to this mulberry tree, 'Pull yourself up by the roots and plant yourself in the sea!' and it would obey you.

A Servant's Duty

7 "Suppose one of you has a servant who is ploughing or looking after the sheep. When he comes in from the field, do you tell him to hurry and eat his meal? [8]Of course not! Instead, you say to him, 'Get my supper ready, then put on your apron and wait on me while I eat and drink; after that you may have your meal.' [9]The servant does not deserve thanks for obeying orders, does he? [10]It is the same with you; when you have done all you have been told to do, say, 'We are ordinary servants; we have only done our duty.' "

Jesus Heals Ten Men

11 As Jesus made his way to Jerusalem, he went along the border between Samaria and Galilee. [12]He was going into a village when he was met by ten men suffering from a dreaded skin disease. They stood at a distance [13]and shouted, "Jesus! Master! Take pity on us!"

14 Jesus saw them and said to them, "Go and let the priests examine you."

On the way they were made clean.[a]
15When one of them saw that he was
healed, he came back, praising God in a
loud voice. 16He threw himself to the
ground at Jesus' feet and thanked him. The
man was a Samaritan. 17Jesus said, "There
were ten men who were healed; where are
the other nine? 18Why is this foreigner the
only one who came back to give thanks to
God?" 19And Jesus said to him, "Get up
and go; your faith has made you well."

The Coming of the Kingdom
(Mt 24.23–28, 37–41)

20 Some Pharisees asked Jesus when the
Kingdom of God would come. His answer
was, "The Kingdom of God does not come
in such a way as to be seen. 21No one will
say, 'Look, here it is!' or, 'There it is!';
because the Kingdom of God is within
you."[b]

22 Then he said to the disciples, "The time
will come when you will wish you could
see one of the days of the Son of Man, but
you will not see it. 23There will be those
who will say to you, 'Look, over there!' or,
'Look, over here!' But don't go out looking
for it. 24As the lightning flashes across the
sky and lights it up from one side to the
other, so will the Son of Man be in his day.
25But first he must suffer much and be
rejected by the people of this day. 26As it
was in the time of Noah so shall it be in the
days of the Son of Man. 27Everybody kept
on eating and drinking, and men and
women married, up to the very day Noah
went into the boat and the flood came and
killed them all. 28It will be as it was in the
time of Lot. Everybody kept on eating and
drinking, buying and selling, planting and
building. 29On the day Lot left Sodom, fire
and sulphur rained down from heaven and
killed them all. 30That is how it will be on
the day the Son of Man is revealed.

31 "On that day someone who is on the
roof of his house must not go down into
the house to get any belongings; in the
same way anyone who is out in the field
must not go back to the house.
32Remember Lot's wife! 33Whoever tries to
save his own life will lose it; whoever loses
his life will save it. 34On that night, I tell
you, there will be two people sleeping in
the same bed: one will be taken away, the
other will be left behind. 35Two women
will be grinding corn together: one will be
taken away, the other will be left behind."[c]

37 The disciples asked him, "Where, Lord?"
Jesus answered, "Wherever there is a
dead body, the vultures will gather."

The Parable of the Widow and the Judge

18 Then Jesus told his disciples a parable
to teach them that they should always
pray and never become discouraged.
2"In a certain town there was a judge who
neither feared God nor respected people.
3And there was a widow in that same town
who kept coming to him and pleading for
her rights, saying, 'Help me against my
opponent!' 4For a long time the judge
refused to act, but at last he said to himself,
'Even though I don't fear God or respect
people, 5yet because of all the trouble this
widow is giving me, I will see to it that she
gets her rights. If I don't, she will keep on
coming and finally wear me out!' "

6 And the Lord continued, "Listen to what
that corrupt judge said. 7Now, will God not
judge in favour of his own people who cry
to him day and night for help? Will he be
slow to help them? 8I tell you, he will judge
in their favour and do it quickly. But will
the Son of Man find faith on earth when he
comes?"

The Parable of the Pharisee and the Tax Collector

9 Jesus also told this parable to people who
were sure of their own goodness and
despised everybody else. 10"Once there
were two men who went up to the Temple
to pray: one was a Pharisee, the other a tax
collector.

11 "The Pharisee stood apart by himself and
prayed,[d] 'I thank you, God, that I am not

[a] **17.14** MADE CLEAN: *See 5.12.*
[b] **17.21** is within you; *or* is among you, *or* will suddenly appear among you.
[c] **17.35** *Some manuscripts add verse 36:* Two men will be working in a field: one will be taken away, the other will be left behind *(see Mt 24.40).*
[d] **18.11** stood apart by himself and prayed; *some manuscripts have* stood up and prayed to himself.

greedy, dishonest, or an adulterer, like
everybody else. I thank you that I am not
like that tax collector over there. [12]I fast two
days a week, and I give you a tenth of all my
income.'
13 "But the tax collector stood at a distance
and would not even raise his face to heaven,
but beat on his breast and said, 'God, have
pity on me, a sinner!' [14]I tell you," said
Jesus, "the tax collector, and not the
Pharisee, was in the right with God when he
went home. For all who make themselves
great will be humbled, and all who humble
themselves will be made great."

Jesus respected the simple trust shown by young children.

Jesus Blesses Little Children

(Mt 19.13–15; Mk 10.13–16)

15 Some people brought their babies to Jesus
for him to place his hands on them. The
disciples saw them and scolded them for
doing so, [16]but Jesus called the children to
him and said, "Let the children come to me
and do not stop them, because the Kingdom
of God belongs to such as these.
[17]Remember this! Whoever does not receive
the Kingdom of God like a child will never
enter it."

The Rich Man

(Mt 19.16–30; Mk 10.17–31)

18 A Jewish leader asked Jesus, "Good
Teacher, what must I do to receive eternal
life?"
19 "Why do you call me good?" Jesus asked
him. "No one is good except God alone.
[20]You know the commandments: 'Do not
commit adultery; do not commit murder;
do not steal; do not accuse anyone falsely;
respect your father and your mother.' "
21 The man replied, "Ever since I was young,
I have obeyed all these commandments."
22 When Jesus heard this, he said to him,
"There is still one more thing you need to
do. Sell all you have and give the money to
the poor, and you will have riches in
heaven; then come and follow me." [23]But
when the man heard this, he became very
sad, because he was very rich.
24 Jesus saw that he was sad and said, "How
hard it is for rich people to enter the
Kingdom of God! [25]It is much harder for a
rich person to enter the Kingdom of God
than for a camel to go through the eye of a
needle."
26 The people who heard him asked, "Who,
then, can be saved?"
27 Jesus answered, "What is humanly
impossible is possible for God."
28 Then Peter said, "Look! We have left our
homes to follow you."
29 "Yes," Jesus said to them, "and I assure you
that anyone who leaves home or wife or
brothers or parents or children for the sake of
the Kingdom of God [30]will receive much
more in this present age and eternal life in
the age to come."

Jesus Speaks a Third Time about his Death

(Mt 20.17–19; Mk 10.32–34)

31 Jesus took the twelve disciples aside and
said to them, "Listen! We are going to
Jerusalem where everything the prophets
wrote about the Son of Man will come true.
[32]He will be handed over to the Gentiles,
who will mock him, insult him, and spit on
him. [33]They will whip him and kill him,
but three days later he will rise to life."

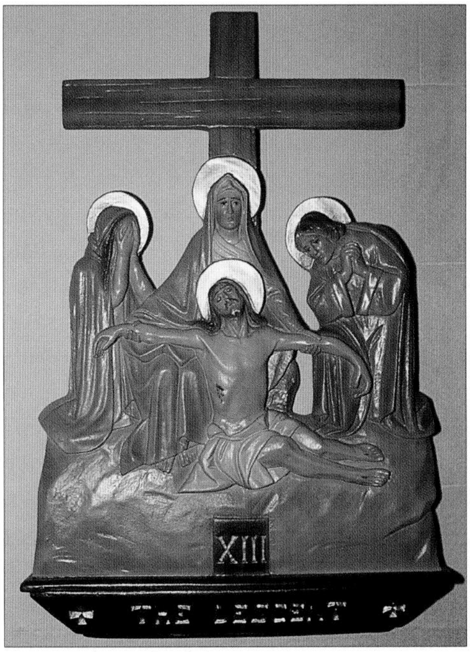

Jesus talked many times to the disciples about his death but they did not understand.

34 But the disciples did not understand any
of these things; the meaning of the words
was hidden from them, and they did not
know what Jesus was talking about.

Jesus Heals a Blind Beggar
(Mt 20.29–34; Mk 10.46–52)

35 As Jesus was coming near Jericho, there
was a blind man sitting by the road,
begging. [36]When he heard the crowd
passing by, he asked, "What is this?"
37 "Jesus of Nazareth is passing by," they
told him.
38 He cried out, "Jesus! Son of David! Take
pity on me!"
39 The people in front scolded him and told
him to be quiet. But he shouted even more
loudly, "Son of David! Take pity on me!"
40 So Jesus stopped and ordered the blind
man to be brought to him. When he came
near, Jesus asked him, [41]"What do you
want me to do for you?"
"Sir," he answered, "I want to see again."
42 Jesus said to him, "Then see! Your faith
has made you well."
43 At once he was able to see, and he
followed Jesus, giving thanks to God.
When the crowd saw it, they all praised
God.

Jesus and Zacchaeus

19 Jesus went on into Jericho and was
passing through. [2]There was a chief
tax collector there named Zacchaeus,
who was rich. [3]He was trying to see who
Jesus was, but he was a little man and could
not see Jesus because of the crowd. [4]So he
ran ahead of the crowd and climbed a
sycomore tree to see Jesus, who was going
to pass that way. [5]When Jesus came to that
place, he looked up and said to Zacchaeus,
"Hurry down, Zacchaeus, because I must
stay in your house today."
6 Zacchaeus hurried down and welcomed
him with great joy. [7]All the people who saw
it started grumbling, "This man has gone as
a guest to the home of a sinner!"
8 Zacchaeus stood up and said to the Lord,
"Listen, sir! I will give half my belongings
to the poor, and if I have cheated anyone, I
will pay back four times as much."
9 Jesus said to him, "Salvation has come to
this house today, for this man, also, is a
descendant of Abraham. [10]The Son of Man
came to seek and to save the lost."

The Parable of the Gold Coins
(Mt 25.14–30)

11 While the people were listening to this,
Jesus continued and told them a parable.
He was now almost at Jerusalem, and they
supposed that the Kingdom of God was
just about to appear. [12]So he said, "There
was once a man of high rank who was
going to a country far away to be made
king, after which he planned to come back
home. [13]Before he left, he called his ten
servants and gave them each a gold coin
and told them, 'See what you can earn
with this while I am gone.' [14]Now, his
own people hated him, and so they sent
messengers after him to say, 'We don't
want this man to be our king.'
15 "The man was made king and came back.
At once he ordered his servants to appear
before him, in order to find out how much
they had earned. [16]The first one came and
said, 'Sir, I have earned ten gold coins with
the one you gave me.' [17]'Well done,' he
said; 'you are a good servant! Since you

were faithful in small matters, I will put
you in charge of ten cities.’ 18The second
servant came and said, ‘Sir, I have earned
five gold coins with the one you gave me.’
19To this one he said, ‘You will be in charge
of five cities.’

20 “Another servant came and said, ‘Sir,
here is your gold coin; I kept it hidden in a
handkerchief. 21I was afraid of you, because
you are a hard man. You take what is not
yours and reap what you did not sow.’ 22He
said to him, ‘You bad servant! I will use
your own words to condemn you! You
know that I am a hard man, taking what is
not mine and reaping what I have not
sown. 23Well, then, why didn’t you put my
money in the bank? Then I would have
received it back with interest when I
returned.’

24 “Then he said to those who were
standing there, ‘Take the gold coin away
from him and give it to the servant who
has ten coins.’ 25But they said to him, ‘Sir,
he already has ten coins!’ 26‘I tell you,’ he
replied, ‘that to all those who have
something, even more will be given; but
those who have nothing, even the little
that they have will be taken away from
them. 27Now, as for those enemies of mine
who did not want me to be their king,
bring them here and kill them in my
presence!’ ”

The Triumphant Approach to Jerusalem
(Mt 21.1–11; Mk 11.1–11; Jn 12.12–19)

28 After Jesus said this, he went on ahead of
them to Jerusalem. 29As he came near
Bethphage and Bethany at the Mount of
Olives, he sent two disciples ahead 30with
these instructions: “Go to the village there
ahead of you; as you go in, you will find a
colt tied up that has never been ridden.
Untie it and bring it here. 31If someone
asks you why you are untying it, tell him
that the Master[a] needs it.”

32 They went on their way and found
everything just as Jesus had told them. 33As
they were untying the colt, its owners said
to them, “Why are you untying it?”

34 “The Master[a] needs it,” they answered,
35and they took the colt to Jesus. Then they
threw their cloaks over the animal and
helped Jesus get on. 36As he rode on,
people spread their cloaks on the road.

37 When he came near Jerusalem, at the
place where the road went down the
Mount of Olives, the large crowd of his
disciples began to thank God and praise
him in loud voices for all the great things
that they had seen: 38“God bless the king
who comes in the name of the Lord! Peace
in heaven and glory to God!”

39 Then some of the Pharisees in the crowd
spoke to Jesus. “Teacher,” they said,
“command your disciples to be quiet!”

40 Jesus answered, “I tell you that if they
keep quiet, the stones themselves will start
shouting.”

Jesus Weeps over Jerusalem

41 He came closer to the city, and when he
saw it, he wept over it, 42saying, “If you
only knew today what is needed for peace!
But now you cannot see it! 43The time will
come when your enemies will surround
you with barricades, blockade you, and
close in on you from every side. 44They
will completely destroy you and the
people within your walls; not a single
stone will they leave in its place, because
you did not recognize the time when God
came to save you!”

Jesus Goes to the Temple
(Mt 21.12–17; Mk 11.15–19; Jn 2.13–22)

45 Then Jesus went into the Temple and
began to drive out the merchants, 46saying
to them, “It is written in the Scriptures that
God said, ‘My Temple will be a house of
prayer.’ But you have turned it into a
hideout for thieves!”

47 Every day Jesus taught in the Temple.
The chief priests, the teachers of the Law,
and the leaders of the people wanted to kill
him, 48but they could not find a way to do
it, because all the people kept listening to
him, not wanting to miss a single word.

[a] **19.31, 19.34** the Master; *or* its owner.

The Question about Jesus' Authority

(Mt 21.23–27; Mk 11.27–33)

20 One day when Jesus was in the Temple
teaching the people and preaching
the Good News, the chief priests and
the teachers of the Law, together with the
elders, came [2]and said to him, "Tell us,
what right have you to do these things?
Who gave you this right?"
3 Jesus answered them, "Now let me ask
you a question. Tell me, [4]did John's right to
baptize come from God or from human
beings?"
5 They started to argue among themselves,
"What shall we say? If we say, 'From God,'
he will say, 'Why, then, did you not believe
John?' [6]But if we say 'From human beings,'
this whole crowd here will stone us,
because they are convinced that John was a
prophet." [7]So they answered, "We don't
know where it came from."
8 And Jesus said to them, "Neither will I
tell you, then, by what right I do these
things."

The Parable of the Tenants in the Vineyard

(Mt 21.33–46; Mk 12.1–12)

9 Then Jesus told the people this parable:
"There was once a man who planted a
vineyard, let it out to tenants, and then left
home for a long time. [10]When the time
came to gather the grapes, he sent a slave to
the tenants to receive from them his share
of the harvest. But the tenants beat the
slave and sent him back without a thing.
[11]So he sent another slave; but the tenants
beat him also, treated him shamefully, and
sent him back without a thing. [12]Then he
sent a third slave; the tenants wounded
him, too, and threw him out. [13]Then the
owner of the vineyard said, 'What shall I
do? I will send my own dear son; surely
they will respect him!' [14]But when the
tenants saw him, they said to one another,
'This is the owner's son. Let's kill him, and
his property will be ours!' [15]So they threw
him out of the vineyard and killed him.
"What, then, will the owner of the
vineyard do to the tenants?" Jesus asked.
[16]"He will come and kill those men, and
hand the vineyard over to other tenants."
When the people heard this, they said,
"Surely not!"
17 Jesus looked at them and asked, "What,
then, does this scripture mean?

> 'The stone which the builders rejected as
> worthless
> turned out to be the most important of
> all.'

18 Everyone who falls on that stone will be
cut to pieces; and if that stone falls on
someone, it will crush him to dust."

The Question about Paying Taxes

(Mt 22.15–22; Mk 12.13–17)

19 The teachers of the Law and the chief
priests tried to arrest Jesus on the spot,
because they knew that he had told this
parable against them; but they were afraid
of the people. [20]So they looked for an
opportunity. They bribed some men to
pretend they were sincere, and they sent
them to trap Jesus with questions, so that
they could hand him over to the authority
and power of the Roman Governor.
[21]These spies said to Jesus, "Teacher, we
know that what you say and teach is right.
We know that you pay no attention to
anyone's status, but teach the truth about
God's will for people. [22]Tell us, is it against
our Law for us to pay taxes to the Roman
Emperor, or not?"
23 But Jesus saw through their trick and said
to them, [24]"Show me a silver coin. Whose
face and name are these on it?"
"The Emperor's," they answered.
25 So Jesus said, "Well, then, pay the
Emperor what belongs to the Emperor, and
pay God what belongs to God."
26 There before the people they could not
catch him out in anything, so they kept
quiet, amazed at his answer.

The Question about Rising from Death
(Mt 22.23–33; Mk 12.18–27)

27 Then some Sadducees, who say that
people will not rise from death, came to
Jesus and said, 28“Teacher, Moses wrote this
law for us: ‘If a man dies and leaves a wife
but no children, that man’s brother must
marry the widow so that they can have
children who will be considered the dead
man’s children.’ 29Once there were seven
brothers; the eldest got married and died
without having children. 30Then the
second one married the woman, 31and
then the third. The same thing happened
to all seven – they died without having
children. 32Last of all, the woman died.
33Now, on the day when the dead rise to
life, whose wife will she be? All seven of
them had married her.”
34 Jesus answered them, “The men and
women of this age marry, 35but the men
and women who are worthy to rise from
death and live in the age to come will not
then marry. 36They will be like angels and
cannot die. They are the children of God,
because they have risen from death. 37And
Moses clearly proves that the dead are
raised to life. In the passage about the
burning bush he speaks of the Lord as ‘the
God of Abraham, the God of Isaac, and the
God of Jacob.’ 38He is the God of the living,
not of the dead, for to him all are alive.”
39 Some of the teachers of the Law spoke
up, “A good answer, Teacher!” 40For they
did not dare ask him any more questions.

The Question about the Messiah
(Mt 22.41–46; Mk 12.35–37)

41 Jesus asked them, “How can it be said
that the Messiah will be the descendant of
David? 42For David himself says in the
book of Psalms,

‘The Lord said to my Lord:
Sit here on my right
43 until I put your enemies as a footstool
under your feet.’

44David called him ‘Lord’; how, then, can
the Messiah be David’s descendant?”

Jesus Warns against the Teachers of the Law
(Mt 23.1–36; Mk 12.38–40)

45 As all the people listened to him, Jesus
said to his disciples, 46“Be on your guard
against the teachers of the Law, who like to
walk about in their long robes and love to
be greeted with respect in the market place;
who choose the reserved seats in the
synagogues and the best places at feasts;
47who take advantage of widows and rob
them of their homes, and then make a
show of saying long prayers! Their
punishment will be all the worse!”

The Widow’s Offering
(Mk 12.41–44)

21 Jesus looked round and saw rich
people dropping their gifts in the
temple treasury, 2and he also saw a
very poor widow dropping in two little
copper coins. 3He said, “I tell you that this
poor widow put in more than all the
others. 4For the others offered their gifts
from what they had to spare of their riches;
but she, poor as she is, gave all she had to
live on.”

Jesus Speaks of the Destruction of the Temple
(Mt 24.1–2; Mk 13.1–2)

5 Some of the disciples were talking about
the Temple, how beautiful it looked with its
fine stones and the gifts offered to God.
Jesus said, 6“All this you see – the time will
come when not a single stone here will be
left in its place; every one will be thrown
down.”

Troubles and Persecutions
(Mt 24.3–14; Mk 13.3–13)

7 “Teacher,” they asked, “when will this be?
And what will happen in order to show that
the time has come for it to take place?”
8 Jesus said, “Be on guard; don’t be
deceived. Many men, claiming to speak for

me, will come and say, 'I am he!' and, 'The
time has come!' But don't follow them.
9Don't be afraid when you hear of wars and
revolutions; such things must happen first,
but they do not mean that the end is near."
10 He went on to say, "Countries will fight
each other; kingdoms will attack one
another. 11There will be terrible
earthquakes, famines, and plagues
everywhere; there will be strange and
terrifying things coming from the sky.
12Before all these things take place, however,
you will be arrested and persecuted; you will
be handed over to be tried in synagogues
and be put in prison; you will be brought
before kings and rulers for my sake. 13This
will be your chance to tell the Good News.
14Make up your minds beforehand not to
worry about how you will defend
yourselves, 15because I will give you such
words and wisdom that none of your
enemies will be able to refute or contradict
what you say. 16You will be handed over by
your parents, your brothers, your relatives,
and your friends; and some of you will be
put to death. 17Everyone will hate you
because of me. 18But not a single hair from
your heads will be lost. 19Stand firm, and
you will save yourselves.

Jesus Speaks of the Destruction of Jerusalem

(Mt 24.15–21; Mk 13.14–19)

20 "When you see Jerusalem surrounded by
armies, then you will know that it will soon
be destroyed. 21Then those who are in Judea
must run away to the hills; those who are in
the city must leave, and those who are out in
the country must not go into the city. 22For
those will be 'The Days of Punishment', to
make all that the Scriptures say come true.
23How terrible it will be in those days for
women who are pregnant and for mothers
with little babies! Terrible distress will come
upon this land, and God's punishment will
fall on this people. 24Some will be killed by
the sword, and others will be taken as
prisoners to all countries; and the heathen
will trample over Jerusalem until their time
is up.

The Coming of the Son of Man

(Mt 24.29–31; Mk 13.24–27)

25 "There will be strange things happening
to the sun, the moon, and the stars. On
earth whole countries will be in despair,
afraid of the roar of the sea and the raging
tides. 26People will faint from fear as they
wait for what is coming over the whole
earth, for the powers in space will be driven
from their courses. 27Then the Son of Man
will appear, coming in a cloud with great
power and glory. 28When these things begin
to happen, stand up and raise your heads,
because your salvation is near."

The Lesson of the Fig Tree

(Mt 24.32–35; Mk 13.28–31)

29 Then Jesus told them this parable: "Think
of the fig tree and all the other trees.
30When you see their leaves beginning to
appear, you know that summer is near. 31In
the same way, when you see these things
happening, you will know that the Kingdom
of God is about to come.
32 "Remember that all these things will take
place before the people now living have all
died. 33Heaven and earth will pass away, but
my words will never pass away.

The Need to Watch

34 "Be on your guard! Don't let yourselves
become occupied with too much feasting
and drinking and with the worries of this
life, or that Day may suddenly catch you
35like a trap. For it will come upon all people
everywhere on earth. 36Be on the alert and
pray always that you will have the strength
to go safely through all those things that will
happen and to stand before the Son of
Man."
37 Jesus spent those days teaching in the
Temple, and when evening came, he would
go out and spend the night on the Mount of
Olives. 38Early each morning all the people
went to the Temple to listen to him.

The Plot against Jesus
(Mt 26.1–5; Mk 14.1–2; Jn 11.45–53)

22 The time was near for the Festival of Unleavened Bread, which is called the Passover. [2]The chief priests and the teachers of the Law were afraid of the people, and so they were trying to find a way of putting Jesus to death secretly.

Judas Agrees to Betray Jesus
(Mt 26.14–16; Mk 14.10–11)

3 Then Satan entered Judas, called Iscariot,
who was one of the twelve disciples. [4]So
Judas went off and spoke with the chief
priests and the officers of the temple guard
about how he could betray Jesus to them.
[5]They were pleased and offered to pay him
money. [6]Judas agreed to it and started
looking for a good chance to hand Jesus over
to them without the people knowing about
it.

Jesus Prepares to Eat the Passover Meal
(Mt 26.17–25; Mk 14.12–21; Jn 13.21–30)

7 The day came during the Festival of
Unleavened Bread when the lambs for the
Passover meal were to be killed. [8]Jesus sent
off Peter and John with these instructions:
"Go and get the Passover meal ready for us
to eat."

9 "Where do you want us to get it ready?"
they asked him.

10 He answered, "As you go into the city, a
man carrying a jar of water will meet you.
Follow him into the house that he enters,
[11]and say to the owner of the house: 'The
Teacher says to you, Where is the room
where my disciples and I will eat the
Passover meal?' [12]He will show you a large
furnished room upstairs, where you will get
everything ready."

13 They went off and found everything just
as Jesus had told them, and they prepared
the Passover meal.

The Lord's Supper
(Mt 26.26–30; Mk 14.22–26; 1 Cor. 11.23–25)

14 When the hour came, Jesus took his place
at the table with the apostles. [15]He said to
them, "I have wanted so much to eat this
Passover meal with you before I suffer! [16]For
I tell you, I will never eat it until it is given
its full meaning in the Kingdom of God."

17 Then Jesus took a cup, gave thanks to
God, and said, "Take this and share it among
yourselves. [18]I tell you that from now on I
will not drink this wine until the Kingdom
of God comes."

19 Then he took a piece of bread, gave
thanks to God, broke it, and gave it to them,
saying, "This is my body, which is given for
you. Do this in memory of me." [20]In the
same way, he gave them the cup after the
supper, saying, "This cup is God's new
covenant sealed with my blood, which is
poured out for you.[a]

21 "But, look! The one who betrays me is
here at the table with me! [22]The Son of
Man will die as God has decided, but how
terrible for that man who betrays him!"

23 Then they began to ask among
themselves which one of them it could be
who was going to do this.

Christians share bread and wine at Holy Communion to remind them of the death of Jesus.

[a] **22.20** *Some manuscripts do not have the words of Jesus after* This is my body *in verse 19, and all of verse 20.*

The Argument about Greatness

24 An argument broke out among the
disciples as to which one of them should be
thought of as the greatest. 25Jesus said to
them, "The kings of the pagans have power
over their people, and the rulers claim the
title 'Friends of the People'. 26But this is
not the way it is with you; rather,
the greatest one among you must be like
the youngest, and the leader must be
like the servant. 27Who is greater, the one
who sits down to eat or the one who
serves? The one who sits down, of course.
But I am among you as one who serves.
28 "You have stayed with me all through
my trials; 29and just as my Father has given
me the right to rule, so I will give you the
same right. 30You will eat and drink at my
table in my Kingdom, and you will sit on
thrones to rule over the twelve tribes of
Israel.

Jesus Predicts Peter's Denial
(Mt 26.31–35; Mk 14.27–31; Jn 13.36–38)

31 "Simon, Simon! Listen! Satan has
received permission to test all of you, to
separate the good from the bad, as a farmer
separates the wheat from the chaff. 32But I
have prayed for you, Simon, that your faith
will not fail. And when you turn back to
me, you must strengthen your brothers."
33 Peter answered, "Lord, I am ready to go
to prison with you and to die with you!"
34 "I tell you, Peter," Jesus said, "the cock
will not crow tonight until you have said
three times that you do not know me."

Purse, Bag, and Sword

35 Then Jesus asked his disciples, "When I
sent you out that time without purse, bag,
or shoes, did you lack anything?"

"Not a thing," they answered.

36 "But now," Jesus said, "whoever has a
purse or a bag must take it; and whoever
has no sword must sell his coat and buy
one. 37For I tell you that the scripture
which says, 'He shared the fate of
criminals,' must come true about me,
because what was written about me is
coming true."

38 The disciples said, "Look! Here are two
swords, Lord!"

"That is enough!"[a] he replied.

Jesus Prays on the Mount of Olives
(Mt 26.36–46; Mk 14.32–42)

39 Jesus left the city and went, as he usually
did, to the Mount of Olives; and the
disciples went with him. 40When he
arrived at the place, he said to them, "Pray
that you will not fall into temptation."
41 Then he went off from them about the
distance of a stone's throw and knelt down
and prayed. 42"Father," he said, "if you
will, take this cup of suffering away from
me. Not my will, however, but your will be
done." 43An angel from heaven appeared
to him and strengthened him. 44In great
anguish he prayed even more fervently; his
sweat was like drops of blood falling to the
ground.[b]
45 Rising from his prayer, he went back to
the disciples and found them asleep, worn
out by their grief. 46He said to them, "Why
are you sleeping? Get up and pray that you
will not fall into temptation."

The Arrest of Jesus
(Mt 26.47–56; Mk 14.43–50; Jn 18.3–11)

47 Jesus was still speaking when a crowd
arrived, led by Judas, one of the twelve
disciples. He came up to Jesus to kiss him.
48But Jesus said, "Judas, is it with a kiss that
you betray the Son of Man?"
49 When the disciples who were with Jesus
saw what was going to happen, they asked,
"Shall we use our swords, Lord?" 50And one
of them struck the High Priest's slave and
cut off his right ear.
51 But Jesus said, "Enough of this!" He
touched the man's ear and healed him.
52 Then Jesus said to the chief priests and
the officers of the temple guard and the
elders who had come there to get him, "Did
you have to come with swords and clubs, as
though I were an outlaw? 53I was with you
in the Temple every day, and you did not
try to arrest me. But this is your hour to act,
when the power of darkness rules."

[a] **22.38** That is enough; *or* Enough of this.

[b] **22.44** *Some manuscripts do not have verses 43–44.*

Peter Denies Jesus
(Mt 26.57–58, 69–75; Mk 14.53–54, 66–72; Jn 18.12–18, 25–27)

54 They arrested Jesus and took him away
into the house of the High Priest; and Peter
followed at a distance. 55A fire had been lit
in the centre of the courtyard, and Peter
joined those who were sitting round it.
56When one of the servant women saw
him sitting there at the fire, she looked
straight at him and said, "This man too was
with Jesus!"
57 But Peter denied it, "Woman, I don't
even know him!"
58 After a little while a man noticed Peter
and said, "You are one of them, too!"
But Peter answered, "Man, I am not!"
59 And about an hour later another man
insisted strongly, "There isn't any doubt
that this man was with Jesus, because he
also is a Galilean!"
60 But Peter answered, "Man, I don't know
what you are talking about!"
At once, while he was still speaking, a
cock crowed. 61The Lord turned round
and looked straight at Peter, and Peter
remembered that the Lord had said to
him, "Before the cock crows tonight, you
will say three times that you do not know
me." 62Peter went out and wept bitterly.

Jesus is Mocked and Beaten
(Mt 26.67–68; Mk 14.65)

63 The men who were guarding Jesus
mocked him and beat him. 64They
blindfolded him and asked him, "Who hit
you? Guess!" 65And they said many other
insulting things to him.

Jesus is Brought before the Council
(Mt 26.59–66; Mk 14.55–64; Jn 18.19–24)

66 When day came, the elders, the chief
priests, and the teachers of the Law met
together, and Jesus was brought before the
Council. 67"Tell us," they said, "are you the
Messiah?"
He answered, "If I tell you, you will not
believe me; 68and if I ask you a question,
you will not answer. 69But from now on the
Son of Man will be seated on the right of
Almighty God."
70 They all said, "Are you, then, the Son of
God?"
He answered them, "You say that I am."
71 And they said, "We don't need any
witnesses! We ourselves have heard what he
said!"

Jesus is Brought before Pilate
(Mt 27.1–2, 11–14; Mk 15.1–5; Jn 18.28–38)

23 The whole group rose up and took
Jesus before Pilate, 2where they began
to accuse him: "We caught this man
misleading our people, telling them not to
pay taxes to the Emperor and claiming that
he himself is the Messiah, a king."
3 Pilate asked him, "Are you the king of
the Jews?"
"So you say," answered Jesus.
4 Then Pilate said to the chief priests and
the crowds, "I find no reason to condemn
this man."

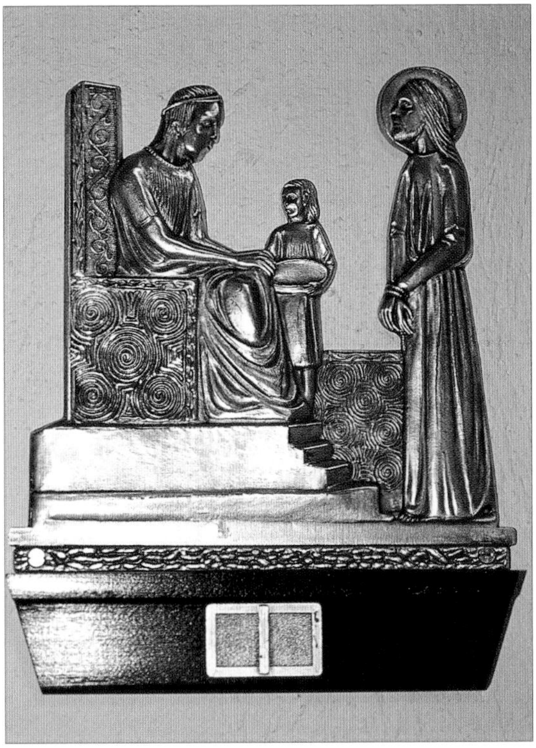

Jesus stood before Pilate on trial.

5 But they insisted even more strongly,
"With his teaching he is starting a riot
among the people all through Judea. He
began in Galilee and now has come here."

Jesus is Sent to Herod

6 When Pilate heard this, he asked, "Is this
man a Galilean?" [7]When he learnt that
Jesus was from the region ruled by Herod,
he sent him to Herod, who was also in
Jerusalem at that time. [8]Herod was very
pleased when he saw Jesus, because he had
heard about him and had been wanting to
see him for a long time. He was hoping to
see Jesus perform some miracle. [9]So Herod
asked Jesus many questions, but Jesus made
no answer. [10]The chief priests and the
teachers of the Law stepped forward and
made strong accusations against Jesus.
[11]Herod and his soldiers mocked Jesus and
treated him with contempt; then they put a
fine robe on him and sent him back to
Pilate. [12]On that very day Herod and Pilate
became friends; before this they had been
enemies.

Jesus is Sentenced to Death

(Mt 27.15–26; Mk 15.6–15; Jn 18.39—19.16)

13 Pilate called together the chief priests, the
leaders, and the people, [14]and said to them,
"You brought this man to me and said that
he was misleading the people. Now, I have
examined him here in your presence, and I
have not found him guilty of any of the
crimes you accuse him of. [15]Nor did Herod
find him guilty, for he sent him back to us.
There is nothing this man has done to
deserve death. [16]So I will have him whipped
and let him go."[a]

18 The whole crowd cried out, "Kill him! Set
Barabbas free for us!" [19](Barabbas had been
put in prison for a riot that had taken place
in the city, and for murder.)

20 Pilate wanted to set Jesus free, so he
appealed to the crowd again. [21]But they
shouted back, "Crucify him! Crucify him!"

22 Pilate said to them the third time, "But
what crime has he committed? I cannot
find anything he has done to deserve death!
I will have him whipped and set him free."

23 But they kept on shouting at the top of
their voices that Jesus should be crucified,
and finally their shouting succeeded. [24]So
Pilate passed the sentence on Jesus that they
were asking for. [25]He set free the man they
wanted, the one who had been put in
prison for riot and murder, and he handed
Jesus over for them to do as they wished.

Jesus is Crucified

(Mt 27.32–44; Mk 15.21–32; Jn 19.17–27)

26 The soldiers led Jesus away, and as they
were going, they met a man from Cyrene
named Simon who was coming into the city
from the country. They seized him, put the
cross on him, and made him carry it behind
Jesus.

27 A large crowd of people followed him;
among them were some women who were
weeping and wailing for him. [28]Jesus turned
to them and said, "Women of Jerusalem!
Don't cry for me, but for yourselves and
your children. [29]For the days are coming
when people will say, 'How lucky are the
women who never had children, who never
bore babies, who never nursed them!'
[30]That will be the time when people will say
to the mountains, 'Fall on us!' and to the
hills, 'Hide us!' [31]For if such things as these
are done when the wood is green, what will
happen when it is dry?"

32 Two other men, both of them criminals,
were also led out to be put to death with
Jesus. [33]When they came to the place called
"The Skull", they crucified Jesus there, and
the two criminals, one on his right and the
other on his left. [34]Jesus said, "Forgive
them, Father! They don't know what they
are doing."[b]

They divided his clothes among
themselves by throwing dice. [35]The people
stood there watching while the Jewish
leaders jeered at him: "He saved others; let
him save himself if he is the Messiah whom
God has chosen!"

36 The soldiers also mocked him: they came
up to him and offered him cheap wine,
[37]and said, "Save yourself if you are the
king of the Jews!"

38 Above him were written these words:
"This is the King of the Jews."

39 One of the criminals hanging there
hurled insults at him: "Aren't you the

[a] **23.16** *Some manuscripts add verse 17:* At every Passover Festival Pilate had to set free one prisoner for them *(see Mk 15.6).*

[b] **23.34** *Some manuscripts do not have* Jesus said, "Forgive them, Father! They don't know what they are doing."

Messiah? Save yourself and us!"
40 The other one, however, rebuked him,
saying, "Don't you fear God? You received
the same sentence he did. [41]Ours, however,
is only right, because we are getting what
we deserve for what we did; but he has
done no wrong." [42]And he said to Jesus,
"Remember me, Jesus, when you come as
King!"
43 Jesus said to him, "I promise you that
today you will be in Paradise with me."

Jesus was put to death on the cross.

The Death of Jesus

(Mt 27.45–56; Mk 15.33–41; Jn 19.28–30)

44–45 It was about twelve o'clock when the
sun stopped shining and darkness covered
the whole country until three o'clock; and
the curtain hanging in the Temple was torn
in two. [46]Jesus cried out in a loud voice,
"Father! In your hands I place my spirit!"
He said this and died.
47 The army officer saw what had
happened, and he praised God, saying,
"Certainly he was a good man!"
48 When the people who had gathered
there to watch the spectacle saw what
happened, they all went back home,
beating their breasts in sorrow. [49]All those
who knew Jesus personally, including the
women who had followed him from
Galilee, stood at a distance to watch.

The Burial of Jesus

(Mt 27.57–61; Mk 15.42–47; Jn 19.38–42)

50–51 There was a man named Joseph from
Arimathea, a town in Judea. He was a good
and honourable man, who was waiting for
the coming of the Kingdom of God.
Although he was a member of the Council,
he had not agreed
with their decision
and action. [52]He
went into the
presence of Pilate
and asked for the
body of Jesus.
[53]Then he took the
body down, wrapped
it in a linen sheet,
and placed it in a
tomb which had
been dug out of solid
rock and which had
never been used. [54]It
was Friday, and the
Sabbath was about to
begin.
55 The women who
had followed Jesus
from Galilee went
with Joseph and saw
the tomb and how
Jesus' body was placed in it. [56]Then they
went back home and prepared the spices
and perfumes for the body.
On the Sabbath they rested, as the Law
commanded.

The Resurrection

(Mt 28.1–10; Mk 16.1–8; Jn 20.1–10)

24 Very early on Sunday morning the
women went to the tomb, carrying the
spices they had prepared. [2]They found
the stone rolled away from the entrance to
the tomb, [3]so they went in; but they did not
find the body of the Lord Jesus. [4]They stood
there puzzled about this, when suddenly two
men in bright shining clothes stood by

them. [5]Full of fear, the women bowed down
to the ground, as the men said to them,
"Why are you looking among the dead for
one who is alive? [6]He is not here; he has
been raised. Remember what he said to you
while he was in Galilee: [7]'The Son of Man
must be handed over to sinners, be crucified,
and three days later rise to life.' "
8 Then the women remembered his words,
[9]returned from the tomb, and told all these
things to the eleven disciples and all the
rest. [10]The women were Mary Magdalene,
Joanna, and Mary the mother of James;
they and the other women with them told
these things to the apostles. [11]But the
apostles thought that what the women said
was nonsense, and they did not believe
them. [12]But Peter got up and ran to the
tomb; he bent down and saw the linen
wrappings but nothing else. Then he went
back home amazed at what had happened.[a]

On Easter Sunday, Christians celebrate Jesus rising from the dead.

The Walk to Emmaus
(Mk 16.12–13)

13 On that same day two of Jesus' followers
were going to a village named Emmaus,
about 11 kilometres from Jerusalem, [14]and
they were talking to each other about all
the things that had happened. [15]As they
talked and discussed, Jesus himself drew
near and walked along with them; [16]they
saw him, but somehow did not recognize
him. [17]Jesus said to them, "What are you
talking about to each other, as you walk
along?"
They stood still, with sad faces. [18]One of
them, named Cleopas, asked him, "Are you
the only visitor in Jerusalem who doesn't
know the things that have been happening
there these last few days?"
19 "What things?" he asked.
"The things that happened to Jesus of
Nazareth," they answered. "This man was a
prophet and was considered by God and by
all the people to be powerful in everything
he said and did. [20]Our chief priests and
rulers handed him over to be sentenced to
death, and he was crucified. [21]And we had
hoped that he would be the one who was
going to set Israel free! Besides all that, this
is now the third day since it happened.
[22]Some of the women of our group
surprised us; they went at dawn to the
tomb, [23]but could not find his body. They
came back saying they had seen a vision of
angels who told them that he is alive.
[24]Some of our group went to the tomb and
found it exactly as the women had said, but
they did not see him."
25 Then Jesus said to them, "How foolish
you are, how slow you are to believe
everything the prophets said! [26]Was it not
necessary for the Messiah to suffer these
things and then to enter his glory?" [27]And
Jesus explained to them what was said
about himself in all the Scriptures,
beginning with the books of Moses and the
writings of all the prophets.
28 As they came near the village to which
they were going, Jesus acted as if he were
going farther; [29]but they held him back,
saying, "Stay with us; the day is almost

[a] **24.12** *Some manuscripts do not have verse 12.*

over and it is getting dark." So he went in
to stay with them. [30]He sat down to eat
with them, took the bread, and said the
blessing; then he broke the bread and gave
it to them. [31]Then their eyes were opened
and they recognized him, but he
disappeared from their sight. [32]They said
to each other, "Wasn't it like a fire burning
in us when he talked to us on the road and
explained the Scriptures to us?"
33 They got up at once and went back to
Jerusalem, where they found the eleven
disciples gathered together with the others
[34]and saying, "The Lord is risen indeed! He
has appeared to Simon!"
35 The two then explained to them what
had happened on the road, and how they
had recognized the Lord when he broke the
bread.

Jesus Appears to his Disciples

(Mt 28.16–20; Mk 16.14–18; Jn 20.19–23; Acts 1.6–8)

36 While the two were telling them this,
suddenly the Lord himself stood among
them and said to them, "Peace be with
you."[a]
37 They were terrified, thinking that they
were seeing a ghost. [38]But he said to them,
"Why are you alarmed? Why are these
doubts coming up in your minds? [39]Look
at my hands and my feet, and see that it is
I myself. Feel me, and you will know, for a
ghost doesn't have flesh and bones, as you
can see I have."
40 He said this and showed them his hands
and his feet.[b] [41]They still could not
believe, they were so full of joy and
wonder; so he asked them, "Have you
anything here to eat?" [42]They gave him a
piece of cooked fish, [43]which he took and
ate in their presence.
44 Then he said to them, "These are the
very things I told you about while I was
still with you: everything written about me
in the Law of Moses, the writings of the
prophets, and the Psalms had to come
true."
45 Then he opened their minds to
understand the Scriptures, [46]and said to
them, "This is what is written: the Messiah
must suffer and must rise from death three
days later, [47]and in his name the message
about repentance and the forgiveness of
sins must be preached to all nations,
beginning in Jerusalem. [48]You are
witnesses of these things. [49]And I myself
will send upon you what my Father has
promised. But you must wait in the city
until the power from above comes down
upon you."

Jesus is Taken Up to Heaven

(Mk 16.19–20; Acts 1.9–11)

50 Then he led them out of the city as far as
Bethany, where he raised his hands and
blessed them. [51]As he was blessing them,
he departed from them and was taken up
into heaven.[c] [52]They worshipped him and
went back into Jerusalem, filled with great
joy, [53]and spent all their time in the
Temple giving thanks to God.

A stained-glass window showing Jesus being taken up to heaven.

[a] **24.36** *Some manuscripts do not have* and said to them, "Peace be with you."

[b] **24.40** *Some manuscripts do not have verse 40.*

[c] **24.51** *Some manuscripts do not have* and was taken up into heaven.

The Gospel According to John

John's Gospel is very different from the other three. It was written much later than the others. We are not sure who the writer was, but he may have been one of the disciples of Jesus.

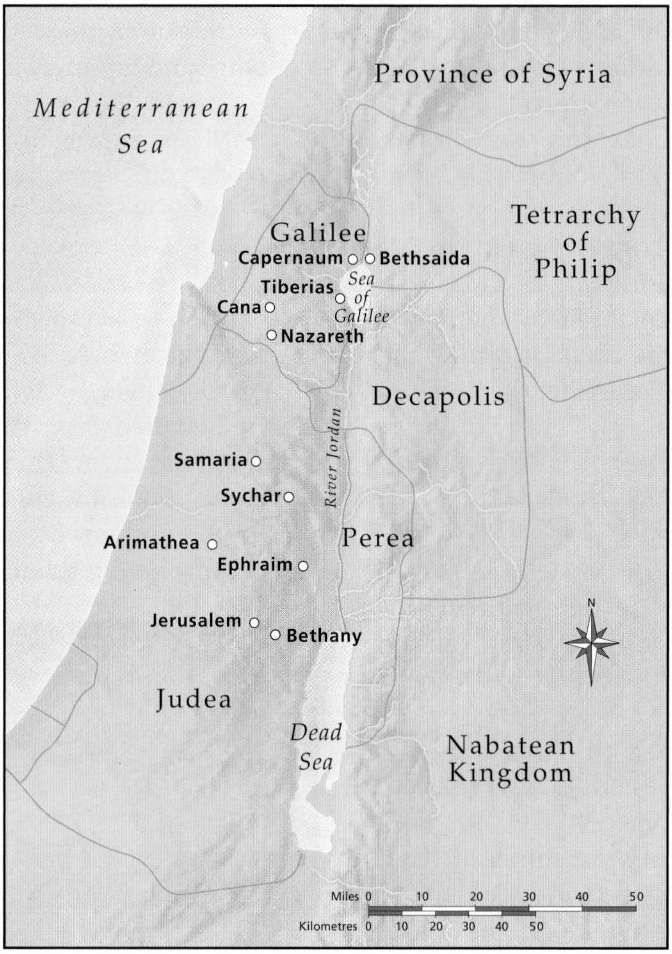

The Life of Jesus

(All dates are approximate)

25 CE
John the Baptist begins his work

Jesus begins his work

Jesus is baptized by John the Baptist

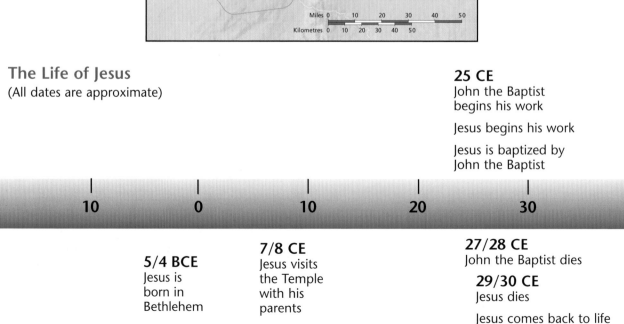

10 | 0 | 10 | 20 | 30

5/4 BCE
Jesus is born in Bethlehem

7/8 CE
Jesus visits the Temple with his parents

27/28 CE
John the Baptist dies

29/30 CE
Jesus dies

Jesus comes back to life

The Word of Life

1 In the beginning the Word already
existed; the Word was with God, and
the Word was God. 2From the very
beginning the Word was with God.
3Through him God made all things; not
one thing in all creation was made without
him. 4The Word was the source of life,[a] and
this life brought light to humanity. 5The
light shines in the darkness, and the
darkness has never put it out.

Jesus was the light that God sent into the world.

6 God sent his messenger, a man named
John, 7who came to tell people about the
light, so that all should hear the message
and believe. 8He himself was not the light;
he came to tell about the light. 9This was
the real light – the light that comes into the
world and shines on everyone.
10 The Word was in the world, and though
God made the world through him, yet the
world did not recognize him. 11He came to
his own country, but his own people did
not receive him. 12Some, however, did
receive him and believed in him; so he gave
them the right to become God's children.
13They did not become God's children by
natural means, that is, by being born as the
children of a human father; God himself
was their Father.
14 The Word became a human being and,
full of grace and truth, lived among us. We
saw his glory, the glory which he received
as the Father's only Son.
15 John spoke about him. He cried out,
"This is the one I was talking about when I
said, 'He comes after me, but he is greater
than I am, because he existed before I was
born.' "
16 Out of the fullness of his grace he has
blessed us all, giving us one blessing after
another. 17God gave the Law through
Moses, but grace and truth came through
Jesus Christ. 18No one has ever seen God.
The only Son, who is the same as God and
is at the Father's side, he has made him
known.

John the Baptist's Message

(Mt 3.1–12; Mk 1.1–8; Lk 3.1–18)

19 The Jewish authorities in Jerusalem sent
some priests and Levites to John, to ask
him, "Who are you?"
20 John did not refuse to answer, but spoke
out openly and clearly, saying: "I am not
the Messiah."
21 "Who are you, then?" they asked. "Are
you Elijah?"
"No, I am not," John answered.
"Are you the Prophet?"[b] they asked.
"No," he replied.
22 "Then tell us who you are," they said.
"We have to take an answer back to those
who sent us. What do you say about
yourself?"
23 John answered by quoting the prophet
Isaiah:

"I am 'the voice of someone shouting in
the desert:
Make a straight path for the Lord to
travel!' "

24 The messengers, who had been sent by
the Pharisees, 25then[c] asked John, "If you
are not the Messiah nor Elijah nor the
Prophet, why do you baptize?"

[a] **1.4** The Word was the source of life; *or* What was made had life in union with the Word.

[b] **1.21** THE PROPHET: *The one who was expected to appear and announce the coming of the Messiah.*

[c] **1.25** The messengers, who had been sent by the Pharisees, then; *or* Those who had been sent were Pharisees; they.

26 John answered, "I baptize with water, but
among you stands the one you do not
know. 27He is coming after me, but I am
not good enough even to untie his
sandals."
28 All this happened in Bethany on the east
side of the River Jordan, where John was
baptizing.

The Lamb of God

29 The next day John saw Jesus coming to
him, and said, "There is the Lamb of God,
who takes away the sin of the world! 30This
is the one I was talking about when I said,
'A man is coming after me, but he is greater
than I am, because he existed before I was
born.' 31I did not know who he would be,
but I came baptizing with water in order
to make him known
to the people of
Israel."
32 And John gave
this testimony: "I
saw the Spirit come
down like a dove
from heaven and
stay on him. 33I still
did not know that
he was the one, but
God, who sent me to
baptize with water,
had said to me, 'You
will see the Spirit
come down and stay
on a man; he is the
one who baptizes
with the Holy Spirit.'
34I have seen it,"
said John, "and I tell
you that he is the
Son of God."

John called Jesus the Lamb of God because he took away the sins of the world.

The First Disciples of Jesus

35 The next day John was standing there
again with two of his disciples, 36when he
saw Jesus walking by. "There is the Lamb of
God!" he said.
37 The two disciples heard him say this and
went with Jesus. 38Jesus turned, saw them
following him, and asked, "What are you
looking for?"
They answered, "Where do you live,
Rabbi?" (This word means "Teacher".)
39 "Come and see," he answered. (It was
then about four o'clock in the afternoon.)
So they went with him and saw where he
lived, and spent the rest of that day with
him.
40 One of them was Andrew, Simon Peter's
brother. 41At once he found his brother
Simon and told him, "We have found the
Messiah." (This word means "Christ".)
42Then he took Simon to Jesus.
Jesus looked at him and said, "Your name
is Simon son of John, but you will be called
Cephas." (This is the same as Peter and
means "a rock".)

Jesus Calls Philip and Nathanael

43 The next day Jesus
decided to go to Galilee.
He found Philip and
said to him, "Come with
me!" 44(Philip was from
Bethsaida, the town
where Andrew and Peter
lived.) 45Philip found
Nathanael and told
him, "We have found
the one whom Moses
wrote about in the book
of the Law and whom
the prophets also wrote
about. He is Jesus son of
Joseph, from Nazareth."
46 "Can anything good
come from Nazareth?"
Nathanael asked.
"Come and see,"
answered Philip.
47 When Jesus saw
Nathanael coming to him, he said about
him, "Here is a real Israelite; there is
nothing false in him!"
48 Nathanael asked him, "How do you
know me?"
Jesus answered, "I saw you when you
were under the fig tree before Philip called
you."

49 "Teacher," answered Nathanael, "you are
the Son of God! You are the King of Israel!"
50 Jesus said, "Do you believe just because I
told you I saw you when you were under
the fig tree? You will see much greater
things than this!" 51And he said to them, "I
am telling you the truth: you will see
heaven open and God's angels going up
and coming down on the Son of Man."

The Wedding in Cana

2 Two days later there was a wedding in
the town of Cana in Galilee. Jesus'
mother was there, 2and Jesus and his
disciples had also been invited to the
wedding. 3When the wine had given out,
Jesus' mother said to him, "They have no
wine left."
4 "You must not tell me what to do," Jesus
replied. "My time has not yet come."
5 Jesus' mother then told the servants,
"Do whatever he tells you."
6 The Jews have rules about ritual
washing, and for this purpose six
stone water jars were there, each one
large enough to hold about a
hundred litres. 7Jesus said to the
servants, "Fill these jars with water."
They filled them to the brim, 8and
then he told them, "Now draw some
water out and take it to the man in
charge of the feast." They took him
the water, 9which now had turned
into wine, and he tasted it. He did not
know where this wine had come from
(but, of course, the servants who had
drawn out the water knew); so he
called the bridegroom 10and said to
him, "Everyone else serves the best
wine first, and after the guests have
had plenty to drink, he serves the
ordinary wine. But you have kept the
best wine until now!"
11 Jesus performed this first miracle in
Cana in Galilee; there he revealed his
glory, and his disciples believed in him.
12 After this, Jesus and his mother,
brothers, and disciples went to
Capernaum and stayed there a few
days.

Jesus Goes to the Temple

(Mt 21.12–13; Mk 11.15–17; Lk 19.45–46)

13 It was almost time for the Passover
Festival, so Jesus went to Jerusalem.
14There in the Temple he found people
selling cattle, sheep, and pigeons, and also
the moneychangers sitting at their tables.
15So he made a whip from cords and drove
all the animals out of the Temple, both the
sheep and the cattle; he overturned the
tables of the moneychangers and scattered
their coins; 16and he ordered those who
sold the pigeons, "Take them out of here!
Stop making my Father's house a market
place!" 17His disciples remembered that the
scripture says, "My devotion to your house,
O God, burns in me like a fire."
18 The Jewish authorities
replied with a question,
"What miracle can you
perform to show us that
you have the right to do
this?"
19 Jesus answered,
"Tear down this
Temple, and in
three days I will
build it again."
20 "Are you going to
build it again in
three days?" they
asked him. "It has
taken forty-six years
to build this
Temple!"
21 But the temple
Jesus was speaking
about was his body.
22So when he
was raised from
death, his disciples
remembered that he
had said this, and
they believed the
scripture and what
Jesus had said.

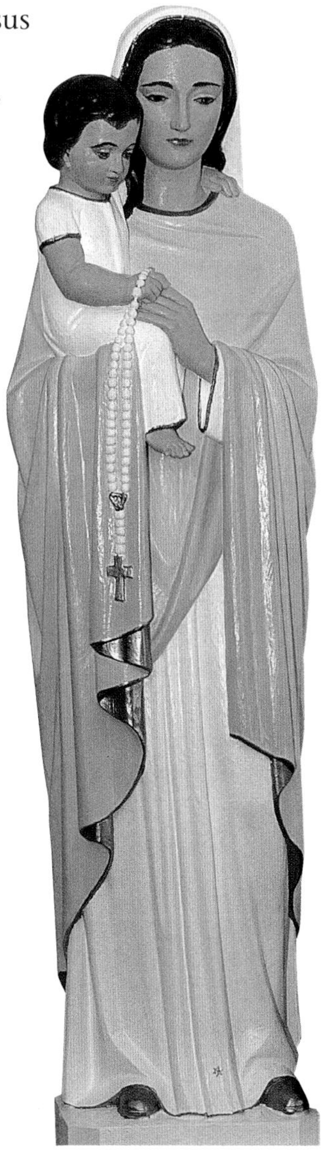

At a wedding feast, Mary told the servants to do what Jesus told them.

Jesus' Knowledge of Human Nature

23 While Jesus was in Jerusalem during the
Passover Festival, many believed in him as
they saw the miracles he performed. [24]But
Jesus did not trust himself to them, because
he knew them all. [25]There was no need for
anyone to tell him about them, because he
himself knew what was in their hearts.

Jesus and Nicodemus

3 There was a Jewish leader named
Nicodemus, who belonged to the party
of the Pharisees. [2]One night he went
to Jesus and said to him, "Rabbi, we know
that you are a teacher sent by God. No one
could perform the miracles you are doing
unless God were with him."
3 Jesus answered, "I am telling you the
truth: no one can see the Kingdom of God
without being born again."[a]
4 "How can a grown man be born again?"
Nicodemus asked. "He certainly cannot
enter his mother's womb and be born a
second time!"
5 "I am telling you the truth," replied Jesus.
"No one can enter the Kingdom of God
without being born of water and the Spirit.
[6]A person is born physically of human
parents, but is born spiritually of the Spirit.
[7]Do not be surprised because I tell you that
you must all be born again.[a] [8]The wind
blows wherever it wishes; you hear the
sound it makes, but you do not know where
it comes from or where it is going. It is like
that with everyone who is born of the
Spirit."
9 "How can this be?" asked Nicodemus.
10 Jesus answered, "You are a great teacher in
Israel, and you don't know this? [11]I am
telling you the truth: we speak of what we
know and report what we have seen, yet
none of you is willing to accept our message.
[12]You do not believe me when I tell you
about the things of this world; how will you
ever believe me, then, when I tell you about
the things of heaven? [13]And no one has ever
gone up to heaven except the Son of Man,
who came down from heaven."[b]
14 As Moses lifted up the bronze snake on a
pole in the desert, in the same way the Son
of Man must be lifted up, [15]so that everyone
who believes in him may have eternal life.
[16]For God loved the world so much that he
gave his only Son, so that everyone who
believes in him may not die but have eternal
life. [17]For God did not send his Son into the
world to be its judge, but to be its saviour.
18 Those who believe in the Son are not
judged; but those who do not believe have
already been judged, because they have not
believed in God's only Son. [19]This is how the
judgement works: the light has come into
the world, but people love the darkness
rather than the light, because their deeds are
evil. [20]All those who do evil things hate the
light and will not come to the light, because
they do not want their evil deeds to be
shown up. [21]But those who do what is true
come to the light in order that the light may
show that what they did was in obedience to
God.

Jesus and John

22 After this, Jesus and his disciples went to
the province of Judea, where he spent some
time with them and baptized. [23]John also
was baptizing in Aenon, not far from Salim,
because there was plenty of water in that
place. People were going to him, and he was
baptizing them. [24](This was before John had
been put in prison.)
25 Some of John's disciples began arguing
with a Jew[c] about the matter of ritual
washing. [26]So they went to John and said,
"Teacher, you remember the man who was
with you on the east side of the Jordan, the
one you spoke about? Well, he is baptizing
now, and everyone is going to him!"
27 John answered, "No one can have
anything unless God gives it to him. [28]You
yourselves are my witnesses that I said, 'I
am not the Messiah, but I have been sent
ahead of him.' [29]The bridegroom is the one
to whom the bride belongs; but the
bridegroom's friend, who stands by and
listens, is glad when he hears the
bridegroom's voice. This is how my own
happiness is made complete. [30]He must
become more important while I become
less important."

[a] **3.3, 3.7** again; *or* from above.
[b] **3.13** *The quotation may continue through verse 21.*
[c] **3.25** a Jew; *some manuscripts have* some Jews.

He who Comes from Heaven

31 He who comes from above is greater
than all. He who is from the earth belongs
to the earth and speaks about earthly
matters, but he who comes from heaven is
above all. [32]He tells what he has seen and
heard, yet no one accepts his message.
[33]But whoever accepts his message
confirms by this that God is truthful.
[34]The one whom God has sent speaks
God's words, because God gives him the
fullness of his Spirit. [35]The Father loves his
Son and has put everything in his power.
[36]Whoever believes in the Son has eternal
life; whoever disobeys the Son will not
have life, but will remain under God's
punishment.

Jesus and the Samaritan Woman

4 The Pharisees heard that Jesus was
winning and baptizing more disciples
than John. [2](Actually, Jesus himself
did not baptize anyone; only his disciples
did.) [3]So when Jesus heard what was being
said, he left Judea and went back to Galilee;
[4]on his way there he had to go through
Samaria.
5 In Samaria he came to a town named
Sychar, which was not far from the field
that Jacob had given to his son Joseph.
[6]Jacob's well was there, and Jesus, tired out
by the journey, sat down by the well. It was
about noon.
7 A Samaritan woman came to draw some
water, and Jesus said to her, "Give me a drink
of water." [8](His disciples had gone into town
to buy food.)
9 The woman answered, "You are a Jew,
and I am a Samaritan – so how can you ask
me for a drink?" (Jews will not use the same
cups and bowls that Samaritans use.)[a]
10 Jesus answered, "If only you knew what
God gives and who it is that is asking you
for a drink, you would ask him, and he
would give you life-giving water."
11 "Sir," the woman said, "you haven't got
a bucket, and the well is deep. Where
would you get that life-giving water? [12]It
was our ancestor Jacob who gave us this
well; he and his sons and his flocks all
drank from it. You don't claim to be greater
than Jacob, do you?"
13 Jesus answered, "All those who drink this
water will be thirsty again, [14]but whoever
drinks the water that I will give him will
never be thirsty again. The water that I will
give him will become in him a spring
which will provide him with life-giving
water and give him eternal life."
15 "Sir," the woman said, "give me that
water! Then I will never be thirsty again,
nor will I have to come here to draw water."
16 "Go and call your husband," Jesus told
her, "and come back."
17 "I haven't got a husband," she answered.
Jesus replied, "You are right when you
say you haven't got a husband. [18]You have
been married to five men, and the man you
live with now is not really your husband.
You have told me the truth."
19 "I see you are a prophet, sir," the woman
said. [20]"My Samaritan ancestors
worshipped God on this mountain, but you
Jews say that Jerusalem is the place where
we should worship God."
21 Jesus said to her, "Believe me, woman,
the time will come when people will not
worship the Father either on this mountain
or in Jerusalem. [22]You Samaritans do not
really know whom you worship; but we
Jews know whom we worship, because it is
from the Jews that salvation comes. [23]But
the time is coming and is already here,
when by the power of God's Spirit people
will worship the Father as he really is,
offering him the true worship that he
wants. [24]God is Spirit, and only by the
power of his Spirit can people worship him
as he really is."
25 The woman said to him, "I know that
the Messiah will come, and when he
comes, he will tell us everything."
26 Jesus answered, "I am he, I who am
talking with you."
27 At that moment Jesus' disciples returned,
and they were greatly surprised to find him
talking with a woman. But none of them
said to her, "What do you want?" or asked
him, "Why are you talking with her?"

[a] **4.9** Jews will not use the same cups and bowls that Samaritans use; *or* Jews will have nothing to do with Samaritans.

28 Then the woman left her water jar, went
back to the town, and said to the people
there, [29]"Come and see the man who told
me everything I have ever done. Could he
be the Messiah?" [30]So they left the town
and went to Jesus.
31 In the meantime the disciples were
begging Jesus, "Teacher, have something to
eat!"
32 But he answered, "I have food to eat that
you know nothing about."
33 So the disciples started asking among
themselves, "Could somebody have
brought him food?"
34 "My food," Jesus said to them, "is to obey
the will of the one who sent me and to
finish the work he gave me to do. [35]You
have a saying, 'Four more months and then
the harvest.' But I tell you, take a good look
at the fields; the crops are now ripe and
ready to be harvested! [36]The one who reaps
the harvest is being paid and gathers the
crops for eternal life; so another who sows
and the one who reaps will be glad together.
[37]The saying is true, 'One sows, another
reaps.' [38]I have sent you to reap a harvest in
a field where you did not work; others
worked there, and you profit from their
work."
39 Many of the Samaritans in that town
believed in Jesus because the woman had
said, "He told me everything I have ever
done." [40]So when the Samaritans came to
him, they begged him to stay with them,
and Jesus stayed there two days.
41 Many more believed because of his
message, [42]and they said to the woman,
"We believe now, not because of what you
said, but because we ourselves have heard
him, and we know that he really is the
Saviour of the world."

Jesus Heals an Official's Son

43 After spending two days there, Jesus left
and went to Galilee. [44]For he himself had
said, "A prophet is not respected in his own
country." [45]When he arrived in Galilee, the
people there welcomed him, because they
had gone to the Passover Festival in
Jerusalem and had seen everything that he
had done during the festival.
46 Then Jesus went back to Cana in Galilee,
where he had turned the water into wine. A
government official was there whose son
was ill in Capernaum. [47]When he heard
that Jesus had come from Judea to Galilee,
he went to him and asked him to go to
Capernaum and heal his son, who was
about to die. [48]Jesus said to him, "None of
you will ever believe unless you see
miracles and wonders."
49 "Sir," replied the official, "come with me
before my child dies."
50 Jesus said to him, "Go, your son will
live!"
The man believed Jesus' words and went.
[51]On his way home his servants met him
with the news, "Your boy is going to live!"
52 He asked them what time it was when
his son got better, and they answered, "It
was one o'clock yesterday afternoon when
the fever left him." [53]Then the father
remembered it was at that very hour that
Jesus had told him, "Your son will live." So
he and all his family believed.
54 This was the second miracle that Jesus
performed after coming from Judea to
Galilee.

The Healing at the Pool

5 After this, Jesus went to Jerusalem for
a religious festival. [2]Near the Sheep
Gate in Jerusalem there is a pool[a] with
five porches; in Hebrew it is called
Bethzatha.[b] [3]A large crowd of sick people
were lying in the porches – the blind, the
lame, and the paralysed.[c] [5]A man was there
who had been ill for 38 years. [6]Jesus saw
him lying there, and he knew that the man
had been ill for such a long time; so he
asked him, "Do you want to get well?"
7 The sick man answered, "Sir, I have no
one here to put me in the pool when the

[a] **5.2** Near the Sheep Gate . . . a pool; *or* Near the Sheep Pool . . . a place.

[b] **5.2** Bethzatha; *some manuscripts have* Bethesda.

[c] **5.3** *Some manuscripts add verses 3b–4:* They were waiting for the water to move, [4]because every now and then an angel of the Lord went down into the pool and stirred up the water. The first sick person to go into the pool after the water was stirred up was healed from whatever disease he had.

water is stirred up; while I am trying to get
in, somebody else gets there first."
8 Jesus said to him, "Get up, pick up your
mat, and walk." [9]Immediately the man got
well; he picked up his mat and started
walking.
The day this happened was a Sabbath,
[10]so the Jewish authorities told the man
who had been healed, "This is a Sabbath,
and it is against our Law for you to carry
your mat."
11 He answered, "The man who made me
well told me to pick up my mat and walk."
12 They asked him, "Who is the man who
told you to do this?"
13 But the man who had been healed did
not know who Jesus was, for there was a
crowd in that place, and Jesus had slipped
away.
14 Afterwards, Jesus found him in the
Temple and said, "Listen, you are well now;
so stop sinning or something worse may
happen to you."
15 Then the man left and told the Jewish
authorities that it was Jesus who had healed
him. [16]So they began to persecute Jesus,
because he had done this healing on a
Sabbath. [17]Jesus answered them, "My
Father is always working, and I too must
work."
18 This saying made the Jewish authorities
all the more determined to kill him; not
only had he broken the Sabbath law, but he
had said that God was his own Father and
in this way had made himself equal with
God.

The Authority of the Son

19 So Jesus answered them, "I am telling
you the truth: the Son can do nothing on
his own; he does only what he sees his
Father doing. What the Father does, the
Son also does. [20]For the Father loves the
Son and shows him all that he himself is
doing. He will show him even greater
things to do than this, and you will all be
amazed. [21]Just as the Father raises the dead
and gives them life, in the same way the
Son gives life to those he wants to. [22]Nor
does the Father himself judge anyone. He
has given his Son the full right to judge,
[23]so that all will honour the Son in the
same way as they honour the Father.
Whoever does not honour the Son does not
honour the Father who sent him.
24 "I am telling you the truth: those who
hear my words and believe in him who
sent me have eternal life. They will not be
judged, but have already passed from
death to life. [25]I am telling you the truth:
the time is coming – the time has already
come – when the dead will hear the voice
of the Son of God, and those who hear it
will come to life. [26]Just as the Father is
himself the source of life, in the same way
he has made his Son to be the source of
life. [27]And he has given the Son the right
to judge, because he is the Son of Man.
[28]Do not be surprised at this; the time is
coming when all the dead will hear his
voice [29]and come out of their graves:
those who have done good will rise and
live, and those who have done evil will
rise and be condemned.

Witnesses to Jesus

30 "I can do nothing on my own authority;
I judge only as God tells me, so my
judgement is right, because I am not trying
to do what I want, but only what he who
sent me wants.
31 "If I testify on my own behalf, what I
say is not to be accepted as real proof.
[32]But there is someone else who testifies
on my behalf, and I know that what he
says about me is true. [33]John is the one to
whom you sent your messengers, and he
spoke on behalf of the truth. [34]It is not
that I must have a human witness; I say
this only in order that you may be saved.
[35]John was like a lamp, burning and
shining, and you were willing for a while
to enjoy his light. [36]But I have a witness
on my behalf which is even greater than
the witness that John gave: what I do, that
is, the deeds my Father gave me to do,
these speak on my behalf and show that
the Father has sent me. [37]And the Father,
who sent me, also testifies on my behalf.
You have never heard his voice or seen his

face, [38]and you do not keep his message
in your hearts, for you do not believe in
the one whom he sent. [39]You study the
Scriptures, because you think that in them
you will find eternal life. And these very
Scriptures speak about me! [40]Yet you are
not willing to come to me in order to have
life.
41 "I am not looking for human praise.
[42]But I know what kind of people you are,
and I know that you have no love for God
in your hearts. [43]I have come with my
Father's authority, but you have not
received me; when, however, someone
comes with his own authority, you will
receive him. [44]You like to receive praise
from one another, but you do not try to
win praise from the one who alone is God;
how, then, can you believe me? [45]Do not
think, however, that I am the one who will
accuse you to my Father. Moses, in whom
you have put your hope, is the very one
who will accuse you. [46]If you had really
believed Moses, you would have believed
me, because he wrote about me. [47]But
since you do not believe what he wrote,
how can you believe what I say?"

Jesus Feeds a Great Crowd
(Mt 14.13–21; Mk 6.30–44; Lk 9.10–17)

6 After this, Jesus went across Lake
Galilee (or, Lake Tiberias, as it is also
called). [2]A large crowd followed him,
because they had seen his miracles of
healing those who were ill. [3]Jesus went up
a hill and sat down with his disciples. [4]The
time for the Passover Festival was near.
[5]Jesus looked round and saw that a large
crowd was coming to him, so he asked
Philip, "Where can we buy enough food to
feed all these people?" [6](He said this to test
Philip; actually he already knew what he
would do.)
7 Philip answered, "For everyone to have
even a little, it would take more than two
hundred silver coins[a] to buy enough
bread."
8 Another of his disciples, Andrew, who
was Simon Peter's brother, said, [9]"There is a
boy here who has five loaves of barley
bread and two fish. But they will certainly
not be enough for all these people."
10 "Make the people sit down," Jesus told
them. (There was a lot of grass there.) So all
the people sat down; there were about
5,000 men. [11]Jesus took the bread, gave
thanks to God, and distributed it to the
people who were sitting there. He did the
same with the fish, and they all had as
much as they wanted. [12]When they were
all full, he said to his disciples, "Gather the
pieces left over; let us not waste any." [13]So
they gathered them all up and filled twelve
baskets with the pieces left over from the
five barley loaves which the people had
eaten.
14 Seeing this miracle that Jesus had
performed, the people there said, "Surely
this is the Prophet[b] who was to come into
the world!" [15]Jesus knew that they were
about to come and seize him in order to
make him king by force; so he went off
again to the hills by himself.

Just as Jesus fed a large crowd, so he feeds his followers in a spiritual way in the service of the Holy Communion.

Jesus Walks on the Water
(Mt 14.22–33; Mk 6.45–52)

16 When evening came, Jesus' disciples went
down to the lake, [17]got into a boat, and
went back across the lake towards
Capernaum. Night came on, and Jesus still

[a] **6.7** SILVER COINS: *A silver coin was the daily wage of a rural worker (see Mt 20.2).*

[b] **6.14** THE PROPHET: *See 1.21.*

had not come to them. [18]By then a strong
wind was blowing and stirring up the water.
[19]The disciples had rowed about five or six
kilometres when they saw Jesus walking on
the water, coming near the boat, and they
were terrified. [20]"Don't be afraid," Jesus told
them, "it is I!" [21]Then they willingly took
him into the boat, and immediately the boat
reached land at the place they were heading
for.

The People Seek Jesus

22 Next day the crowd which had stayed on
the other side of the lake realized that there
had been only one boat there. They knew
that Jesus had not gone in it with his
disciples, but that they had left without
him. [23]Other boats, which were from
Tiberias, came to shore near the place
where the crowd had eaten the bread after
the Lord had given thanks. [24]When the
crowd saw that Jesus was not there, nor his
disciples, they got into those boats and
went to Capernaum, looking for him.

Jesus the Bread of Life

25 When the people found Jesus on the
other side of the lake, they said to him,
"Teacher, when did you get here?"

26 Jesus answered, "I am telling you the
truth: you are looking for me because you
ate the bread and had all you wanted, not
because you understood my miracles. [27]Do
not work for food that goes bad; instead,
work for the food that lasts for eternal life.
This is the food which the Son of Man will
give you, because God, the Father, has put
his mark of approval on him."

28 So they asked him, "What can we do in
order to do what God wants us to do?"

29 Jesus answered, "What God wants you to
do is to believe in the one he sent."

30 They replied, "What miracle will you
perform so that we may see it and believe
you? What will you do? [31]Our ancestors ate
manna in the desert, just as the scripture
says, 'He gave them bread from heaven to
eat.' "

32 "I am telling you the truth," Jesus said.
"What Moses gave you was not[a] the bread
from heaven; it is my Father who gives you
the real bread from heaven. [33]For the bread
that God gives is he who comes down from
heaven and gives life to the world."

34 "Sir," they asked him, "give us this bread
always."

35 "I am the bread of life," Jesus told them.
"Those who come to me will never be
hungry; those who believe in me will never
be thirsty. [36]Now, I told you that you have
seen me but will not believe. [37]Everyone
whom my Father gives me will come to me.
I will never turn away anyone who comes
to me, [38]because I have come down from
heaven to do not my own will but the will
of him who sent me. [39]And it is the will of
him who sent me that I should not lose any
of all those he has given me, but that I
should raise them all to life on the last day.
[40]For what my Father wants is that all who
see the Son and believe in him should have
eternal life. And I will raise them to life on
the last day."

41 The people started grumbling about him,
because he said, "I am the bread that came
down from heaven." [42]So they said, "This
man is Jesus son of Joseph, isn't he? We
know his father and mother. How, then,
does he now say he came down from
heaven?"

43 Jesus answered, "Stop grumbling among
yourselves. [44]No one can come to me
unless the Father who sent me draws him
to me; and I will raise him to life on the last
day. [45]The prophets wrote, 'Everyone will
be taught by God.' Anyone who hears the
Father and learns from him comes to me.
[46]This does not mean that anyone has seen
the Father; he who is from God is the only
one who has seen the Father. [47]I am telling
you the truth: he who believes has eternal
life. [48]I am the bread of life. [49]Your
ancestors ate manna in the desert, but they
died. [50]But the bread that comes down
from heaven is of such a kind that whoever
eats it will not die. [51]I am the living bread
that came down from heaven. If anyone
eats this bread, he will live for ever. The
bread that I will give him is my flesh,
which I give so that the world may live."

[a] **6.32** What Moses gave you was not; *or* It was not Moses who gave you.

52 This started an angry argument among
them. "How can this man give us his flesh
to eat?" they asked.
53 Jesus said to them, "I am telling you the
truth: if you do not eat the flesh of the Son
of Man and drink his blood, you will not
have life in yourselves. 54 Those who eat my
flesh and drink my blood have eternal life,
and I will raise them to life on the last day.
55 For my flesh is the real food; my blood is
the real drink. 56 Those who eat my flesh
and drink my blood live in me, and I live in
them. 57 The living Father sent me, and
because of him I live also. In the same way
whoever eats me will live because of me.
58 This, then, is the bread that came down
from heaven; it is not like the bread that
your ancestors ate. They later died, but
those who eat this bread will live for ever."
59 Jesus said this as he taught in the
synagogue in Capernaum.

The Words of Eternal Life

60 Many of his followers heard this and said,
"This teaching is too hard. Who can listen to
it?"
61 Without being told, Jesus knew that they
were grumbling about this, so he said to
them, "Does this make you want to give
up? 62 Suppose, then, that you should see
the Son of Man go back up to the place
where he was before? 63 What gives life is
God's Spirit; human power is of no use at
all. The words I have spoken to you bring
God's life-giving Spirit. 64 Yet some of you
do not believe." (Jesus knew from the very
beginning who were the ones that would
not believe and which one would betray
him.) 65 And he added, "This is the very
reason I told you that no one can come to
me unless the Father makes it possible for
him to do so."
66 Because of this, many of Jesus' followers
turned back and would not go with him
any more. 67 So he asked the twelve
disciples, "And you – would you also like to
leave?"
68 Simon Peter answered him, "Lord, to
whom would we go? You have the words
that give eternal life. 69 And now we believe
and know that you are the Holy One who
has come from God."
70 Jesus replied, "I chose the twelve of you,
didn't I? Yet one of you is a devil!" 71 He
was talking about Judas, the son of Simon
Iscariot. For Judas, even though he was one
of the twelve disciples, was going to betray
him.

Jesus and his Brothers

7 After this, Jesus travelled in Galilee; he
did not want to travel in Judea,
because the Jewish authorities there
were wanting to kill him. 2 The time for the
Festival of Shelters was near, 3 so Jesus'
brothers said to him, "Leave this place and
go to Judea, so that your followers will see
the things that you are doing. 4 No one
hides what he is doing if he wants to be
well known. Since you are doing these
things, let the whole world know about
you!" 5 (Not even his brothers believed in
him.)
6 Jesus said to them, "The right time for
me has not yet come. Any time is right for
you. 7 The world cannot hate you, but it
hates me, because I keep telling it that its
ways are bad. 8 You go on to the festival. I
am not going[a] to this festival, because the
right time has not come for me." 9 He said
this, and then stayed on in Galilee.

Jesus at the Festival of Shelters

10 After his brothers had gone to the
festival, Jesus also went; however, he did
not go openly, but secretly. 11 The Jewish
authorities were looking for him at the
festival. "Where is he?" they asked.
12 There was much whispering about him
in the crowd. "He is a good man," some
people said. "No," others said, "he is
misleading the people." 13 But no one
talked about him openly, because they were
afraid of the Jewish authorities.
14 The festival was nearly half over when
Jesus went to the Temple and began
teaching. 15 The Jewish authorities were
greatly surprised and said, "How does this
man know so much when he has never had
any training?"

[a] **7.8** I am not going; *some manuscripts have* I am not yet going.

16 Jesus answered, "What I teach is not my
own teaching, but it comes from God, who
sent me. [17]Whoever is willing to do what
God wants will know whether what I teach
comes from God or whether I speak on my
own authority. [18]A person who speaks on
his own authority is trying to gain glory for
himself. But he who wants glory for the
one who sent him is honest, and there is
nothing false in him. [19]Moses gave you the
Law, didn't he? But not one of you obeys
the Law. Why are you trying to kill me?"
20 "You have a demon in you!" the crowd
answered. "Who is trying to kill you?"
21 Jesus answered, "I performed one
miracle, and you were all surprised.
[22]Moses ordered you to circumcise your
sons (although it was not Moses but your
ancestors who started it), and so you
circumcise a boy on the Sabbath. [23]If a boy
is circumcised on the Sabbath so that
Moses' Law is not broken, why are you
angry with me because I made a man
completely well on the Sabbath? [24]Stop
judging by external standards, and judge by
true standards."

Is he the Messiah?

25 Some of the people of Jerusalem said,
"Isn't this the man the authorities are
trying to kill? [26]Look! He is talking in
public, and they say nothing against him!
Can it be that they really know that he is
the Messiah? [27]But when the Messiah
comes, no one will know where he is from.
And we all know where this man comes
from."
28 As Jesus taught in the Temple, he said in
a loud voice, "Do you really know me and
know where I am from? I have not come on
my own authority. He who sent me,
however, is truthful. You do not know him,
[29]but I know him, because I come from
him and he sent me."
30 Then they tried to seize him, but no one
laid a hand on him, because his hour had
not yet come. [31]But many in the crowd
believed in him and said, "When the
Messiah comes, will he perform more
miracles than this man has?"

Guards are Sent to Arrest Jesus

32 The Pharisees heard the crowd
whispering these things about Jesus, so
they and the chief priests sent some guards
to arrest him. [33]Jesus said, "I shall be with
you a little while longer, and then I shall go
away to him who sent me. [34]You will look
for me, but you will not find me, because
you cannot go where I will be."
35 The Jewish authorities said among
themselves, "Where is he about to go so
that we shall not find him? Will he go to
the Greek cities where our people live, and
teach the Greeks? [36]He says that we will
look for him but will not find him, and that
we cannot go where he will be. What does
he mean?"

Streams of Life-giving Water

37 On the last and most important day of
the festival Jesus stood up and said in a
loud voice, "Whoever is thirsty should
come to me, and [38]whoever believes in me
should drink. As the scripture says, 'Streams
of life-giving water will pour out from his
side.' "[a] [39]Jesus said this about the Spirit,
which those who believed in him were
going to receive. At that time the Spirit had
not yet been given, because Jesus had not
been raised to glory.

Division among the People

40 Some of the people in the crowd heard
him say this and said, "This man is really
the Prophet!"[b]
41 Others said, "He is the Messiah!"
But others said, "The Messiah will not
come from Galilee! [42]The scripture says
that the Messiah will be a descendant of
King David and will be born in Bethlehem,
the town where David lived." [43]So there
was a division in the crowd because of
Jesus. [44]Some wanted to seize him, but no
one laid a hand on him.

[a] **7.38** *Jesus' words in verses 37–38 may be translated:* "Whoever is thirsty should come to me and drink. [38]As the scripture says, 'Streams of life-giving water will pour out from within anyone who believes in me.' "

[b] **7.40** THE PROPHET: *See 1.21.*

The Unbelief of the Jewish Authorities

45 When the guards went back, the chief
priests and Pharisees asked them, “Why
did you not bring him?”
46 The guards answered, “Nobody has ever
talked like this man!”
47 “Did he fool you, too?” the Pharisees
asked them. 48“Have you ever known one
of the authorities or one Pharisee to believe
in him? 49This crowd does not know the
Law of Moses, so they are under God’s
curse!”
50 One of the Pharisees there was
Nicodemus, the man who had gone to see
Jesus before. He said to the others,
51“According to our Law we cannot
condemn anyone before hearing him and
finding out what he has done.”
52 “Well,” they answered, “are you also
from Galilee? Study the
Scriptures and you will learn
that no prophet ever comes[a]
from Galilee.”

The Woman Caught in Adultery

8 [Then everyone went
home, but Jesus went to
the Mount of Olives.
2Early the next morning he
went back to the Temple. All
the people gathered round
him, and he sat down and
began to teach them. 3The
teachers of the Law and the
Pharisees brought in a woman
who had been caught
committing adultery, and they made her
stand before them all. 4“Teacher,” they said
to Jesus, “this woman was caught in the
very act of committing adultery. 5In our
Law Moses commanded that such a
woman must be stoned to death. Now,
what do you say?” 6They said this to trap
Jesus, so that they could accuse him. But he
bent over and wrote on the ground with
his finger.
7 As they stood there asking him
questions, he straightened himself up and
said to them, “Whichever one of you has
committed no sin may throw the first
stone at her.” 8Then he bent over again
and wrote on the ground. 9When they
heard this, they all left, one by one, the
older ones first. Jesus was left alone, with
the woman still standing there. 10He
straightened himself up and said to her,
“Where are they? Is there no one left to
condemn you?”
11 “No one, sir,” she answered.
“Well, then,” Jesus said, “I do not
condemn you either. Go, but do not sin
again.”][b]

Jesus the Light of the World

12 Jesus spoke to the Pharisees again. “I am
the light of the world,” he said. “Whoever
follows me will have the light of life and
will never walk in darkness.”

Christians hold lighted candles to remind themselves that Jesus was the Light of the World.

13 The Pharisees said to him, “Now you are
testifying on your own behalf; what you
say proves nothing.”
14 “No,” Jesus answered, “even though I do
testify on my own behalf, what I say is
true, because I know where I came from
and where I am going. You do not know
where I came from or where I am going.
15You make judgements in a purely human
way; I pass judgement on no one. 16But if

[a] **7.52** no prophet ever comes; *one manuscript has* the Prophet will not come.

[b] **8.11** *Many manuscripts and early translations do not have this passage (8.1–11); others have it after Jn 21.24; others have it after Lk 21.38; one manuscript has it after Jn 7.36.*

I were to do so, my judgement would be
true, because I am not alone in this; the
Father who sent me is with me. [17]It is
written in your Law that when two
witnesses agree, what they say is true. [18]I
testify on my own behalf, and the Father
who sent me also testifies on my behalf."
19 "Where is your father?" they asked him.
"You know neither me nor my Father,"
Jesus answered. "If you knew me, you
would know my Father also."
20 Jesus said all this as he taught in the
Temple, in the room where the offering
boxes were placed. And no one arrested
him, because his hour had not come.

You cannot Go Where I am Going

21 Again Jesus said to them, "I will go away;
you will look for me, but you will die in
your sins. You cannot go where I am
going."
22 So the Jewish authorities said, "He says
that we cannot go where he is going. Does
this mean that he will kill himself?"
23 Jesus answered, "You belong to this
world here below, but I come from above.
You are from this world, but I am not from
this world. [24]That is why I told you that
you will die in your sins. And you will die
in your sins if you do not believe that 'I Am
Who I Am'."
25 "Who are you?" they asked him.
Jesus answered, "What I have told you
from the very beginning.[a] [26]I have much to
say about you, much to condemn you for.
The one who sent me, however, is truthful,
and I tell the world only what I have heard
from him."
27 They did not understand that Jesus was
talking to them about the Father. [28]So he
said to them, "When you lift up the Son of
Man, you will know that 'I Am Who I Am';
then you will know that I do nothing on
my own authority, but I say only what the
Father has instructed me to say. [29]And he
who sent me is with me; he has not left me
alone, because I always do what pleases
him."
30 Many who heard Jesus say these things
believed in him.

The Truth will Set you Free

31 So Jesus said to those who believed in
him, "If you obey my teaching, you are
really my disciples; [32]you will know the
truth, and the truth will set you free."
33 "We are the descendants of Abraham,"
they answered, "and we have never been
anybody's slaves. What do you mean, then,
by saying, 'You will be free'?"
34 Jesus said to them, "I am telling you the
truth: everyone who sins is a slave of sin.
[35]A slave does not belong to a family
permanently, but a son belongs there for
ever. [36]If the Son sets you free, then you
will be really free. [37]I know you are
Abraham's descendants. Yet you are trying
to kill me, because you will not accept my
teaching. [38]I talk about what my Father has
shown me, but you do what your father has
told you."
39 They answered him, "Our father is
Abraham."
"If you really were Abraham's children,"
Jesus replied, "you would do[b] the same
things that he did. [40]All I have ever done is
to tell you the truth I heard from God, yet
you are trying to kill me. Abraham did
nothing like this! [41]You are doing what
your father did."
"God himself is the only Father we
have," they answered, "and we are his true
children."
42 Jesus said to them, "If God really were
your Father, you would love me, because I
came from God and now I am here. I did
not come on my own authority, but he sent
me. [43]Why do you not understand what I
say? It is because you cannot bear to listen
to my message. [44]You are the children of
your father, the Devil, and you want to
follow your father's desires. From the very
beginning he was a murderer and has never
been on the side of truth, because there is
no truth in him. When he tells a lie, he is
only doing what is natural to him, because
he is a liar and the father of all lies. [45]But I
tell the truth, and that is why you do not
believe me. [46]Which one of you can prove
that I am guilty of sin? If I tell the truth,
then why do you not believe me? [47]He who

[a] **8.25** What I have told you from the very beginning; *or* Why should I speak to you at all?

[b] **8.39** If you really were . . . you would do; *some manuscripts have* If you are . . . do.

comes from God listens to God's words.
You, however, are not from God, and that is
why you will not listen."

Jesus and Abraham

48 They asked Jesus, "Were we not right in
saying that you are a Samaritan and have a
demon in you?"
49 "I have no demon," Jesus answered. "I
honour my Father, but you dishonour me.
50I am not seeking honour for myself. But
there is one who is seeking it and who
judges in my favour. 51I am telling you the
truth: whoever obeys my teaching will
never die."
52 They said to him, "Now we are certain
that you have a demon! Abraham died, and
the prophets died, yet you say that whoever
obeys your teaching will never die. 53Our
father Abraham died; you do not claim to be
greater than Abraham, do you? And the
prophets also died. Who do you think you
are?"
54 Jesus answered, "If I were to honour
myself, that honour would be worth
nothing. The one who honours me is my
Father – the very one you say is your God.
55You have never known him, but I know
him. If I were to say that I do not know him,
I would be a liar like you. But I do know
him, and I obey his word. 56Your father
Abraham rejoiced that he was to see the
time of my coming; he saw it and was glad."
57 They said to him, "You are not even fifty
years old – and you have seen Abraham?"[a]
58 "I am telling you the truth," Jesus replied.
"Before Abraham was born, 'I Am'."
59 Then they picked up stones to throw at
him, but Jesus hid himself and left the
Temple.

Jesus Heals a Man Born Blind

9 As Jesus was walking along, he saw a
man who had been born blind. 2His
disciples asked him, "Teacher, whose
sin caused him to be born blind? Was it his
own or his parents' sin?"
3 Jesus answered, "His blindness has
nothing to do with his sins or his parents'
sins. He is blind so that God's power might
be seen at work in him. 4As long as it is day,
we must keep on doing the work of him
who sent me; night is coming when no one
can work. 5While I am in the world, I am
the light for the world."
6 After he said this, Jesus spat on the
ground and made some mud with the
spittle; he rubbed the mud on the man's
eyes 7and said, "Go and wash your face in
the Pool of Siloam." (This name means
"Sent".) So the man went, washed his face,
and came back seeing.
8 His neighbours, then, and the people
who had seen him begging before this,
asked, "Isn't this the man who used to sit
and beg?"
9 Some said, "He is the one," but others
said, "No he isn't; he just looks like him."
So the man himself said, "I am the man."
10 "How is it that you can now see?" they
asked him.
11 He answered, "The man called Jesus made
some mud, rubbed it on my eyes, and told
me to go to Siloam and wash my face. So I
went, and as soon as I washed, I could see."
12 "Where is he?" they asked.
"I don't know," he answered.

The Pharisees Investigate the Healing

13 Then they took to the Pharisees the man
who had been blind. 14The day that Jesus
made the mud and cured him of his
blindness was a Sabbath. 15The Pharisees,
then, asked the man again how he had
received his sight. He told them, "He put
some mud on my eyes; I washed my face,
and now I can see."
16 Some of the Pharisees said, "The man
who did this cannot be from God, for he
does not obey the Sabbath law."
Others, however, said, "How could a man
who is a sinner perform such miracles as
these?" And there was a division among
them.
17 So the Pharisees asked the man once
more, "You say he cured you of your
blindness – well, what do you say about
him?"

[a] **8.57** you have seen Abraham?; *some manuscripts have* has Abraham seen you?

"He is a prophet," the man answered.
18 The Jewish authorities, however, were not
willing to believe that he had been blind and
could now see, until they called his parents
19and asked them, "Is this your son? You say
that he was born blind; how is it, then, that
he can now see?"
20 His parents answered, "We know that he
is our son, and we know that he was born
blind. 21But we do not know how it is that
he is now able to see, nor do we know who
cured him of his blindness. Ask him; he is
old enough, and he can answer for himself!"
22His parents said this because they were
afraid of the Jewish authorities, who had
already agreed that anyone who said he
believed that Jesus was the Messiah would
be expelled from the synagogue. 23That is
why his parents said, "He is old enough; ask
him!"
24 A second time they called back the man
who had been born blind, and said to him,
"Promise before God that you will tell the
truth! We know that this man who cured
you is a sinner."
25 "I do not know if he is a sinner or not,"
the man replied. "One thing I do know: I
was blind, and now I see."
26 "What did he do to you?" they asked.
"How did he cure you of your blindness?"
27 "I have already told you," he answered,
"and you would not listen. Why do you
want to hear it again? Maybe you, too,
would like to be his disciples?"
28 They cursed him and said, "You are that
fellow's disciple; but we are Moses'
disciples. 29We know that God spoke to
Moses; as for that fellow, however, we do
not even know where he comes from!"
30 The man answered, "What a strange thing
that is! You do not know where he comes
from, but he cured me of my blindness!
31We know that God does not listen to
sinners; he does listen to people who respect
him and do what he wants them to do.
32Since the beginning of the world nobody
has ever heard of anyone giving sight to a
person born blind. 33Unless this man came
from God, he would not be able to do a
thing."
34 They answered, "You were born and
brought up in sin – and you are trying to
teach us?" And they expelled him from the
synagogue.

Spiritual Blindness

35 When Jesus heard what had happened,
he found the man and asked him, "Do you
believe in the Son of Man?"
36 The man answered, "Tell me who he is,
sir, so that I can believe in him!"
37 Jesus said to him, "You have already seen
him, and he is the one who is talking with
you now."
38 "I believe, Lord!" the man said, and knelt
down before Jesus.
39 Jesus said, "I came to this world to judge,
so that the blind should see and those who
see should become blind."
40 Some Pharisees who were there with him
heard him say this and asked him, "Surely
you don't mean that we are blind, too?"
41 Jesus answered, "If you were blind, then
you would not be guilty; but since you
claim that you can see, this means that you
are still guilty."

The Parable of the Shepherd

10 Jesus said, "I am telling you the truth:
the man who does not enter the
sheepfold by the gate, but climbs in
some other way, is a thief and a robber.
2The man who goes in through the gate is
the shepherd of the sheep. 3The gatekeeper
opens the gate for him; the sheep hear his
voice as he calls his own sheep by name,
and he leads them out. 4When he has
brought them out, he goes ahead of them,
and the sheep follow him, because they
know his voice. 5They will not follow
someone else; instead, they will run away
from such a person, because they do not
know his voice."
6 Jesus told them this parable, but they did
not understand what he meant.

Jesus the Good Shepherd

7 So Jesus said again, "I am telling you the
truth: I am the gate for the sheep. 8All
others who came before me are thieves and

robbers, but the sheep did not listen to
them. [9]I am the gate. Whoever comes in by
me will be saved; they will come in and go
out and find pasture. [10]The thief comes
only in order to steal, kill, and destroy. I
have come in order that you might have
life – life in all its fullness.
11 "I am the good shepherd, who is willing
to die for the sheep. [12]When the hired
man, who is not a shepherd and does not
own the sheep, sees a wolf coming, he
leaves the sheep and runs away; so the
wolf snatches the sheep and scatters them.
[13]The hired man runs away because he is
only a hired man and does not care about
the sheep. [14–15]I am the good shepherd. As
the Father knows me and I know the
Father, in the same way I know my sheep
and they know me. And I am willing to die
for them. [16]There are other sheep which
belong to me that are not in this
sheepfold. I must bring them, too; they
will listen to my voice, and they will
become[a] one flock with one shepherd.

17 "The Father loves me because I am willing
to give up my life, in order that I may receive
it back again. [18]No one takes my life away
from me. I give it up of my own free will. I
have the right to give it up, and I have the
right to take it back. This is what my Father
has commanded me to do."
19 Again there was a division among the
people because of these words. [20]Many of
them were saying, "He has a demon! He is
mad! Why do you listen to him?"
21 But others were saying, "A man with a
demon could not talk like this! How could
a demon give sight to blind people?"

Jesus is Rejected

22 It was winter, and the Festival of the
Dedication of the Temple was being
celebrated in Jerusalem. [23]Jesus was
walking in Solomon's Porch in the Temple,
[24]when the people gathered round him
and asked, "How long are you going to
keep us in suspense? Tell us the plain
truth: are you the Messiah?"
25 Jesus answered, "I have already
told you, but you would not believe
me. The things I do by my Father's
authority speak on my behalf; [26]but
you will not believe, for you are not
my sheep. [27]My sheep listen to my
voice; I know them, and they follow
me. [28]I give them eternal life, and
they shall never die. No one can
snatch them away from me. [29]What
my Father has given me is greater[b]
than everything, and no one can
snatch them away from the Father's
care. [30]The Father and I are one."
31 Then the people again picked up
stones to throw at him. [32]Jesus said
to them, "I have done many good
deeds in your presence which the
Father gave me to do; for which one
of these do you want to stone me?"

Jesus said he was a good shepherd who looked after his sheep very carefully.

[a] **10.16** they will become; *some manuscripts have* there will be.

[b] **10.29** What my Father has given me is greater; *some manuscripts have* My Father, who gave them to me, is greater.

33 They replied, "We do not want to stone
you because of any good deeds, but because
of your blasphemy! You are only a man, but
you are trying to make yourself God!"
34 Jesus answered, "It is written in your own
Law that God said, 'You are gods.' 35We
know that what the scripture says is true for
ever; and God called those people gods, the
people to whom his message was given. 36As
for me, the Father chose me and sent me
into the world. How, then, can you say that
I blaspheme because I said that I am the Son
of God? 37Do not believe me, then, if I am
not doing the things my Father wants me to
do. 38But if I do them, even though you do
not believe me, you should at least believe
my deeds, in order that you may know once
and for all that the Father is in me and that
I am in the Father."
39 Once more they tried to seize Jesus, but
he slipped out of their hands.
40 Jesus then went back again across the
River Jordan to the place where John had
been baptizing, and he stayed there.
41Many people came to him. "John
performed no miracles," they said, "but
everything he said about this man was
true." 42And many people there believed in
him.

The Death of Lazarus

11 A man named Lazarus, who lived in
Bethany, was ill. Bethany was the town
where Mary and her sister Martha
lived. 2(This Mary was the one who poured
the perfume on the Lord's feet and wiped
them with her hair; it was her brother
Lazarus who was ill.) 3The sisters sent Jesus
a message: "Lord, your dear friend is ill."
4 When Jesus heard it, he said, "The final
result of this illness will not be the death of
Lazarus; this has happened in order to bring
glory to God, and it will be the means by
which the Son of God will receive glory."
5 Jesus loved Martha and her sister and
Lazarus. 6Yet when he received the news
that Lazarus was ill, he stayed where he was
for two more days. 7Then he said to the
disciples, "Let us go back to Judea."
8 "Teacher," the disciples answered, "just a
short time ago the people there wanted to
stone you; and are you planning to go
back?"
9 Jesus said, "A day has twelve hours,
hasn't it? So whoever walks in broad
daylight does not stumble, for they see the
light of this world. 10But if they walk
during the night they stumble, because
they have no light." 11Jesus said this and
then added, "Our friend Lazarus has fallen
asleep, but I will go and wake him up."
12 The disciples answered, "If he is asleep,
Lord, he will get well."
13 Jesus meant that Lazarus had died, but
they thought he meant natural sleep. 14So
Jesus told them plainly, "Lazarus is dead,
15but for your sake I am glad that I was not
with him, so that you will believe. Let us go
to him."
16 Thomas (called the Twin) said to his
fellow-disciples, "Let us all go with the
Teacher, so that we may die with him!"

Jesus the Resurrection and the Life

17 When Jesus arrived, he found that
Lazarus had been buried four days before.
18Bethany was less than three kilometres
from Jerusalem, 19and many Judeans had
come to see Martha and Mary to comfort
them over their brother's death.
20 When Martha heard that Jesus was
coming, she went out to meet him, but
Mary stayed in the house. 21Martha said to
Jesus, "If you had been here, Lord, my
brother would not have died! 22But I know
that even now God will give you whatever
you ask him for."
23 "Your brother will rise to life," Jesus told
her.
24 "I know," she replied, "that he will rise to
life on the last day."
25 Jesus said to her, "I am the resurrection
and the life. Those who believe in me will
live, even though they die; 26and all those
who live and believe in me will never die.
Do you believe this?"
27 "Yes, Lord!" she answered. "I do believe
that you are the Messiah, the Son of God,
who was to come into the world."

Jesus Weeps

28 After Martha said this, she went back and
called her sister Mary privately. "The
Teacher is here," she told her, "and is
asking for you." 29 When Mary heard this,
she got up and hurried out to meet him.
30 (Jesus had not yet arrived in the village,
but was still in the place where Martha had
met him.) 31 The people who were in the
house with Mary, comforting her, followed
her when they saw her get up and hurry
out. They thought that she was going to
the grave to weep there.
32 Mary arrived where Jesus was, and as
soon as she saw him, she fell at his feet.
"Lord," she said, "if you had been here, my
brother would not have died!"
33 Jesus saw her weeping, and he saw how
the people who were with her were
weeping also; his heart was touched, and
he was deeply moved. 34 "Where have you
buried him?" he asked them.

"Come and see, Lord," they answered.

35 Jesus wept. 36 "See how much he loved
him!" the people said.
37 But some of them said, "He gave sight to
the blind man, didn't he? Could he not
have kept Lazarus from dying?"

Lazarus is Brought to Life

38 Deeply moved once more, Jesus went to
the tomb, which was a cave with a stone
placed at the entrance. 39 "Take the stone
away!" Jesus ordered.

Martha, the dead man's sister, answered,
"There will be a bad smell, Lord. He has
been buried four days!"

40 Jesus said to her, "Didn't I tell you that
you would see God's glory if you believed?"
41 They took the stone away. Jesus looked
up and said, "I thank you, Father, that you
listen to me. 42 I know that you always
listen to me, but I say this for the sake of
the people here, so that they will believe
that you sent me." 43 After he had said this,
he called out in a loud voice, "Lazarus,
come out!" 44 He came out, his hands and
feet wrapped in grave clothes, and with a
cloth round his face. "Untie him," Jesus
told them, "and let him go."

The Plot against Jesus

(Mt 26.1–5; Mk 14.1–2; Lk 22.1–2)

45 Many of the people who had come to
visit Mary saw what Jesus did, and they
believed in him. 46 But some of them
returned to the Pharisees and told them
what Jesus had done. 47 So the Pharisees
and the chief priests met with the Council
and said, "What shall we do? Look at all the
miracles this man is performing! 48 If we let
him go on in this way, everyone will
believe in him, and the Roman authorities
will take action and destroy our Temple
and our nation!"
49 One of them, named Caiaphas, who was
High Priest that year, said, "What fools you
are! 50 Don't you realize that it is better for
you to let one man die for the people,
instead of having the whole nation
destroyed?" 51 Actually, he did not say this
of his own accord; rather, as he was High
Priest that year, he was prophesying that
Jesus was going to die for the Jewish people,
52 and not only for them, but also to bring
together into one body all the scattered
people of God.
53 From that day on the Jewish authorities
made plans to kill Jesus. 54 So Jesus did not
travel openly in Judea, but left and went to
a place near the desert, to a town named
Ephraim, where he stayed with the
disciples.
55 The time for the Passover Festival was
near, and many people went up from the
country to Jerusalem to perform the ritual
of purification before the festival. 56 They
were looking for Jesus, and as they gathered
in the Temple, they asked one another,
"What do you think? Surely he will not
come to the festival, will he?" 57 The chief
priests and the Pharisees had given orders
that if anyone knew where Jesus was, he
must report it, so that they could arrest
him.

Jesus is Anointed at Bethany

(Mt 26.6–13; Mk 14.3–9)

12 Six days before the Passover, Jesus
went to Bethany, the home of Lazarus,
the man he had raised from death.

[2]They prepared a dinner for him there,
which Martha helped to serve; Lazarus was
one of those who were sitting at the table
with Jesus. [3]Then Mary took half a litre of a
very expensive perfume made of pure nard,
poured it on Jesus' feet, and wiped them
with her hair. The sweet smell of the
perfume filled the whole house. [4]One of
Jesus' disciples, Judas Iscariot – the one who
was going to betray him – said, [5]"Why
wasn't this perfume sold for three hundred
silver coins[a] and the money given to the
poor?" [6]He said this, not because he cared
about the poor, but because he was a thief.
He carried the money bag and would help
himself from it.
7 But Jesus said, "Leave her alone! Let her
keep what she has for the day of my burial.
[8]You will always have poor people with
you, but you will not always have me."

The Plot against Lazarus

9 A large number of people heard that
Jesus was in Bethany, so they went there,
not only because of Jesus but also to see
Lazarus, whom Jesus had raised from death.
[10]So the chief priests made plans to kill
Lazarus too, [11]because on his account
many Jews were rejecting them and
believing in Jesus.

The Triumphant Entry into Jerusalem

(Mt 21.1–11; Mk 11.1–11; Lk 19.28–40)

12 The next day the large crowd that had
come to the Passover Festival heard that
Jesus was coming to Jerusalem. [13]So they
took branches of palm trees and went out
to meet him, shouting, "Praise God! God
bless him who comes in the name of the
Lord! God bless the King of Israel!"
14 Jesus found a donkey and rode on it, just
as the scripture says,

15 "Do not be afraid, city of Zion!
Here comes your king,
riding on a young donkey."

16 His disciples did not understand this at
the time; but when Jesus had been raised to
glory, they remembered that the scripture
said this about him and that they had done
this for him.
17 The people who had been with Jesus
when he called Lazarus out of the grave and
raised him from death had reported what
had happened. [18]That was why the crowd
met him – because they heard that he had
performed this miracle. [19]The Pharisees
then said to one another, "You see, we are
not succeeding at all! Look, the whole
world is following him!"

Some Greeks Seek Jesus

20 Some Greeks were among those who had
gone to Jerusalem to worship during the
festival. [21]They went to Philip (he was from
Bethsaida in Galilee) and said, "Sir, we want
to see Jesus."
22 Philip went and told Andrew, and the
two of them went and told Jesus. [23]Jesus
answered them, "The hour has now come
for the Son of Man to receive great glory.
[24]I am telling you the truth: a grain of
wheat remains no more than a single grain
unless it is dropped into the ground and
dies. If it does die, then it produces many
grains. [25]Those who love their own life will
lose it; those who hate their own life in
this world will keep it for life eternal.
[26]Whoever wants to serve me must follow
me, so that my servant will be with me
where I am. And my Father will honour
anyone who serves me.

Jesus Speaks about his Death

27 "Now my heart is troubled – and what
shall I say? Shall I say, 'Father, do not let
this hour come upon me'? But that is why
I came – so that I might go through this
hour of suffering. [28]Father, bring glory to
your name!"
Then a voice spoke from heaven, "I have
brought glory to it, and I will do so again."
29 The crowd standing there heard the
voice, and some of them said it was
thunder, while others said, "An angel spoke
to him!"
30 But Jesus said to them, "It was not for my
sake that this voice spoke, but for yours.

[a] **12.5** SILVER COINS: *See 6.7.*

[31]Now is the time for this world to be
judged; now the ruler of this world will be
overthrown. [32]When I am lifted up from
the earth, I will draw everyone to me."
[33](In saying this he indicated the kind of
death he was going to suffer.)
34 The crowd answered, "Our Law tells us
that the Messiah will live for ever. How,
then, can you say that the Son of Man must
be lifted up? Who is this Son of Man?"
35 Jesus answered, "The light will be among
you a little longer. Continue on your way
while you have the light, so that the
darkness will not come upon you; for the
one who walks in the dark does not know
where he is going. [36]Believe in the light,
then, while you have it, so that you will be
the people of the light."

The Unbelief of the People

After Jesus said this, he went off and hid
himself from them. [37]Even though he had
performed all these miracles in their
presence, they did not believe in him, [38]so
that what the prophet Isaiah had said
might come true:

"Lord, who believed the message we
told?
To whom did the Lord reveal his
power?"

39 And so they were not able to believe,
because Isaiah also said:

40 "God has blinded their eyes
and closed their minds,
so that their eyes would not see,
and their minds would not
understand,
and they would not turn to me, says
God,
for me to heal them."

41 Isaiah said this because he saw Jesus'
glory and spoke about him.
42 Even then, many of the Jewish
authorities believed in Jesus; but because of
the Pharisees they did not talk about it
openly, so as not to be expelled from the
synagogue. [43]They loved human approval
rather than the approval of God.

Judgement by Jesus' Words

44 Jesus said in a loud voice, "Whoever
believes in me believes not only in me but
also in him who sent me. [45]Whoever sees
me sees also him who sent me. [46]I have
come into the world as light, so that
everyone who believes in me should not
remain in the darkness. [47]If anyone hears
my message and does not obey it, I will not
judge him. I came, not to judge the world,
but to save it. [48]Those who reject me and
do not accept my message have one who
will judge them. The words I have spoken
will be their judge on the last day! [49]This is
true, because I have not spoken on my own
authority, but the Father who sent me has
commanded me what I must say and speak.
[50]And I know that his command brings
eternal life. What I say, then, is what the
Father has told me to say."

Jesus Washes his Disciples' Feet

13 It was now the day before the Passover
Festival. Jesus knew that the hour had
come for him to leave this world and
go to the Father. He had always loved those
in the world who were his own, and he
loved them to the very end.
2 Jesus and his disciples were at supper. The
Devil had already put into the heart of Judas,
the son of Simon Iscariot, the thought of
betraying Jesus.[a] [3]Jesus knew that the Father
had given him complete power; he knew
that he had come from God and was going
to God. [4]So he rose from the table, took off
his outer garment, and tied a towel round
his waist. [5]Then he poured some water into
a basin and began to wash the disciples' feet
and dry them with the towel round his
waist. [6]He came to Simon Peter, who said to
him, "Are you going to wash my feet, Lord?"
7 Jesus answered him, "You do not
understand now what I am doing, but you
will understand later."
8 Peter declared, "Never at any time will
you wash my feet!"

[a] **13.2** The Devil . . . betraying Jesus; *or* The Devil had already decided that Judas, the son of Simon Iscariot, would betray Jesus.

"If I do not wash your feet," Jesus
answered, "you will no longer be my
disciple."
9 Simon Peter answered, "Lord, do not
wash only my feet, then! Wash my hands
and head, too!"
10 Jesus said, "Those who have had a bath
are completely clean and do not have to
wash themselves, except for their feet.[a] All
of you are clean – all except one." [11](Jesus
already knew who was going to betray him;
that is why he said, "All of you, except one,
are clean.")
12 After Jesus had washed their feet, he put
his outer garment back on and returned to
his place at the table. "Do you understand
what I have just done to you?" he asked.
[13]"You call me Teacher and Lord, and it is
right that you do so, because that is what I
am. [14]I, your Lord and Teacher, have just
washed your feet. You, then, should wash
one another's feet. [15]I have set an example
for you, so that you will do just what I have
done for you. [16]I am telling you the truth:
slaves are never greater than their master,
and messengers are never greater than the
one who sent them. [17]Now that you
know this truth, how happy you will
be if you put it into practice!
18 "I am not talking about all of you;
I know those I have chosen. But the
scripture must come true that says,
'The man who shared my food
turned against me.' [19]I tell you this
now before it happens, so that
when it does happen, you will
believe that 'I Am Who I Am.' [20]I
am telling you the truth:
whoever receives anyone I
send receives me also; and
whoever receives me
receives him who sent me."

Jesus Predicts his Betrayal

(Mt 26.20–25; Mk 14.17–21; Lk
22.21–23)

21 After Jesus had said this,
he was deeply troubled and
declared openly, "I am telling you the
truth: one of you is going to betray me."
22 The disciples looked at one another,
completely puzzled about whom he meant.
[23]One of the disciples, the one whom Jesus
loved, was sitting next to Jesus. [24]Simon
Peter motioned to him and said, "Ask him
whom he is talking about."
25 So that disciple moved closer to Jesus'
side and asked, "Who is it, Lord?"
26 Jesus answered, "I will dip some bread in
the sauce and give it to him; he is the
man." So he took a piece of bread, dipped
it, and gave it to Judas, the son of Simon
Iscariot. [27]As soon as Judas took the bread,
Satan entered him. Jesus said to him, "Be
quick about what you are doing!" [28]None
of the others at the table understood why
Jesus said this to him. [29]Since Judas was in
charge of the money bag, some of the
disciples thought that Jesus had told him to
go and buy what they needed for the
festival, or to give something to the poor.
30 Judas accepted the bread and went out at
once. It was night.

The New Commandment

31 After Judas had left, Jesus said, "Now
the Son of Man's glory is revealed; now
God's glory is revealed through
him. [32]And if God's glory is
revealed through him,
then God will reveal
the glory of the Son
of Man in himself,
and he will do so at
once.[33]My children,
I shall not be with
you very much
longer. You will look
for me; but I tell
you now what I
told the Jewish
authorities,
'You cannot go
where I am
going.' [34]And
now I give
you a new

Jesus washed the disciples' feet to show them that all people should be equal.

[a] **13.10** *Some manuscripts do not have* except for their feet.

commandment: love one another. As I have
loved you, so you must love one another.
[35]If you have love for one another, then
everyone will know that you are my
disciples."

Jesus Predicts Peter's Denial

(Mt 26.31–35; Mk 14.27–31; Lk 22.31–34)

36 "Where are you going, Lord?" Simon
Peter asked him.
"You cannot follow me now where I am
going," answered Jesus; "but later you will
follow me."
37 "Lord, why can't I follow you now?"
asked Peter. "I am ready to die for you!"
38 Jesus answered, "Are you really ready to
die for me? I am telling you the truth:
before the cock crows you will say three
times that you do not know me.

Jesus the Way to the Father

14 "Do not be worried and upset," Jesus
told them. "Believe[a] in God and
believe also in me. [2]There are many
rooms in my Father's house, and I am going
to prepare a place for you. I would not tell
you this if it were not so.[b] [3]And after I go
and prepare a place for you, I will come
back and take you to myself, so that you
will be where I am. [4]You know the way that
leads to the place where I am going."
5 Thomas said to him, "Lord, we do not
know where you are going; so how can we
know the way to get there?"
6 Jesus answered him, "I am the way, the
truth, and the life; no one goes to the
Father except by me. [7]Now that you have
known me," he said to them, "you will
know[c] my Father also, and from now on
you do know him and you have seen him."
8 Philip said to him, "Lord, show us the
Father; that is all we need."
9 Jesus answered, "For a long time I have
been with you all; yet you do not know me,
Philip? Whoever has seen me has seen the
Father. Why, then, do you say, 'Show us the
Father'? [10]Do you not believe, Philip, that I
am in the Father and the Father is in me?
The words that I have spoken to you," Jesus
said to his disciples, "do not come from me.
The Father, who remains in me, does his
own work. [11]Believe me when I say that I
am in the Father and the Father is in me. If
not, believe because of the things I do. [12]I
am telling you the truth: those who believe
in me will do what I do – yes, they will do
even greater things, because I am going to
the Father. [13]And I will do whatever you
ask for in my name, so that the Father's
glory will be shown through the Son. [14]If
you ask me[d] for anything in my name, I
will do it.

The Promise of the Holy Spirit

15 "If you love me, you will obey my
commandments. [16]I will ask the Father,
and he will give you another Helper, who
will stay with you for ever. [17]He is the Spirit
who reveals the truth about God. The
world cannot receive him, because it
cannot see him or know him. But you
know him, because he remains with you
and is[e] in you.
18 "When I go, you will not be left all alone;
I will come back to you. [19]In a little while
the world will see me no more, but you will
see me; and because I live, you also will live.
[20]When that day comes, you will know that
I am in my Father and that you are in me,
just as I am in you.
21 "Those who accept my commandments
and obey them are the ones who love me.
My Father will love those who love me; I
too will love them and reveal myself to
them."
22 Judas (not Judas Iscariot) said, "Lord,
how can it be that you will reveal yourself
to us and not to the world?"
23 Jesus answered him, "Whoever loves me
will obey my teaching. My Father will love
him, and my Father and I will come to him
and live with him. [24]Whoever does not
love me does not obey my teaching. And
the teaching you have heard is not mine,
but comes from the Father, who sent me.

[a] **14.1** Believe; *or* You believe.
[b] **14.2** There are . . . were not so; *or* There are many rooms in my Father's house; if it were not so, would I tell you that I am going to prepare a place for you?
[c] **14.7** Now that you have known me . . . you will know; *some manuscripts have* If you had known me . . . you would know.
[d] **14.14** *Some manuscripts do not have* me.
[e] **14.17** is; *some manuscripts have* will be.

25 “I have told you this while I am still with
you. [26]The Helper, the Holy Spirit, whom
the Father will send in my name, will teach
you everything and make you remember all
that I have told you.
27 “Peace is what I leave with you; it is my
own peace that I give you. I do not give it
as the world does. Do not be worried and
upset; do not be afraid. [28]You heard me say
to you, ‘I am leaving, but I will come back
to you.’ If you loved me, you would be glad
that I am going to the Father; for he is
greater than I. [29]I have told you this now
before it all happens, so that when it does
happen, you will believe. [30]I cannot talk
with you much longer, because the ruler of
this world is coming. He has no power over
me, [31]but the world must know that I love
the Father; that is why I do everything as
he commands me.
“Come, let us go from this place.

Jesus the Real Vine

15 “I am the real vine, and my Father is
the gardener. [2]He breaks off every
branch in me that does not bear fruit,
and he prunes every branch that does bear
fruit, so that it will be clean and bear more
fruit. [3]You have been made clean already
by the teaching I have given you. [4]Remain
united to me, and I will remain united to
you. A branch cannot bear fruit by itself; it
can do so only if it remains in the vine. In
the same way you cannot bear fruit unless
you remain in me.
5 “I am the vine, and you are the
branches. Those who remain in me, and I
in them, will bear much fruit; for you can
do nothing without me. [6]Whoever does
not remain in me is thrown out like a
branch and dries up; such branches are
gathered up and thrown into the fire,
where they are burnt. [7]If you remain in
me and my words remain in you, then you
will ask for anything you wish, and you
shall have it. [8]My Father’s glory is shown
by your bearing much fruit; and in this
way you become my disciples. [9]I love you
just as the Father loves me; remain in my
love. [10]If you obey my commands, you
will remain in my love, just as I have
obeyed my Father’s commands and
remain in his love.
11 “I have told you this so that my joy may
be in you and that your joy may be
complete. [12]My commandment is this:
love one another, just as I love you. [13]The
greatest love a person can have for his
friends is to give his life for them. [14]And
you are my friends if you do what I
command you. [15]I do not call you servants
any longer, because servants do not know
what their master is doing. Instead, I call
you friends, because I have told you
everything I have heard from my Father.
[16]You did not choose me; I chose you and
appointed you to go and bear much fruit,
the kind of fruit that endures. And so the
Father will give you whatever you ask of
him in my name. [17]This, then, is what I
command you: love one another.

The World’s Hatred

18 “If the world hates you, just remember
that it has hated me first. [19]If you
belonged to the world, then the world
would love you as its own. But I chose you
from this world, and you do not belong to
it; that is why the world hates you.
[20]Remember what I told you: ‘Slaves are
not greater than their master.’ If people
persecuted me, they will persecute you
too; if they obeyed my teaching, they will
obey yours too. [21]But they will do all this
to you because you are mine; for they do
not know the one who sent me. [22]They
would not have been guilty of sin if I had
not come and spoken to them; as it is,
they no longer have any excuse for their
sin. [23]Whoever hates me hates my Father
also. [24]They would not have been guilty
of sin if I had not done among them the
things that no one else ever did; as it is,
they have seen what I did, and they hate
both me and my Father. [25]This, however,
was bound to happen so that what is
written in their Law may come true: ‘They
hated me for no reason at all.’
26 “The Helper will come – the Spirit, who
reveals the truth about God and who comes

from the Father. I will send him to you from
the Father, and he will speak about me.
[27]And you, too, will speak about me,
because you have been with me from the
very beginning.

16 "I have told you this, so that you will
not give up your faith. [2]You will be
expelled from the synagogues, and the
time will come when anyone who kills you
will think that by doing this he is serving
God. [3]People will do these things to you
because they have not known either the
Father or me. [4]But I have told you this, so
that when the time comes for them to do
these things, you will remember that I told
you.

The Work of the Holy Spirit

"I did not tell you these things at the
beginning, for I was with you. [5]But now I
am going to him who sent me, yet none of
you asks me where I am going. [6]And now
that I have told you, your hearts are full of
sadness. [7]But I am telling you the truth: it
is better for you that I go away, because if I
do not go, the Helper will not come to you.
But if I do go away, then I will send him to
you. [8]And when he comes, he will prove to
the people of the world that they are
wrong about sin and about what is right
and about God's judgement. [9]They are
wrong about sin, because they do not
believe in me; [10]they are wrong about
what is right, because I am going to the
Father and you will not see me any more;
[11]and they are wrong about judgement,
because the ruler of this world has already
been judged.
12 "I have much more to tell you, but now it
would be too much for you to bear.
[13]When, however, the Spirit comes, who
reveals the truth about God, he will lead
you into all the truth. He will not speak on
his own authority, but he will speak of what
he hears, and will tell you of things to
come. [14]He will give me glory, because he
will take what I say and tell it to you. [15]All
that my Father has is mine; that is why I
said that the Spirit will take what I give him
and tell it to you.

Sadness and Gladness

16 "In a little while you will not see me any
more, and then a little while later you will
see me."
17 Some of his disciples asked among
themselves, "What does this mean? He tells
us that in a little while we will not see him,
and then a little while later we will see him;
and he also says, 'It is because I am going to
the Father.' [18]What does this 'a little while'
mean? We don't know what he is talking
about!"
19 Jesus knew that they wanted to question
him, so he said to them, "I said, 'In a little
while you will not see me, and then a little
while later you will see me.' Is this what you
are asking about among yourselves? [20]I am
telling you the truth: you will cry and weep,
but the world will be glad; you will be sad,
but your sadness will turn into gladness.
[21]When a woman is about to give birth, she
is sad because her hour of suffering has
come; but when the baby is born, she
forgets her suffering, because she is happy
that a baby has been born into the world.
[22]That is how it is with you: now you are
sad, but I will see you again, and your hearts
will be filled with gladness, the kind of
gladness that no one can take away from
you.
23 "When that day comes, you will not ask
me for anything. I am telling you the truth:
the Father will give you whatever you ask
him for in my name.[a] [24]Until now you have
not asked for anything in my name; ask and
you will receive, so that your happiness may
be complete.

Victory over the World

25 "I have used figures of speech to tell you
these things. But the time will come when I
will not use figures of speech, but will speak
to you plainly about the Father. [26]When
that day comes, you will ask him in my
name; and I do not say that I will ask him
on your behalf, [27]for the Father himself
loves you. He loves you because you love
me and have believed that I came from
God. [28]I did come from the Father, and I

[a] **16.23** the Father will give you whatever you ask him for in my name; *some manuscripts have* if you ask the Father for anything, he will give it to you in my name.

came into the world; and now I am leaving
the world and going to the Father."
29 Then his disciples said to him, "Now you
are speaking plainly, without using figures
of speech. 30We know now that you know
everything; you do not need someone to
ask you questions. This makes us believe
that you came from God."
31 Jesus answered them, "Do you believe
now? 32The time is coming, and is already
here, when all of you will be scattered, each
of you to your own home, and I will be left
all alone. But I am not really alone, because
the Father is with me. 33I have told you this
so that you will have peace by being united
to me. The world will make you suffer. But
be brave! I have defeated the world!"

Jesus Prays for his Disciples

17 After Jesus finished saying this, he
looked up to heaven and said, "Father,
the hour has come. Give glory to your
Son, so that the Son may give glory to you.
2For you gave him authority over all
humanity, so that he might give eternal life
to all those you gave him. 3And eternal life
means knowing you, the only true God, and
knowing Jesus Christ, whom you sent. 4I
have shown your glory on earth; I have
finished the work you gave me to do.
5Father! Give me glory in your presence
now, the same glory I had with you before
the world was made.
6 "I have made you known to those you
gave me out of the world. They belonged to
you, and you gave them to me. They have
obeyed your word, 7and now they know
that everything you gave me comes from
you. 8I gave them the message that you
gave me, and they received it; they know
that it is true that I came from you, and they
believe that you sent me.
9 "I pray for them. I do not pray for the
world but for those you gave me, for they
belong to you. 10All I have is yours, and all
you have is mine; and my glory is shown
through them. 11And now I am coming to
you; I am no longer in the world, but they
are in the world. Holy Father! Keep them
safe by the power of your name, the name
you gave me,[a] so that they may be one just
as you and I are one. 12While I was with
them, I kept them safe by the power of your
name, the name you gave me.[b] I protected
them, and not one of them was lost, except
the man who was bound to be lost – so that
the scripture might come true. 13And now I
am coming to you, and I say these things in
the world so that they might have my joy in
their hearts in all its fullness. 14I gave them
your message, and the world hated them,
because they do not belong to the world,
just as I do not belong to the world. 15I do
not ask you to take them out of the world,
but I do ask you to keep them safe from the
Evil One. 16Just as I do not belong to the
world, they do not belong to the world.
17Dedicate them to yourself by means of
the truth; your word is truth. 18I sent them
into the world, just as you sent me into the
world. 19And for their sake I dedicate myself
to you, in order that they, too, may be truly
dedicated to you.
20 "I pray not only for them, but also for
those who believe in me because of their
message. 21I pray that they may all be one.
Father! May they be in us, just as you are in
me and I am in you. May they be one, so
that the world will believe that you sent me.
22I gave them the same glory you gave me,
so that they may be one, just as you and I
are one: 23I in them and you in me, so that
they may be completely one, in order that
the world may know that you sent me and
that you love them as you love me.
24 "Father! You have given them to me, and
I want them to be with me where I am, so
that they may see my glory, the glory you
gave me; for you loved me before the world
was made. 25Righteous Father! The world
does not know you, but I know you, and
these know that you sent me. 26I made you
known to them, and I will continue to do
so, in order that the love you have for me
may be in them, and so that I also may be
in them."

[a] **17.11** Keep them safe by the power of your name, the name you gave me; *some manuscripts have* By the power of your name keep safe those you have given me.
[b] **17.12** I kept them safe by the power of your name, the name you gave me; *some manuscripts have* By the power of your name I kept safe those you have given me.

The Arrest of Jesus
(Mt 26.47–56; Mk 14.43–50; Lk 22.47–53)

18 After Jesus had said this prayer, he left
with his disciples and went across the
brook called Kidron. There was a
garden in that place, and Jesus and his
disciples went in. [2]Judas, the traitor, knew
where it was, because many times Jesus had
met there with his disciples. [3]So Judas went
to the garden, taking with him a group of
Roman soldiers, and some temple guards
sent by the chief priests and the Pharisees;
they were armed and carried lanterns and
torches. [4]Jesus knew everything that was
going to happen to him, so he stepped
forward and asked them, "Who is it you are
looking for?"
5 "Jesus of Nazareth," they answered.
"I am he," he said.
Judas, the traitor, was standing there
with them. [6]When Jesus said to them, "I
am he," they moved back and fell to the
ground. [7]Again Jesus asked them, "Who is
it you are looking for?"
"Jesus of Nazareth," they said.
8 "I have already told you that I am he,"
Jesus said. "If, then, you are looking for me,
let these others go." [9](He said this so that
what he had said might come true: "Father,
I have not lost even one of those you gave
me.")
10 Simon Peter, who had a sword, drew it
and struck the High Priest's slave, cutting
off his right ear. The name of the slave was
Malchus. [11]Jesus said to Peter, "Put your
sword back in its place! Do you think that I
will not drink the cup of suffering which
my Father has given me?"

Jesus before Annas

12 Then the Roman soldiers with their
commanding officer and the Jewish guards
arrested Jesus, bound him, [13]and took him
first to Annas. He was the father-in-law of
Caiaphas, who was High Priest that year.
[14]It was Caiaphas who had advised the
Jewish authorities that it was better that
one man should die for all the people.

Peter Denies Jesus
(Mt 26.69–70; Mk 14.66–68; Lk 22.55–57)

15 Simon Peter and another disciple
followed Jesus. That other disciple was well
known to the High Priest, so he went with
Jesus into the courtyard of the High Priest's
house, [16]while Peter stayed outside by the
gate. Then the other disciple went back out,
spoke to the girl at the gate, and brought
Peter inside. [17]The girl at the gate said to
Peter, "Aren't you also one of the disciples
of that man?"
"No, I am not," answered Peter.
18 It was cold, so the servants and guards
had built a charcoal fire and were standing
round it, warming themselves. So Peter
went over and stood with them, warming
himself.

The High Priest Questions Jesus
(Mt 26.59–66; Mk 14.55–64; Lk 22.66–71)

19 The High Priest questioned Jesus about
his disciples and about his teaching.
[20]Jesus answered, "I have always spoken
publicly to everyone; all my teaching was
done in the synagogues and in the
Temple, where all the people come
together. I have never said anything in
secret. [21]Why, then, do you question me?
Question the people who heard me. Ask
them what I told them – they know what
I said."
22 When Jesus said this, one of the guards
there slapped him and said, "How dare you
talk like that to the High Priest!"
23 Jesus answered him, "If I have said
anything wrong, tell everyone here what it
was. But if I am right in what I have said,
why do you hit me?"
24 Then Annas sent him, still bound, to
Caiaphas the High Priest.

Peter Denies Jesus Again
(Mt 26.71–75; Mk 14.69–72; Lk 22.58–62)

25 Peter was still standing there keeping
himself warm. So the others said to him,
"Aren't you also one of the disciples of that
man?"
But Peter denied it. "No, I am not," he
said.

26 One of the High Priest's slaves, a relative
of the man whose ear Peter had cut off,
spoke up. "Didn't I see you with him in the
garden?" he asked.
27 Again Peter said "No" – and at once a
cock crowed.

Jesus is Brought before Pilate

(Mt 27.1–2, 11–14; Mk 15.1–5; Lk 23.1–5)

28 Early in the morning Jesus was taken
from Caiaphas' house to the governor's
palace. The Jewish authorities did not go
inside the palace, for they wanted to keep
themselves ritually clean, in order to be
able to eat the Passover meal. [29]So Pilate
went outside to them and asked, "What
do you accuse this man of?"
30 Their answer was, "We would not have
brought him to you if he had not
committed a crime."
31 Pilate said to them, "Then you
yourselves take him and try him according
to your own law."
They replied, "We are not allowed to
put anyone to death." [32](This happened
in order to make the words of Jesus come
true, the words he used when he indicated
the kind of death he would die.)
33 Pilate went back into the palace and
called Jesus. "Are you the King of the
Jews?" he asked him.
34 Jesus answered, "Does this question
come from you or have others told you
about me?"
35 Pilate replied, "Do you think I am a Jew?
It was your own people and the chief
priests who handed you over to me. What
have you done?"
36 Jesus said, "My kingdom does not belong
to this world; if my kingdom belonged to
this world, my followers would fight to
keep me from being handed over to the
Jewish authorities. No, my kingdom does
not belong here!"
37 So Pilate asked him, "Are you a king, then?"
Jesus answered, "You say that I am a king.
I was born and came into the world for this
one purpose, to speak about the truth.
Whoever belongs to the truth listens to me."
38 "And what is truth?" Pilate asked.

Jesus is Sentenced to Death

(Mt 27.15–31; Mk 15.6–20; Lk 23.13–25)

Then Pilate went back outside to the
people and said to them, "I cannot find any
reason to condemn him. [39]But according
to the custom you have, I always set free a
prisoner for you during the Passover. Do
you want me to set free for you the King of
the Jews?"
40 They answered him with a shout, "No,
not him! We want Barabbas!" (Barabbas was
a bandit.)

Pontius Pilate sent Jesus to his death.

19 Then Pilate took Jesus and had him
whipped. [2]The soldiers made a crown
out of thorny branches and put it on
his head; then they put a purple robe on
him [3]and came to him and said, "Long live
the King of the Jews!" And they went up
and slapped him.
4 Pilate went out once more and said to
the crowd, "Look, I will bring him out here
to you to let you see that I cannot find any
reason to condemn him." [5]So Jesus came
out, wearing the crown of thorns and the
purple robe. Pilate said to them, "Look!
Here is the man!"
6 When the chief priests and the temple
guards saw him, they shouted, "Crucify
him! Crucify him!"

Pilate said to them, "You take him, then,
and crucify him. I find no reason to
condemn him."
7 The crowd answered back, "We have a
law that says he ought to die, because he
claimed to be the Son of God."
8 When Pilate heard this, he was even more
afraid. [9]He went back into the palace and
asked Jesus, "Where do you come from?"
But Jesus did not answer. [10]Pilate said to
him, "You will not speak to me? Remember,
I have the authority to set you free and also
to have you crucified."
11 Jesus answered, "You have authority over
me only because it was given to you by God.
So the man who handed me over to you is
guilty of a worse sin."
12 When Pilate heard this, he tried to find a
way to set Jesus free. But the crowd shouted
back, "If you set him free, that means that
you are not the Emperor's friend! Anyone
who claims to be a king is a rebel against the
Emperor!"
13 When Pilate heard these words, he took
Jesus outside and sat down on the judge's
seat in the place called "The Stone
Pavement". (In Hebrew the name is
"Gabbatha".) [14]It was then almost noon of
the day before the Passover. Pilate said to
the people, "Here is your king!"
15 They shouted back, "Kill him! Kill him!
Crucify him!"
Pilate asked them, "Do you want me to
crucify your king?"
The chief priests answered, "The only king we have is the Emperor!"
16 Then Pilate handed Jesus over to them to be crucified.

Jesus is Crucified

(Mt 27.32–44; Mk 15.21–32; Lk 23.26–43)

So they took charge of Jesus. [17]He went
out, carrying his cross, and came to "The
Place of the Skull", as it is called. (In Hebrew
it is called "Golgotha".) [18]There they
crucified him; and they also crucified two
other men, one on each side, with Jesus
between them. [19]Pilate wrote a notice and
had it put on the cross. "Jesus of Nazareth,
the King of the Jews", is what he wrote.
[20]Many people read it, because the place
where Jesus was crucified was not far from
the city. The notice was written in Hebrew,
Latin, and Greek. [21]The chief priests said to
Pilate, "Do not write 'The King of the Jews',
but rather, 'This man said, I am the King of
the Jews.' "
22 Pilate answered, "What I have written
stays written."
23 After the soldiers had crucified Jesus, they
took his clothes and divided them into four
parts, one part for each soldier. They also
took the robe, which was made of one piece
of woven cloth without any seams in it.
[24]The soldiers said to one another, "Let's
not tear it; let's throw dice to see who will
get it." This happened in order to make the
scripture come true:

"They divided my clothes among
themselves
and gambled for my robe."

And this is what the soldiers did.
25 Standing close to Jesus' cross were his mother, his mother's sister, Mary the wife of Clopas, and Mary Magdalene. [26]Jesus saw his mother and the disciple he loved standing there; so he said to his mother, "He is your son."

The soldiers made Jesus wear a crown of thorns.

27 Then he said to the disciple, "She is your
mother." From that time the disciple took
her to live in his home.

As he died on the cross, Jesus asked John to look after his mother, Mary.

The Death of Jesus
(Mt 27.45–56; Mk 15.33–41; Lk 23.44–49)

28 Jesus knew that by now everything had
been completed; and in order to make the
scripture come true, he said, "I am thirsty."
29 A bowl was there, full of cheap wine; so
a sponge was soaked in the wine, put on a
stalk of hyssop, and lifted up to his lips.
30Jesus drank the wine and said, "It is
finished!"
Then he bowed his head and died.

Jesus' Side is Pierced

31 Then the Jewish authorities asked Pilate
to allow them to break the legs of the men
who had been crucified, and to take the
bodies down from the crosses. They
requested this because it was Friday, and
they did not want the bodies to stay on the
crosses on the Sabbath, since the coming
Sabbath was especially holy. 32So the
soldiers went and broke the legs of the first
man and then of the other man who had
been crucified with Jesus. 33But when they
came to Jesus, they saw that he was already
dead, so they did not break his legs. 34One
of the soldiers, however, plunged his spear
into Jesus' side, and at once blood and
water poured out. 35(The one who saw this
happen has spoken of it, so that you also
may believe.[a] What he said is true, and he
knows that he speaks the truth.) 36This was
done to make the scripture come true: "Not
one of his bones will be broken." 37And
there is another scripture that says, "People
will look at him whom they pierced."

The Burial of Jesus
(Mt 27.57–61; Mk 15.42–47; Lk 23.50–56)

38 After this, Joseph, who was from the
town of Arimathea, asked Pilate if he could
take Jesus' body. (Joseph was a follower of
Jesus, but in secret, because he was afraid of
the Jewish authorities.) Pilate told him he
could have the body, so Joseph went and
took it away. 39Nicodemus, who at first had
gone to see Jesus at night, went with
Joseph, taking with him about 30
kilogrammes of spices, a mixture of myrrh
and aloes. 40The two men took Jesus' body
and wrapped it in linen with the spices
according to the Jewish custom of
preparing a body for burial. 41There was a
garden in the place where Jesus had been
put to death, and in it there was a new
tomb where no one had ever been buried.
42Since it was the day before the Sabbath
and because the tomb was close by, they
placed Jesus' body there.

The Empty Tomb
(Mt 28.1–8; Mk 16.1–8; Lk 24.1–12)

20 Early on Sunday morning, while it was
still dark, Mary Magdalene went to the
tomb and saw that the stone had been
taken away from the entrance. 2She went
running to Simon Peter and the other
disciple, whom Jesus loved, and told them,
"They have taken the Lord from the tomb,
and we don't know where they have put
him!"
3 Then Peter and the other disciple went to
the tomb. 4The two of them were running,
but the other disciple ran faster than Peter
and reached the tomb first. 5He bent over
and saw the linen wrappings, but he did

[a] **19.35** believe; *some manuscripts have* continue to believe.

not go in. 6Behind him came Simon Peter,
and he went straight into the tomb. He saw
the linen wrappings lying there 7and the
cloth which had been round Jesus' head. It
was not lying with the linen wrappings but
was rolled up by itself. 8Then the other
disciple, who had reached the tomb first,
also went in; he saw and believed. 9(They
still did not understand the scripture which
said that he must rise from death.) 10Then
the disciples went back home.

Jesus Appears to Mary Magdalene
(Mt 28.9–10; Mk 16.9–11)

11 Mary stood crying outside the tomb.
While she was still crying, she bent over and
looked in the tomb 12and saw two angels
there dressed in white, sitting where the
body of Jesus had been, one at the head and
the other at the feet. 13"Woman, why are
you crying?" they asked her.
She answered, "They have taken my Lord
away, and I do not know where they have
put him!"
14 Then she turned round and saw Jesus
standing there; but she did not know that it
was Jesus. 15"Woman, why are you crying?"
Jesus asked her. "Who is it that you are
looking for?"
She thought he was the gardener, so she
said to him, "If you took him away, sir, tell
me where you have put him, and I will go
and get him."
16 Jesus said to her, "Mary!"
She turned towards him and said in
Hebrew, "Rabboni!" (This means "Teacher".)
17 "Do not hold on to me," Jesus told her,
"because I have not yet gone back up to the
Father. But go to my brothers and tell them
that I am returning to him who is my Father
and their Father, my God and their God."
18 So Mary Magdalene went and told the
disciples that she had seen the Lord and
related to them what he had told her.

Jesus Appears to his Disciples
(Mt 28.16–20; Mk 16.14–18; Lk 24.36–49)

19 It was late that Sunday evening, and the
disciples were gathered together behind
locked doors, because they were afraid of
the Jewish authorities. Then Jesus came and
stood among them. "Peace be with you," he
said. 20After saying this, he showed them
his hands and his side. The disciples were
filled with joy at seeing the Lord. 21Jesus
said to them again, "Peace be with you. As
the Father sent me, so I send you." 22Then
he breathed on them and said, "Receive the
Holy Spirit. 23If you forgive people's sins,
they are forgiven; if you do not forgive
them, they are not forgiven."

Jesus and Thomas

24 One of the twelve disciples, Thomas
(called the Twin), was not with them when
Jesus came. 25So the other disciples told
him, "We have seen the Lord!"
Thomas said to them, "Unless I see the
scars of the nails in his hands and put my
finger on those scars and my hand in his
side, I will not believe."
26 A week later the disciples were together
again indoors, and Thomas was with them.
The doors were locked, but Jesus came and
stood among them and said, "Peace be with
you." 27Then he said to Thomas, "Put your
finger here, and look at my hands; then
stretch out your hand and put it in my side.
Stop your doubting, and believe!"
28 Thomas answered him, "My Lord and my
God!"
29 Jesus said to him, "Do you believe
because you see me? How happy are those
who believe without seeing me!"

The Purpose of this Book

30 In his disciples' presence Jesus performed
many other miracles which are not written
down in this book. 31But these have been
written in order that you may believe[a] that
Jesus is the Messiah, the Son of God, and
that through your faith in him you may
have life.

Jesus Appears to Seven Disciples

21 After this, Jesus appeared once more to
his disciples at Lake Tiberias. This is
how it happened. 2Simon Peter,
Thomas (called the Twin), Nathanael (the
one from Cana in Galilee), the sons of

[a] **20.31** believe; *some manuscripts have* continue to believe.

Zebedee, and two other disciples of Jesus
were all together. [3]Simon Peter said to the
others, "I am going fishing."
"We will come with you," they told him.
So they went out in a boat, but all that night
they did not catch a thing. [4]As the sun was
rising, Jesus stood at the water's edge, but the
disciples did not know that it was Jesus.
[5]Then he asked them, "Young men, haven't
you caught anything?"
"Not a thing," they answered.
6 He said to them, "Throw your net out on
the right side of the boat, and you will catch
some." So they threw the net out and could
not pull it back in, because they had caught
so many fish.
7 The disciple whom Jesus loved said to
Peter, "It is the Lord!" When Peter heard
that it was the Lord, he wrapped his outer
garment round him (for he had taken his
clothes off) and jumped into the water.
[8]The other disciples came to shore in the
boat, pulling the net full of fish. They were
not very far from land, about a hundred
metres away. [9]When they stepped ashore,
they saw a charcoal fire there with fish on it
and some bread. [10]Then Jesus said to them,
"Bring some of the fish you have just
caught."
11 Simon Peter went aboard and dragged the
net ashore full of big fish, 153 in all; even
though there were so many, still the net did
not tear. [12]Jesus said to them, "Come and
eat." None of the disciples dared ask him,
"Who are you?" because they knew it was
the Lord. [13]So Jesus went over, took the
bread, and gave it to them; he did the same
with the fish.
14 This, then, was the third time Jesus
appeared to the disciples after he was raised
from death.

Jesus and Peter

15 After they had eaten, Jesus said to Simon
Peter, "Simon son of John, do you love me
more than these others do?"
"Yes, Lord," he answered, "you know that I
love you."
Jesus said to him, "Take care of my
lambs." [16]A second time Jesus said to him,
"Simon son of John, do you love me?"
"Yes, Lord," he answered, "you know that
I love you."
Jesus said to him, "Take care of my
sheep." [17]A third time Jesus said, "Simon
son of John, do you love me?"
Peter was sad because Jesus asked him the
third time, "Do you love me?" so he said to
him, "Lord, you know everything; you
know that I love you!"
Jesus said to him, "Take care of my sheep.
[18]I am telling you the truth: when you were
young, you used to get ready and go
anywhere you wanted to; but when you are
old, you will stretch out your hands and
someone else will bind you and take you
where you don't want to go." [19](In saying
this, Jesus was indicating the way in which
Peter would die and bring glory to God.)
Then Jesus said to him, "Follow me!"

Jesus and the Other Disciple

20 Peter turned round and saw behind him
that other disciple, whom Jesus loved – the
one who had leaned close to Jesus at the
meal and had asked, "Lord, who is going to
betray you?" [21]When Peter saw him, he
asked Jesus, "Lord, what about this man?"
22 Jesus answered him, "If I want him to live
until I come, what is that to you? Follow
me!"
23 So a report spread among the followers of
Jesus that this disciple would not die. But
Jesus did not say that he would not die; he
said, "If I want him to live until I come,
what is that to you?"
24 He is the disciple who spoke of these
things, the one who also wrote them down;
and we know that what he said is true.

Conclusion

25 Now, there are many other things that
Jesus did. If they were all written down one
by one, I suppose that the whole world
could not hold the books that would be
written.

Angel Messenger sent by God to men and women. An angel appeared to Mary telling her that she was going to give birth to Jesus.

Baptism A ceremony performed by John the Baptist. He plunged people beneath the waters of the River Jordan to show that they were sorry for their sins. Jesus was baptized by John.

Bethlehem A small town close to Jerusalem. The place where Jesus was born.

Devil The evil force in the Gospels who was opposed to all that God did. The Devil is also called Satan.

Disciple A word used in the Gospels to speak of the twelve men that Jesus chose to follow him. The disciples were also sometimes called 'apostles' in the Gospels.

Gentile In the time of Jesus this was the name given to people who were not Jews.

Gethsemane The garden just outside Jerusalem where Jesus prayed before he was arrested.

Golgotha The hill on which Jesus was put to death.

Herod the Great The governor of Palestine for the Romans between 40 and 4 BCE. Herod was king when Jesus was born. He was a very wicked king who tried to kill Jesus when he was a baby.

Gospel A book which tells the 'Good News'. There are four Gospels in the New Testament which tell the story of Jesus: Matthew, Mark, Luke and John.

High Priest The religious leader of the Jews at the time of Jesus. Annas and Caiaphas are the two High Priests mentioned in the Gospels.

Holy Spirit Christians believe in one God who takes three forms. These are God the Father, God the Son (Jesus Christ) and God the Holy Spirit. The Holy Spirit is often mentioned in the Gospels.

Israel The country where Jesus was born. Israel was also known as Palestine.

James One of the twelve disciples of Jesus. His brother, John, was also a disciple.

Jerusalem The most important city in Israel. The Temple stood in Jerusalem and Jesus was put to death in the city.

John One of the twelve disciples of Jesus, along with his brother James. James and John, together with Peter, were the closest friends of Jesus.

John the Baptist The cousin of Jesus. He began preaching to the people to prepare them for the coming of Jesus.

Joseph The husband of Mary.

Judas Iscariot The disciple who betrayed Jesus to the Romans.

Kingdom of God Jesus told many parables about the Kingdom of God. This Kingdom was the rule of God on earth which Jesus had come to set up.

Matthew One of the twelve disciples of Jesus. Before following Jesus he was a tax-collector working for the Romans. Matthew was also called 'Levi'.

Mary The mother of Jesus and the wife of Joseph.

Messiah The title given to a leader that the Jews expected God to send, who would deliver them from their enemies. Christians believed that Jesus was the Messiah.

Mary Magdalene A female follower of Jesus who was present at his death and resurrection.

Nazareth The town in which Jesus grew up.

Parable A story told by Jesus to teach a religious truth. The Gospels are full of these stories which Jesus told to teach people about God.

Passover The most important Jewish festival which was celebrated each year. It reminded everyone of the delivery of the Israelites from slavery in Egypt centuries earlier. Jews still celebrate the Passover today.

Peter A fisherman who became the leading disciple of Jesus. He denied that he knew Jesus three times before Jesus was put to death.

Pharisees The Jewish leaders who are mentioned most often in the Gospels. Jesus was very critical of the Pharisees.

Pontius Pilate The procurator (governor) of Palestine and the man responsible for condemning Jesus to death.

Resurrection The return of Jesus to life three days after he was put to death. Jesus then appeared to many different people.

River Jordan The river that runs from north to south in Israel, ending in the Dead Sea. It is 1200 feet below sea-level.

Sabbath Saturday, the weekly day of rest for all Jews, when they remember the seventh day of creation on which God rested.

Sadducees A small group of Jewish leaders who often worked together with the Pharisees. They strongly opposed Jesus.

Son of David A title that was sometimes given to Jesus. David was the most popular Jewish king in the Old Testament. Only the Messiah was called the Son of David.

Son of God A title that was sometimes given to Jesus in the Gospels. God called Jesus his Son after Jesus had been baptized by John the Baptist in the River Jordan.

Son of Man The favourite title used by Jesus to describe himself. In the Gospels Jesus is both God and man.

Synagogue Jewish meeting house and place of worship. Jesus sometimes worshipped in a synagogue.

Temple The most important place of worship in Jerusalem for all Jews at the time of Jesus.